RURAL DEVELOPMENT AND TECHNO-INNOVATIONS

ENV BOOKS SERIES

RURAL DEVELOPMENT AND TECHNO-INNOVATIONS

Editors

Dr. Alka Chauhan

Society for Environment, Health
Awareness of Nutrition & Toxicology (SEHAT)
B-225/5D, Top Floor, Subhash Gali, Road No. 7, Block B
Ashok Nagar, Shahdara, Delhi - 110 093
(India)

Er. Chhavi Kumar 'Bharti'

M.Tech., NET
Assistant Professor
ARSD College, University of Delhi (India)

&

Dr. Pawan Kumar 'Bharti'

Society for Environment, Health Awareness of
Nutrition & Toxicology (SEHAT)
B-225/5D, Top Floor, Subhash Gali, Road No. 7, Block B
Ashok Nagar, Shahdara, Delhi - 110 093
(India)

DPH

DISCOVERY PUBLISHING HOUSE PVT. LTD.
INDIA

Published by:
Namit Wasan
DISCOVERY PUBLISHING HOUSE PVT. LTD.
4383/4B, Ansari Road, Darya Ganj
New Delhi-110 002 (India)
Phone : +91-11-23279245; 23253475; 43596065
E-mail : discoverybooksindia@gmail.com
discoverypublishinghouse@gmail.com
namitwasan9@gmail.com
web : www.discoverypublishinggroup.com

***First Edition:* 2019**

ISBN: 978-93-88854-07-8

Rural Development and Techno-Innovations

Printed at:
Infinity Imaging Systems
Delhi

Preface

Rural development actions are intended to further the social and economic development of rural communities. Rural development programs have historically been top-down from local or regional authorities, regional development agencies, NGOs, national governments or international development organizations. Local populations can also bring about endogenous initiatives for development. The term is not limited to issues of developing countries. In fact many developed countries have very active rural development programs.

Rural development aims at finding ways to improve rural lives with participation of rural people themselves, so as to meet the required needs of rural communities. The outsider may not understand the setting, culture, language and other things prevalent in the local area. As such, rural people themselves have to participate in their sustainable rural development. In developing countries like Nepal, Pakistan, India, Bangladesh, China, integrated development approaches are being followed up. In this context, many approaches and ideas have been developed and implemented, for instance, bottom-up approach, PRA-Participatory Rural Appraisal, RRA- Rapid Rural Appraisal, etc.

The present book updates the subject content of business development in fishery and aquaculture sectors, Promotion of cultural and natural heritage as a potential tourism destination, life cycle assessment for leather products, upliftment of tribal people, empowerment of farm women groups in agrarian economy, strategies for growth of vegetable seed industry, nanotechnology in smart agriculture development, geoexchanger system for buildings and gender empowerment from millennium development goals to sustainable development goals.

Thanks are due to publisher and contributors from various institutions and universities.

The book will be helpful for the researchers, academia working in the field of business development in fishery, Promotion of cultural and natural heritage as potential tourism destination, life cycle assessment for leather products, upliftment of tribal people, empowerment of farm women groups, strategies for growth of vegetable seed industry, nanotechnology in smart agriculture development, gender empowerment and sustainable development goals.

–Editors

(envbooks@gmail.com)

Contents

Pages: 1-7

Rural Development and Techno-Innovations

Edited by: Dr. Alka Chauhan; Er. Chhavi Kumar 'Bharti' & Dr. Pawan Kumar 'Bharti'

ISBN: 978-93-88854-07-8

Edition: 2019

Published by: Discovery Publishing House Pvt. Ltd., New Delhi (India)

1

Introduction

Rural development is the process of improving the quality of life and economic well-being of people living in rural areas, often relatively isolated and sparsely populated areas.

Rural development has traditionally centered on the exploitation of land-intensive natural resources such as agriculture and forestry. However, changes in global production networks and increased urbanization have changed the character of rural areas. Increasingly tourism, niche manufacturers, and recreation have replaced resource extraction and agriculture as dominant economic drivers. The need for rural communities to approach development from a wider perspective has created more focus on a broad range of development goals rather than merely creating incentive for agricultural or resource based businesses. Education, entrepreneurship, physical infrastructure, and social infrastructure all play an important role in developing rural regions. Rural development is also characterized by its emphasis on locally produced economic development strategies. In contrast to urban regions, which have many similarities, rural areas are highly distinctive from one another. For this reason there are a large variety of rural development approaches used globally.

Rural development can be understood as the unfolding of capitalism in rural areas, and as that package of policy and project interventions that aim to foster socio-economic change and human improvement in rural areas. Some writing on 'rural development' thus addresses general issues of agrarian change, peasant economy, and rural politics. Other writing, more applied in focus, addresses project impacts on rural people and environments, asking how these impacts might be improved and enhanced. Between these two bodies of work is that which focuses on interventions, but with a critical eye, inquiring into the ways in which projects themselves foster capitalist development, facilitate state and social control of rural populations, and constitute processes of rural modernization. Analytical frameworks have been drawn variously from Marxist political economy, neoclassical and institutional economics, institutional analysis, actor-oriented and structuration theory, poststructuralism and pragmatism. The rural development literature is thus diverse. However, within this diversity certain patterns are apparent. First, writing on rural development has followed broader trends in social theory. Second, theory and practice have informed each other. Third, debates on theory and practice have been informed by broader shifts in the global economy. This reflects the interactive nature of the relationship between rural development as capitalist development and rural development as intervention.

Rural development is a comprehensive term. It essentially focuses on action for the development of areas outside the mainstream urban economic system, we should think of what type of rural development is needed because modernization of village leads to urbanization and village environment disappears.

Rural development actions are intended to further the social and economic development of rural communities. Rural development programs have historically been top-down from local or regional authorities, regional development agencies, NGOs, national governments or international development organizations. Local populations can also bring about endogenous initiatives for development. The term is not limited to issues of developing countries. In fact many developed countries have very active rural development programs.

Rural development aims at finding ways to improve rural lives with participation of rural people themselves, so as to meet the required needs of rural communities. The outsider may not understand the setting, culture, language and other things prevalent in the local area. As such, rural people themselves have to participate in their sustainable rural development. In developing countries like Nepal, Pakistan, India, Bangladesh, China, integrated development approaches are being followed up. In this context, many approaches and ideas have been developed and implemented, for instance, bottom-up approach, PRA- Participatory Rural Appraisal, RRA- Rapid Rural Appraisal, etc. The New Rural Reconstruction Movement in China has been actively promoting rural development through their ecological farming projects.

URBAN DEVELOPMENT

Urban planning is a technical and political process concerned with the development and design of land use and the built environment, including air, water, and the infrastructure passing into and out of urban areas, such as transportation, communications, and distribution networks. Urban planning deals with physical layout of human settlements. The primary concern is the public welfare, which includes considerations of efficiency, sanitation, protection and use of the environment, as well as effects on social and economic activities. Urban planning is considered an interdisciplinary field that includes social, engineering and design sciences. It is closely related to the field of urban design and some urban planners provide designs for streets, parks, buildings and other urban areas. Urban planning is also referred to as urban and regional planning, regional planning, town planning, city planning, rural planning, urban development or some combination in various areas worldwide.

Urban planning guides orderly development in urban, suburban and rural areas. Although predominantly concerned with the planning of settlements and communities, urban planning is also responsible for the planning and development of water use and resources, rural and agricultural land, parks and conserving areas of natural environmental significance. Practitioners of urban planning are concerned with research and analysis, strategic thinking, architecture, urban design, public consultation, policy recommendations, implementation and management. Enforcement methodologies include governmental zoning, planning permissions, and building codes, as well as private easements and restrictive covenants.

Urban planners work with the cognate fields of architecture, landscape architecture, civil engineering, and public administration to achieve strategic, policy and sustainability goals. Early urban planners were often members of these cognate fields. Today urban planning is a separate, independent professional discipline. The discipline is the broader category that includes different sub-fields such as land-use planning, zoning, economic development, environmental planning, and transportation planning.

Planning theory is the body of scientific concepts, definitions, behavioral relationships, and assumptions that define the body of knowledge of urban planning. There are eight procedural theories of planning that remain the principal theories of planning procedure today: the rational-comprehensive approach, the incremental approach, the transactive approach, the communicative approach, the advocacy approach, the equity approach, the radical approach, and the humanist or phenomenological approach.

TECHNICAL ASPECTS

Technical aspects of urban planning involve the applying scientific, technical processes, considerations and features that are involved in planning for land use, urban design, natural resources, transportation, and infrastructure. Urban planning includes techniques such as: predicting population growth, zoning, geographic mapping and analysis, analyzing park space, surveying the water supply, identifying transportation patterns, recognizing food supply demands, allocating healthcare and social services, and analyzing the impact of land use.

In order to predict how cities will develop and estimate the effects of their interventions, planners use various models. These models can be used to indicate relationships and patterns in demographic, geographic, and economic data. They might deal with short-term issues such as how people move through cities, or long-term issues such as land use and growth.

Building codes and other regulations dovetail with urban planning by governing how cities are constructed and used from the individual level.

Technological innovation is an extended concept of innovation. While innovation is a rather-well defined concept, it has a broad meaning to many people, and especially numerous understanding in the academic and business world. Innovation, refers to adding extra steps of developing new services and products in the marketplace or in the public that fulfill undressed needs or solve problems that were not in the past. Technological Innovation, however focuses on the technological aspects of a product or service rather than covering the entire organization business model. It is important to clarify that Innovation is not only driven by technology.

Technological innovation is the process where an organization (or a group of people working outside a structured organization) embarks in a journey where the importance of technology as a source of innovation has been identified as a critical success factor for increased market competitiveness. The wording "technological innovation" is preferred to "technology innovation". "Technology innovation" gives a sense of working on technology for the sake of technology. "Technological innovation" better reflects the business consideration of improving business value by working on technological aspects of the product or services. Moreover, in a vast majority of products and services, there is not one unique technology at the heart of the system. It is the combination, the integration and interaction of different technologies that make the product or service successful.

The concept of a technological innovation system was introduced as part of a wider theoretical school, called the innovation system approach. The central idea behind this approach is that determinants of technological change are not only to be found in individual firms or in research institutes, but also in a broad societal structure in which firms, as well as knowledge institutes, are embedded. Since the 1980s, innovation system studies have pointed out the influence of societal structures on technological change, and indirectly on long-term economic growth, within nations, sectors or technological fields. The purpose of analyzing a Technological Innovation System is to analyze and evaluate the development of a particular technological field in terms of the structures and processes that support or hamper it. Besides its particular focus, there are two, more analytical, features that set the Technological Innovation System approach apart from other innovation system approaches.

SEVEN SYSTEM FUNCTIONS

As an example, the seven system functions defined by Hekkert are explained here:

F1. Entrepreneurial activities: The classic role of the entrepreneur is to translate knowledge into business opportunities, and eventually innovations. The entrepreneur does this by performing market-oriented experiments that establish change, both to the emerging technology and to the institutions that surround it. The Entrepreneurial Activities involve projects aimed to prove the usefulness of the emerging technology in a practical and/or commercial environment. Such projects typically take the form of experiments and demonstrations.

F2. Knowledge development: The Knowledge Development function involves learning activities, mostly on the emerging technology, but also on markets, networks, users etc. There are various types of learning activities, the most important categories being learning-by-searching and learning-by-doing. The former concerns R&D activities in basic science, whereas the latter involves learning activities in a practical context, for example in the form of laboratory experiments or adoption trials.

F3. Knowledge diffusion/knowledge exchange through networks: The characteristic organization structure of a Technological Innovation System is that of the network. The primary function of networks is to facilitate the exchange of knowledge between all the actors involved in it. Knowledge Diffusion activities involve partnerships between actors, for example technology developers, but also meetings like workshops and conferences. The important role of Knowledge Diffusion stems from Lundvall's notion of interactive learning as the raison-d'être of any innovation system. The innovation system approach stresses that innovation happens only where actors of different backgrounds interact. A special form of interactive learning is learning-by-using, which involves learning activities based on the experience of users of technological innovations, for example through user-producer interactions.

F4. Guidance of the search: The Guidance of the Search function refers to activities that shape the needs, requirements and expectations of actors with respect to their (further) support of the emerging technology. Guidance of the Search refers to individual choices related to the technology but it may also take the form of hard institutions, for example policy targets. It also refers to promises and expectations as expressed by various actors in the community. Guidance of the Search can be positive or negative. A positive Guidance of the Search means a convergence of positive signals - expectations, promises, policy directives - in a particular direction of technology development. If negative, there will be a digression, or, even worse, a rejection of development altogether. This convergence is important since, usually, various technological options exist within an emerging technological field, all of which require investments in order to develop further. Since resources are usually limited, it is important that specific foci are chosen. After all, without any focus there will be a dilution of resources, preventing all options from prospering. On the other hand, too much focus may result in the loss of variety. A healthy Technological Innovation System will strike a balance between creating and reducing variety.

F5. Market formation: Emerging technologies cannot be expected to compete with incumbent technologies. In order to stimulate innovation, it is usually necessary to create artificial (niche) markets. The Market Formation function involves activities that contribute to the creation of a demand for the emerging technology, for example by financially supporting the use of the emerging technology, or by taxing the use of competing technologies. Market Formation is especially important in the field of sustainable energy technologies, since, in this case, there usually is a strong normative legitimation for the intervention in market dynamics.

F6. Resource mobilization: Resource Mobilization refers to the allocation of financial, material and human capital. The access to such capital factors is necessary for all other developments. Typical activities involved in this system function are investments and subsidies. They can also involve the deployment of generic infrastructures such as educational systems, large R&D facilities or refueling infrastructures. In some cases, the mobilization of natural resources, such as biomass, oil or natural gas is important as well. The Resource Mobilization function represents a basic economic variable. Its importance is obvious: an emerging technology cannot be supported in any way if there are no financial or natural means, or if there are no actors present with the right skills and competences.

F7. Support from advocacy coalitions: The rise of an emerging technology often leads to resistance from actors with interests in the incumbent energy system. In order for a Technological Innovation System to develop, other actors must counteract this inertia. This can be done by urging authorities to reorganize the institutional configuration of the system. The Support from Advocacy Coalitions function involves political lobbies and advice activities on behalf of interest groups. This system function may be regarded as a special form of Guidance of the Search. After all, lobbies and advices are pleas in favor of particular technologies. The essential feature which sets this category apart is that advocacy coalitions do not have the power, like for example governments, to change formal institutions directly. Instead, they employ the power of persuasion. The notion of the advocacy coalition is based on the work of Sabatier, who introduced the idea within the context of political science. The concept stresses the idea that structural change within a system is the outcome of competing interest groups, each representing a separate system of values and ideas. The outcome is determined by political power.

ACQUIRING NEW TECHNOLOGIES AND CAPABILITIES

To improve competitiveness and retain sustainability, firms require new technologies and capabilities. In this age of rapid innovation and complexity, it is challenging for the firms to develop internally and remain competitive at the same time. Merger, acquisition and alliance are some of the ways to achieve this, but the primary driver is the desire to obtain valuable resources. Many acquisitions failed to achieve their objectives and resulted in poor performance because of improper implementation.

1. Improper documentation and changing implicit knowledge makes it difficult to share information during acquisition.
2. For acquired firm symbolic and cultural independence which is the base of technology and capabilities are more important than administrative independence.
3. Detailed knowledge exchange and integrations are difficult when the acquired firm is large and high performing.
4. Management of executives from acquired firm is critical in terms of promotions and pay incentives to utilize their talent and value their expertise.
5. Transfer of technologies and capabilities are most difficult task to manage because of complications of acquisition implementation. The risk of losing implicit knowledge is always associated with the fast pace acquisition.

Preservation of tacit knowledge, employees and literature are always delicate during and after acquisition. Strategic management of all these resources is a very important factor for a successful acquisition.

Increase in acquisitions in our global business environment has pushed us to evaluate the key stake holders of acquisition very carefully before implementation. It is imperative for the acquirer to understand this relationship and apply it to its advantage. Retention is only possible when resources are exchanged and managed without affecting their independence.

REFERENCES

https://en.wikipedia.org/wiki/Rural_development

https://en.wikipedia.org/wiki/Urban_planning

https://www.sciencedirect.com/topics/agricultural-and-biological-sciences/rural-development

https://en.wikipedia.org/wiki/Technological_innovation

https://en.wikipedia.org/wiki/Technological_innovation_system

Pages: 8-27

Rural Development and Techno-Innovations
Edited by: Dr. Alka Chauhan; Er. Chhavi Kumar 'Bharti' & Dr. Pawan Kumar 'Bharti'
ISBN: 978-93-88854-07-8
Edition: **2019**
Published by: **Discovery Publishing House Pvt. Ltd., New Delhi (India)**

2

Promotion of Cultural and Natural Heritage of the Tribal District of Lahaul and Spiti as a Potential Tourism Destination in Northwestern Himalaya

Kesar Chand[1]; Sarla Shashni[*1]
Sumati Rathore[1]; Sagar Sood[1]
Renu Lata[1] and Rakesh Chand Sundriyal[2]

ABSTRACT

The trend of ingenious economy concept has created an example for a new kind of tourism all over the world so as in the tribal regions of the Himalayas. This is a kind of tourism that is directed towards and engaged an authentic experience with participative learning in the arts, heritage or specific character of a place between tourists and local people. This new paradigm of tourism has been used as a tool to develop sustainable tourism to keep the equilibrium between economy, society and environment. The tribal district of Lahaul and Spiti of North Western Himalayan state of Himachal Pradesh is known for its natural beauty and unique cultural heritage. Due to hard terrains, environmental conditions and inaccessibility to the region, tourism is still in its initial stage but is continuously increasing. Therefore, it is very important to analyse pros and cons of the present tourism activities which will help in developing sustainable tourism in future. Current chapter documents the list of cultural and natural attractions in the region which can be promoted as potential tourism destinations.

Keywords: Tourism, Society and Environment, Tradition, Tribal, Himalaya.

1 G.B. Pant National Institute of Himalayan Environment and Sustainable Development, Himachal Regional Centre, Mohal-Kullu - 175 126 Himachal Pradesh (India)

2 G.B. Pant National Institute of Himalayan Environment and Sustainable Development, Kosi-Katarmal, Almora - 263 643 Uttarakhand (India)

INTRODUCTION

Traditional knowledge in terms of cultural and natural resource management plays an important role in socio-economic development of any area. In higher or remote area of Himalaya, people have very unique knowledge and faith system in terms of conserving their traditional heritage. The main purpose of the current study is to document the potential of cultural and natural resources of these remote areas to promote as sustainable tourism destinations which has a very intact traditional knowledge system from the centuries. In North-Western Himalayan state, Himachal Pradesh is one of the famous tourist destinations all over the World which attracts millions of tourists every year. According to the Statistical Department of HP total 1,84,50,520 visitors visited the state during the year 2015-16 (Economic and Statistical Department, 2016). The state offers a wide range of tourism products to the visitors for rest, solitude, recreation, adventure and scenic beauty. The state has 12 districts, with people holding some unique features about their communities, tribes, traditions and cultures. There are millions of tourists visiting the state on annual basis in popular tourist destinations. Knowledge and values are the keystones for the decision making in the social development of any communities so as in the tourism development.

Knowledge in this context is not only knowledge of indigenous people as many non-indigenous groups are also involved in decisions about tourism development of any area (Gillespie, 2000; Stockton, 1995; Sullivan, 2004). Indigenous people here refer to the local community of any specific location which represents their culture as a fascinating frontier for tourists. Destinations associated with the culture of communities tend to be unique places, which can enrich the way tourists understand the world. In general, most indigenous people would prefer to be identified specifically by their tribe, group, clan, or nation (Waitt, 1997). However, the phrase "indigenous people" is increasingly used in reference to communities, peoples, and nations that have historical continuity with pre-invasion and pre-colonial societies. It generally refers to people who: consider themselves distinct from other sectors of societies now prevailing in those territories, or parts of them. They form at present non-dominant sectors of society and are determined to preserve, develop, and transmit to future generations their ancestral territories, and their ethnic identity, as the basis of their continued existence as peoples, in accordance with their own cultural patterns, social institutions, and legal systems. Indigenous tourism refers to tourism activities in which indigenous people are directly involved either through control and/or by having their culture serve as the essence of the attraction (Hinch and Butler 1996).

Himachal Pradesh is the third largest state in the western Himalayan region. The state offers tremendous tourist potentialities and is blessed with all the necessary resources, which helps in flourishing tourism activities like geographical and cultural variety, clean, calm and beautiful streams, sacred shrines, famous historic monuments and simple, peace-loving and hospitable people. In the state, tourism has been recognized as one of the most important sectors of the economy as it is being realized as a major engine of growth for future and as such contribution of the tourism sector to the state GDP is significant.

Lahaul and Spiti district is the largest districts among all districts of Himachal Pradesh. This district is home to various beautiful snow clad and barren mountain ranges, glaciers which attracts various tourists every year. There are several places to visit in this beautiful snow-covered mountain region like, Rohtang Pass, Sissu, Tandi Sangam, Shishur monastery, Goshal village, Guru Ghantal monastery, Keylong, Miyar village, Udaipur, Trilokinath, Jispa, Lady of Keylong Glacier, Kaza, Tabo, Hikkim, Langza village and other routes etc. Spiti region is rich in monasteries, therefore, it is known as "Land of the Lamas". All these places have immense tourism potential. After 1995, this tribal region was opened for tourists. Afterwards, percentage of tourists especially inbound is increasing gradually. This circuit is having treasure of tourism resources; like 1000 years old monasteries, CDBR (Cold Deserts Biosphere Reserve), Ajanta of Himalaya i.e. *Tabo* etc. In this Valley, every year various tourists from across the world come and go for camping, climbing, trekking, astrophotography, religious visits, visiting wildlife sanctuaries etc. All these sports and adventure activities have been attracting enthusiastic people from the country and all around the globe. There are various tiny tourism units come up to Lahaul and Spiti and also offer conveniences to the guests and various domestic tourists visit religiously important destinations and temples to worship all over the year. (Agarwal *et al.*, 2013, Salerno and Quarto, 2014). This district is also regarded as "the magical showcase of Nature's splendour". The fragile ecosystem of these remote regions is very sensitive to tourist activity because resources are limited (Sood, 2010). This mountain tourism is multifaceted and may entail farm/agricultural tourism, cultural tourism, nature tourism, adventure tourism, and ecotourism in the countryside. On the other hand, tourism also helps to improve the infrastructure, roads, transportation, air connectivity, water, and sewerage system and hospitability facilities, etc. which ultimately uplift the livelihood system of the local population (Jreat and Manoj, 2004). Himachal Pradesh Tourism Development Corporation is also taking important steps for the growth of healthy tourism in the state. A large number of tourists visit these sacred century old monasteries and temples throughout the year. The Himachal government also maintains the beautification around the temples, provides clean drinking water, a proper mechanism for garbage disposal etc. But due to various geographical barriers, their efforts have not made more developed in the tribal area.

(Manjit Singh, 2004). This sector also opens various business opportunities for natives in the countryside. With the increase in tourist influx, pressure on natural resources, is posing threat to rivers and mountains of these fragile and sensitive areas. The indigenous-themed tourism, with the question of control, or the ability of indigenous people to influence sustainable tourism development is one of the major aspects which needs to be taken care of while promoting such tourism destinations (Zeppel 1998, Hinch 2001). The current chapter also describes and lists the potential destinations of the tribal district of Lahaul and Spiti which can be promoted as major and unique tourist destinations.

STUDY SITE

Lahaul and Spiti district of Himachal Pradesh is very rich and prosperous in traditional knowledge and located between 31°44′57″ and 32°59′57″ N latitude to 76°46′29″ and 78°41′34″ E longitude. This district is different in geographical point of view. Lahaul and Spiti is inhabited by two major ethnic groups, namely, *Lahaulas* in Lahaul and Bodhs (*Bhotias*) in Spiti. *Lahaulas* are of Tibetan and Indo-Aryan descent, while the Spiti area inhabited by *Bhotia* owing to their proximity to Tibet. These two sub-divisions are quite different in character. Spiti is more barren, desert-like and difficult to cross with an average elevation of the valley floor of 4270 m (14,009 ft). The winter season lasts from November to April. The temperature falls below freezing often and the average snowfall is about 7 feet. Down the ages, the people of Lahaul and Spiti have retained trade and cultural links across the border with Tibet and with neighbouring Ladakh in Jammu & Kashmir. At the crossroads of important trade routes, the Hindustan-Tibet road passes through this district and is the lifeline of its people. Due to the inaccessible terrain, the entire region remained insulated from external influences, untouched by modern life. All the above characteristics are presenting different lives and traditions with help to increases the tourism opportunities in the cold desert area. Lahaul and Spiti are perfect locations for nature lovers and trekkers too. Located at an altitude ranges up to 4500 m above mean sea level (amsl) in the north-eastern corner, these are the two remote valleys of Himachal Pradesh. Before these two districts were combined, the Lahaul capital was *Kardang* and *Dhankar* was the capital of Spiti. But now, these are spread over an area of 13835 sq. km and as per 2011 census, the total populations of these districts were recorded around 31,564 (Fig. 2.1). The breathtaking snow-capped hills and the craggy beauty of these regions lure the travellers. A beautiful land of captivating Buddhist art and culture-Lahaul is distinguished by inflicting mountains and glaciers while the vegetation, climate and the landscape of Spiti are similar to that of Tibet. That's why the village of Spiti is also popular as 'Little Tibet'. However, Lahaul and Spiti are the famous attractions in Himachal Pradesh that offer a wonderful experience to all the tourists who visit these places. The lush green valley, the cold desert and the blend of Buddhism and Hinduism make Lahaul and Spiti a worth place visiting in India.

POTENTIAL TOURISM ATTRACTIONS

Economic and Statistics Department of Himachal Pradesh (2014-15) shows that there is an allotment of 3,481.04 lakh for the development of tourism in the state. According to the Directorate of tourism 2015 report, total 1, 75, 31,153 tourists visited the state during the year 2015-16 in which the lowest number of 91,203 tourists visited the Lahaul & Spiti district. This is the lowest 0.52% of the total number of tourists visited the state with 19.53% highest for the Kullu district. The reason for the lesser visitors in the region may be due to inaccessibility, harsh climatic condition, seasonality, fewer tourism products, and unavailability of infrastructure, etc. Our current efforts are to document the potential sites of the region which can be promoted as a tourism destination. Tourist can visit these areas during June to September to take a break from the summer heat and enjoy the mystic location as their perfect getaway.

TOURISM ATTRACTION OF LAHAUL AND SPITI

Monasteries

Every village or a hamlet has prayer flags fluttering over the Buddhist monastery. These shrines are centres of the cultural life of people and have influenced their religious beliefs for centuries and around which their social life revolves. Here's a glimpse of spiritual wonders of Lahaul and Spiti.

Guru Ghantal Monastery

This monastery is situated on a hill above the Tupchiling village at the confluence of the rivers Chandra and Bhaga. The monastery was founded by Padma Sambhava and is more than 800 years old. The peculiar feature of the monastery is the wooden idols as distinguished from the clay idols found in other monasteries. This monastery has idols of Guru Padma Sambhava, Brijeshwari Devi and several other *lamas* (monk). One can visit the monastery with a small trek witnessing wide lush green valley with the Chandra-Bhaga River.

Kardang Monastery

Kardang Monastery is located in the village of Kardang which was once the capital of Lahaul. It is the most popular and the biggest monastery in the area. The monastery is situated on the left bank of the river Bhaga just above the village of Kardang. It was founded about 900 years ago and stood in ruins up to 1912 when *lama* Norbu of Kardang renovated it. Kardang monastery is located against the backdrop of the bare mountains of the Rangcha massif which rises above the valley like a giant cobra standing on its tail with hood outspread, ready to strike.

Kibber Monastery

The village of Kibber is located at a height of about 14,200 ft in a narrow valley on the summit of a limestone rock. The monastery in Kibber which is named after Serkang Rimpochhe of Tabo. The remarkable feature about the architecture of this *gompa* is the use of stone instead of mud or adobe brick used extensively in the valley. The *lama* breathed his last in Kibber in 1983. It is believed that when he was being cremated a water source erupted from that spot. Even today that water source is being used by the villagers.

Shashur Monastery

Shashur in the local Spiti parlance means in the blue pines. This is very apt as good patches of blue pine can still be seen around the monastery. Shashur monastery was founded in the 17th C. AD by *Lama* Deva Gyatsho of Zanskar. In the month of June/July *Chham* (mask dance) is performed in the monastery which is the most popular *Chham* in Lahaul.

Kye Monastery

Overlooking Kaza from a height of about 13,500 ft, the Kye monastery is the largest in the valley and holds a powerful sway over the most populous part of the valley around Kaza (Fig 2.2b). The *gompa* is an irregular heap of low rooms and narrow corridors on a monolithic conical hill. It is also known for its beautiful murals, *thankas,* rare manuscripts, stucco images and peculiar wind instruments that form part of the orchestra whenever *Chham* is enacted in the *gompa* in summer. Another interesting aspect of the *gompa* is its collection of weapons which may have been used to ward off marauders as also to maintain its control over people betraying a church-militant character.

Tabo Monastery

Tabo also known as the Ajanta of Himalayas is an ancient village located 46 km away from Kaza, on the left bank of the Piti River at an altitude of 10004 feet. The biggest attraction of this village, for that matter of the whole valley, is the Tabo monastery, called Chogs-hkhor ('doctrinal circle' or 'doctrinal enclave') is a complex that holds nine temples, 23 chortens, a monks' chamber and an extension that houses the nuns chamber. Tabo holds the distinction of being the largest monastic complex in Spiti. (Fig. 2.3. a & b, 2.5. a)

Dhankar Monastery

Dhankar is a village in Spiti valley of Lahaul and Spiti district; there is a Buddhist temple in the village also known as Dhankar *Gompa* (Fig. 2.4. a & b). It is built at the highest place of the valley. It is situated at an elevation of 3,852 meters. Locally, Dhang or *dang* means cliff, and *kar* or *khar* means fort. Hence, Dhankar means fort on a cliff. Dhankar, like Kye Monastery in Spiti, and Thiksey, Likir and Rangdum monasteries in Ladakh, was built as a fort monastery on the Central Tibetan pattern. It was reported to have 90 monks in 1855. In the 17th century, Dhankar was the capital of all Spiti Valley Kingdom. It was the seat of the early rulers of Spiti, the Nonos, who had the right to cultivate the government lands nearby and were required to keep the fort in repair. They also dispensed justice to the people and were noted for their harsh penalties until the British replaced them.

Tangyud/Komic Monastery

This castle monastery is situated on the edge of a deep canyon. The wall of the structure is made up of mud and stones. It is located at an altitude of 4516 m amsl.

Mrikula Devi Temple

This temple is situated in Udaipur, dedicated to Goddess Kali. It is constructed in 11th century AD. The silver idol of Kali (Mahishasurmardini) was installed by Thakur in 1569-70. Temple is also rich in wood and stone artwork. Wall of this temple also showing the fine wood carving and also depicting the various stories of Mahabharata and Ramayana. This temple is also under ASI (Archeological Survey of India).

Trilokinath Temple

It is situated in Udaipur, Lahual sub-division of the district. This temple is dedicated to *Avalokiteshwar Bhagwan*. This is the only temple where both Hindu and Buddhist worship to the same deity. The temple is visited by the followers from all over the state and considered as one of the main pilgrims in the state.

Fairs and Festival

Fairs and festival days are observed with singing, dancing, and merry-making. At some festivals, people of Spiti valley dress in queer costumes like masks with horns and fancy dress and amuse them.

Chandra-Bhaga Sangam Parv

This parv is celebrated at Tandi (Altitude: 2875 m amsl; 33°33′03.35″N and 76° 58′30.29″E) in Lahaul & Spiti district locally named cha-cha parv. Tandi (Tan-Deh) is a place where Draupadi has given up her body. Chandra-Bhaga River in Lahaul-Spiti district had historical significance. Many monks and sages meditated on the banks of the river. It had been a holy river as their mortal remains were immersed in the river over the centuries, tribals of Lahaul-Spiti would celebrate the Sangam Parv in the Chandra-Bhaga River. Panchayat representatives from all 28-gram panchayats of Lahaul constitute a committee for this purpose (Fig. 2.7).

Ladarcha Fair

It is a popular means of celebration to the people of Spiti valley. Before the closure of the Tibetan traders, the fair used to be held at Kibbarmaidan in Spiti in the month of July. This used to be the meeting point for traders from Ladakh, Rampur Busher, and Spiti. It used to offer a good barter ground for them of their production. But now, the fair is celebrated at Kaza, the headquarters of Spiti Sub Division. The fair is usually held in the 3rd week of August. The fair now observes a get together of visitors and traders from Kullu, Lahaul, and Kinnaur. The fair has thus gradually become a conference of Spiti, Ladakh & Kinnaur cultures along with that of the Indian plains.

Pouri Fair

It has its magnanimous celebration during the months of summer in the third week of August every year. This fair used to be the most prominent among the other fairs of Lahaul where rustic folks irrespective of all casts and creed gathered not only from Lahaul but from Chamba and Kullu too. The fair demarcates the synthesis of pilgrimage and festive activities. Preparations are made at least a week in advance and most of the people leave their homes a day before the celebrations for the darshan of the idol of Triloknath (Lord Shiva of Three Worlds) or Avalokiteshvara as it is regarded by Buddhist. After paying their obeisance, the people visit parikrama gallery between the inner and outside walls of the temple. Pilgrims or devotees usually complete three or seven clockwise circumambulations of the gallery or the rotating the prayer wheels and murmuring Mantras every morning and evening till they stay there. An ambiance of holistic spirituality provokes the religious consciousness of the people as *ghee* and mustard oil lamps are lighted inside incessantly. People even donate money and *ghee* or oil to maintain the lamps, one of which is so big as to accommodate 16 Kgs. of *ghee* or oil. After the completion of prayer and rituals, the fair begins with pomp and glory. For the relaxation and breaks a wide range of temporary shops, tea stalls and hotels are established at the fairground. As soon as darkness dawns upon there is an aura of spiritual festivity in a huge circle to the melody of folk songs devotional or otherwise. On the second morning, a traditional procession is taken out, which is headed by the Thakur of Trilokinath riding on a tinted horse. Their targeted destination is the region whereas per the traditional lore, seven gods, and the youngest of who was Trilokinath had appeared from seven springs in the past. This thrives to be the most important ritual of the fair. The procession then returns to the fairground for further festivities. Some people for their native places leave as soon as the procession disperses, while others stay until the third day when the fair is over.

Keylong Fair

Tribal fair of Keylong coinciding with Independence Day is celebrated with great pomp and show from 14th to 16th August, at Keylong the headquarters of the district. People from each and every nooks and corner of the valley congregate in their queer disposition and a large number of Indian and foreign tourists assemble here to witness the fair. It is being celebrated as at State level fair. In order to make the fair colourful, artists and cultural troupes are invited from Chandigarh, Dharamshala, Leh, Chamba, Kullu, Spiti in addition to local artists.

Halda Festival

The First festival, celebrated in the month of January. This is a Buddhist event that is celebrated in the Lahaul region of Himachal Pradesh. During this festival, a person with Cedar twigs moving to a place that has been selected by the *lama* is called *Sheeskareppa* (A patch of round circle made on the wall of the house). It is usually the symbol of winter goddess. Halda festival is the religious festival that rejoiced by the Lahaul district's peoples, usually, it is the festival of light and during the festival, the spots of *ghee* and *sattu* drew on the patch. The Cedar twigs are then thrown in a bonfire and various dancing acts are performed for many days.

Lossar/Fagdi Festival

This festival is held in a midnight towards the end of the month of *Poush* (December and January). A local deity is worshipped in hope of restoring the bliss and prosperity through the winter season. This basically marks the beginning of the Tibetan year by the kindling of the lamps by the natives. After singing the religious songs in the morning, the people offer their prayers to god. On this day Lord Shiva, Naga and goddess Hidimba are worshiped, and the younger generation also marks the moment by venerating village elders. *Chaang* and *Lugri*, locally brewed liquors flow freely in this day and ritual dishes are eaten. During the time monasteries have some of the spectacular dance and stylized *Chhamm* dance, with elaborate costumes and masks, commemorates the assassination of the cruel Tibetan King, Lang drama in the ninth century.

Tsheshu Fair

This is celebrated in Shashur Monastery, Gemur Monastery, Kye Monastery, Kardang Monastery, Tabo Monastery and Mane Monastery in the months of June. A large number of devotees and people gather on these occasions. Devil dance is performed by the *lamas* bedecked in colorful dresses and wearing masks of different birds and animals.

Traditional Mud House Architecture

Traditional houses are one of the main attractions of tourism in cold desert. Dryness of the local climate is reflected in the architecture of this construction typology which consists of thick mud walls with small openings in order to insulate the interior from the harsh outside climate. This style of construction which is predominantly used for residential houses and temples is still being practiced though it shows high seismic vulnerability. Buildings of this construction type can be found in the Spiti river valley of the districts Lahaul and Spiti. As a specific term has not yet been coined for these houses, it was decided to name this construction type 'Spitian architecture'. The region is a desert area where timber is scarce and mud is the main locally available construction material. The buildings are therefore made of rammed earthen walls and timber is solely used for floors and roofs as well as for door and window frames (Fig. 2.8 a & b). Natural stones are also scarce and are thus only used for foundations. This type of housing construction is commonly found in both rural and sub-urban areas. This construction type has been in practice for more than 200 years. Locally available stone is used for foundation. A trench is dug about 300 mm in depth and 500 mm in width. Courses of stones with mud mortar are then laid in the trench up to the ground level. The same courses are then taken up to 600 to 900 mm above the ground in order to form the lower portion of the walls. Through this procedure the walls are protected from direct rain water splashes and snow. These buildings are typically found on both sloped and hilly terrain. They do not share common walls with adjacent buildings. Houses in the valley are built on flat lands while those on slopes and ridges are located on flat plateaus that are artificially cut into the topographical feature. In the Spiti river valley, the village Lossar is characterized by an entirely flat topography whereas the village Kibber is located on slopes. When separated from adjacent buildings, the typical distance from a neighbouring building is a minimum. The houses are generally rectangular in plan without any *verandah* (balcony). A typical house is of two to three storeys with the lower storey used for cattle and the upper storey(s) for the family. Openings are generally of small size. In some cases, skylights are provided in the roof in order to provide natural light to the interior corridors and staircases. The main function of this building typology is a single-family house. In a typical building of this type, there are no elevators and no fire-protected exit staircases. The typical building has generally one door other than the main entrance door which can be considered as an escape route at the buildings rear. On contoured sites, these doors may be located at different levels. Now a days most of the tourist preferred to live in these houses.

Gondhla Palace

Besides, these there are number of palaces which can be promoted as a tourism destination in the valley which has its own heritage importance. It is also known as House of Thakur of Gondhla or Gondhla castle or fort, attracts many tourists across the world. This structure is situated along the right bank of the Chandra River. This seven-story castle is the best example of indigenous masonry. According to the native people of this village, the fort was built in 1700 A.D. by Raja Man Singh of Kullu. He also married a daughter of the Gondhla family to cement relations with the Thakur.

Natural Lakes

Chander Taal

Chandra stands for the moon and the word *taal* stands for a lake. The meaning of Chandertaal is "lake of the moon". Its shape is almost like a crescent. It is in the Spiti valley of the district at an altitude of 4300 m. This beautiful Himalayan freshwater lake spread in 2 to 3 km. area and is surrounded by beautiful large brown mountains, which in winter season turn white. Crystal clear water of the lake attracts various nature lovers, photographers, trekker, and campers. It is one the high-altitude wetlands of India. This region is the favorite spot of shepherds because of ample grass. This is the source of Chandra river in the district. This lake is worshipped by both Hinduism and Buddhism people. This place is the very beautiful tourist destination.

Deepak Taal

This Lake is on the way to Keylong - Leh road at an altitude of 3750 m. The water of this tiny lake is so clear it gives the mirror image of the surrounding.

Suraj Taal

This sacred water body situated at an altitude of 4870 m in the Lahaul and Spiti district. The Suraj *taal* is the lake dedicated to Sun God from the origins of Bhaga River can be traced down. This is third highest lakes of the India which remain snow bounded from the month of November to April.

The Fossil Village in Spiti Valley: Langza

Spiti valley is full of isolated villages blessed with ancient monasteries. Langza village is also one of them. It is located at an altitude of 4338 m (amsl), 32°16.568′N; 78° 05.039′ E in Spiti Valley. This village also known as 'Switzerland of Spiti' because of its natural beauty. Langza is also considered to be one of the highest villages in the world with a motorable road. The population of the village is predominantly Buddhist and belongs to the Sakyapa sect of Tibetan Buddhism. The village has a population of about 137 people living in 33 houses. Langza is divided into two sections; Langza Yongma (Lower) and Langza Gongma (Upper). In the olden days, the major livelihood option of the villagers was mud craft. Various kinds of utensils are produced and sold in Kaja fair and also across the country. A huge golden color Buddha statue is built over the head of the villages. The main attraction of this village is the fossil. These millions of years old fossils of marine creatures are found in abundance in Langza village (Fig. 2.6 a & b). Small children from the village sell these fossils to visitors. Various people visit to this village and tourism are also becoming an income source for the people.

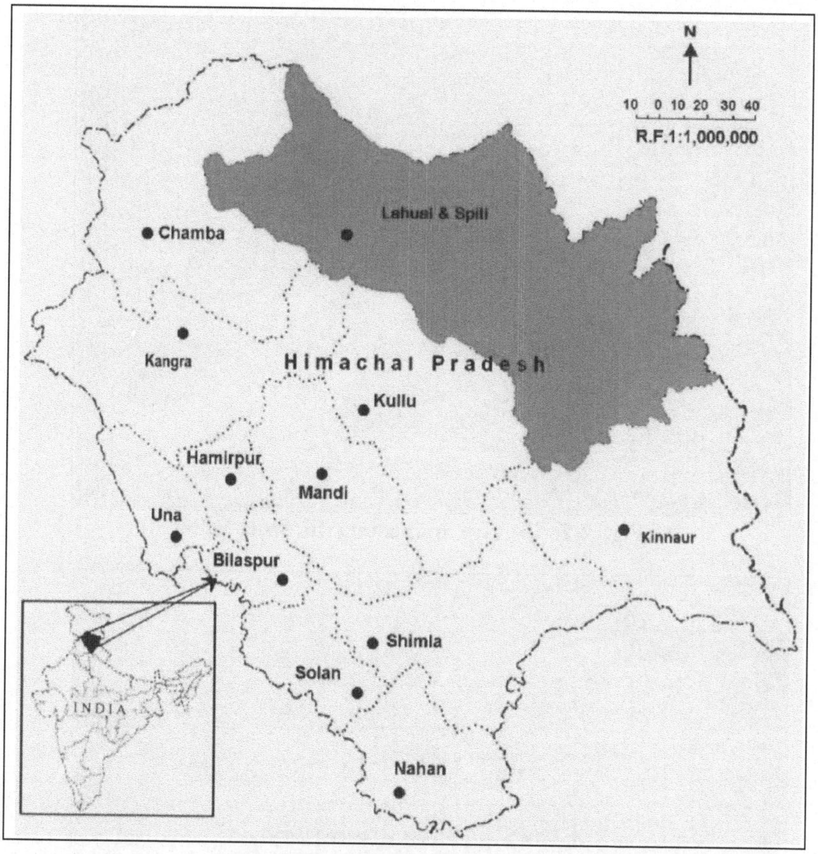

Fig. 2.1: Location of study site

Fig. 2.2: (a) Tupchiling monastery in Lahaul Valley

Fig. 2.2: (b) Kye monastery in Spiti Valley

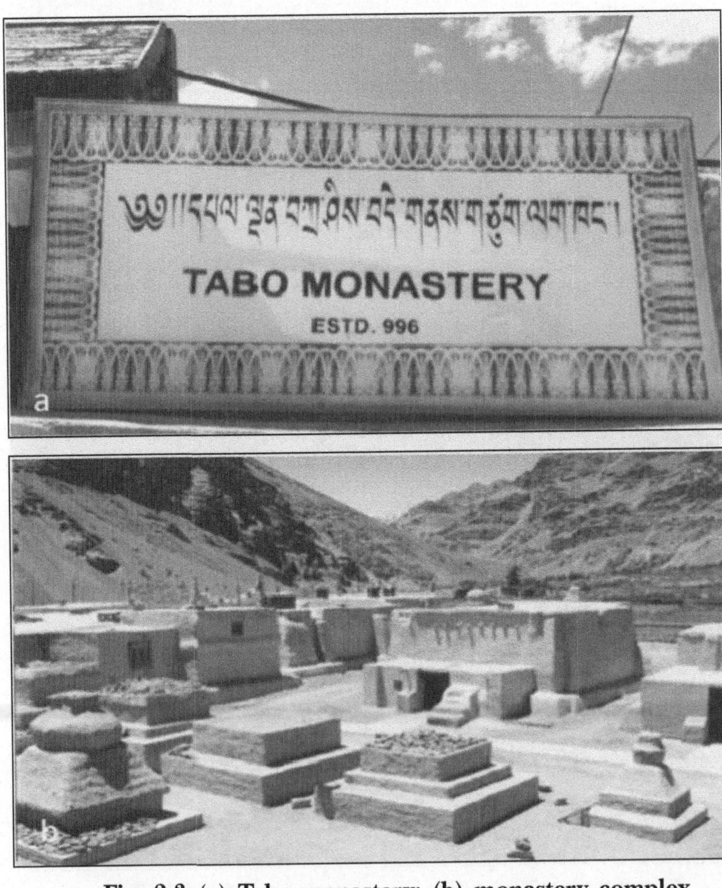

Fig. 2.3 (a) Tabo monastery; (b) monastery complex

Fig. 2.4: (a) Dhankar Monastery
(b) Goat in Dhankar Monastery covered with prayer flags

Fig. 2.5: (a) 1000 years' old monastery in Tabo; (b) Komic monastery

Fig. 2.6: (a) Fossil village Langza; (b) Fossils rocks

Fig. 2.7: (a, b, c, d) Sangam Parv celebrated at the Confluence of Chandra Bhaga River in Lahual & Spiti

Fig. 2.8: (a & b). Mud house architecture in Spiti Valley

CONCLUSION

Indigenous tourism has come a long way since it simply meant tourists coming to an area to watch at natives posing in traditional dress. There are a number of enterprises and opportunities that are coming up for the tourism development with the community. Above mentioned tourism destinations of the Lahaul and Spiti district has a vast potential to develop a tourism destination in the region. This traditional cultural and natural heritage of the region can be promoted as a primary attraction point for the visitors visiting the district. At the same time, its sustainability and conservation are the issue which needs to be taken care of while its promotion. Tourism in Lahaul and Spiti district is still in the nascent stage and it should be regulated in beginning to sustain its ecological and cultural values for long. Development and promotion of tourism activities in the region can be a good livelihood option for the locals, especially youth by creating awareness about their ancestral tradition and culture. In Lahaul and Spiti district, the tourist visits only in six months. After the opening of the Rohtang tunnel to the Lahaul and Spiti district, will boost the tourism activity in the region. This will help in the promotion of the winter tourism while enjoying various traditional fairs and festivals of the valley celebrated during winter.

Thus, Lahaul and Spiti have immense potential for cultural and natural tourism and this activity may be said to be one of the safest means of sustaining local and indigenous livelihoods, traditions and cultural heritage.

RECOMMENDATIONS

Tourism can be an important point of economy of any region because of the number of tourists visiting the region to spend some quality time with nature and learn about the culture of the community living in. At the same point, there can be some threats to the environmental and socio-cultural aspects of the region. Therefore, to minimize these threats several initiatives needs to be taken, which are as:

- Tourism training centres for the sensitization of the tourists visiting the area.
- Community museum needs to be developed with the repository of the collection of various aspects from the past.
- Capacity building of the community for the promotion of sustainable tourism while conserving natural and cultural heritage with maximum benefit to the locals.
- List of do's and don'ts to the tourists.
- Carrying capacity should be identified.
- Implementation of the ecotourism policy of Himachal Pradesh, 2017 in the developmental activities.
- Along with this, also use the ideas of native host communities and stakeholders for the sustainable tourism development.

REFERENCES

Agarwal, S., Bhatt, A., Kapoor, N., Moutinho, T., Van Herwarde, G., & Walker, K. (2013). Promoting Ecotourism in Himachal Pradesh.

Gillespie, D. (2000). Tourism in Kakadu National Park. In D. Wade-Marshall and P. Loveday (Eds.), (1998) Northern Australia: Progress and Prospects: Vol. 1: Contemporary Issues in Development, (pp. 224-250). Darwin: North Australia Research Unit.

Hinch, T., & Butler, R. (1996). Indigenous Tourism: A Common Ground for Discussion. In R. Butler & T. Hinch, (Eds.), Tourism and Indigenous Peoples, 3-21. London: International Thomson Business Press.

Jreat & Manoj. (2004). Tourism in Himachal Pradesh. New Delhi, India: Indus Publishing House.

Salerno, I. & Quarto, A. (2014) Rivista di ScienzedelTurismo. (pp. 69-71). LED EdizioniUniversitarie: Milano.

Singh, M. (2004). Management of State Tourism Development Corporations. New Delhi, India: Deep and Deep Publications.

Sood, V.K. (2000). Dynamics of Tourism Development and Aspects of Sustainability: A Case Study of Ladakh. Tourism Recreation Research, 25(3): 115-127.

Statistical Abstract of Himachal Pradesh 2015-16. Department of Economics and Statistics, Himachal Pradesh.

Stockton, E. (1995). The Aboriginal Gift, Spirituality for a Nation. Sydney: Millenium Books.

Sullivan, H. (2004). Visitors to Aboriginal Sites: Access, Control, and Management. Proceedings of the 2003 Ubirr workshop. Canberra, ANPWS.

Waitt, G. (1997). Selling Paradise and Adventure: Representations of the Landscape in the Tourist Advertising of Australia. Australian Geographic Studies, 35(1).

Zeppel, H. (1998b). Selling the Dreamtime: Aboriginal Culture in Australian Tourism. In D. Rowe & G. Lawrence (Eds.), Tourism, leisure, Sport, Critical Perspectives (pp. 23-38). Sydney: Hodder Headline.

Pages: 28-45

Rural Development and Techno-Innovations
Edited by: Dr. Alka Chauhan; Er. Chhavi Kumar 'Bharti' & Dr. Pawan Kumar 'Bharti'
ISBN: 978-93-88854-07-8
Edition: 2019
Published by: Discovery Publishing House Pvt. Ltd., New Delhi (India)

3

Problem and Prospectus of MGNREGP in Kerala

Dr. Lawrence Prabu C.
Dr. Esakkimuthu M*
Dr. Shilaja S

ABSTRACT

Poverty eradication is a long term goal of India. Since independence number of poverty alleviation programmes were launched. It would be incorrect to say that all the poverty alleviation programmes had shown the result much expected. In this way the ongoing programme the Mahatma Gandhi National Rural Employment Guarantee Programme is a flagship programme of Government of India. It is launched on February 2006 with the aim of enhancing livelihood security and poverty reduction.

Key words: Alleviation, eradication, flagship, Kerala, livelihood security, MGNREFP and Poverty

INTRODUCTION

In a rural agrarian labour and rural population depend on the wages they earn through unskilled, casual manual labour. They are vulnerable to the possibility of sinking from transient to chronic poverty in the event of inadequate labour demand or in the face of unpredictable crises that may be general in nature, like natural disasters or personal, like ill-health, all of which adversely impact their employment opportunities. In a context of poverty and unemployment, the intervention of wage employment programme in developed as well as developing countries is perceived as boon for unemployed rural poor. These programmes typically provide unskilled manual workers with short-term employment on public works such as irrigation, infrastructure, afforestation, soil conservation and road

Kerala Agricultural University, Vellayani, Kerala (India)

construction. The programmes provide income source to poor households during critical times and therefore enable consumption smoothing specially during slack agricultural seasons or years. In such a way that with the aim of providing an employment to needy poor, there are number of rural development programmes have been carved with the different objectives and dimensions among those "The Mahatma Gandhi National Rural Employment Guarantee Programme" is a flagship programme of government of India made a paradigm shift by providing hundred days guaranteed wage employment in a financial year to every households whose adult members are volunteer to do unskilled manual work. It is designed as a safety net to reduce migration in rural areas in the lean period.

Jobless growth is a joy less growth of any country especially developing and population rich country like India. At overall level the unemployment rate is estimated at 94, which imply that 9.4 per cent of the labour force is unemployed and looking for jobs. In absolute terms about 40 million persons are found unemployed and majority of the estimated unemployed persons (80 per cent) is in the rural sector at overall level (Ministry of Labour and Employment 2010). In the midst of unemployment and distress migration the happy bells started to jingle in rural areas when the Government of India announced that "You have the right" to get an employment for hundred days in a financial year through "Mahatma Gandhi National Rural Employment Guarantee Programme".

The Rural India constitutes 72 per cent of the total population of India and scattered in more than six lakh villages. It plays a major role in shaping the democratic India economically, socially and culturally. The majority of the rural population depends on agriculture as a source of livelihood, however increasing real estate business, shrinkage of paddy cultivation, mechanization interventions, natural disasters etc., adversely affect the employment opportunity of casual women and men labourers who depend on agriculture and displace them for searching other employment sources. Due to inadequate employment opportunity the rural people become vulnerable to the possibility of sinking from transient to chronic poverty.

The poverty eradication is a challenging task which is placed before India when it freed from British rule. It is said to be that India still having the world's largest number of poverty affected people. It has been estimated that 350-400 million are below poverty line, of which 75 per cent of them in rural areas. Poverty and unemployment is not a straightforward issue, requires to be addressed by targeted, time bounded and specifically designed law or policy or else it could lead to multidimensional poverty and distress migration of rural poor people from villages to city. In order to address this crucial issue, the Government of India has taken various experiments such as five year plans, poverty alleviation and developmental programmes for the last five decades. The emerging threat such as poverty, distress migration, unemployment, inequalities etc., emphasis and invite the era of rural development.

In the context of poverty and unemployment, generation of productive and gainful employment with decent working conditions through the wage employment programmes in developed and developing countries are perceived as a boon for the unemployed rural poor and also as crucial strategy for 'inclusive growth' as well as it is equally important to make the employment opportunities accessible to all, especially poor and weaker sections of the society.

Since Independence, number of rural development programmes were implemented by the Government of India with the different perspectives and goals. But all the programmes did not bring the expected result and also some of the sections especially women, unskilled casual labourers remain unaffected by those programmes. Among those, the "Mahatma Gandhi National Rural Employment Guarantee Programme" is the flagship programme of the Government of India. The programme was launched by the Prime Minister Dr. Manmohan Singh on 2nd February 2006 based on the Mahatma Gandhi National Rural Employment Guarantee Act 2005. The historic legislation was passed by the Government of India on 23rd August 2005 and it was promulgated on 7th September 2005. It was enacted by the parliament to address the crucial issues of unemployment and poverty in rural India.

The ultimate objective of the programme is to enhance the livelihood security in rural areas by providing at least hundred days guaranteed wage employment in every financial year to every household whose adult members volunteer to do unskilled manual work. The programme provides unskilled manual works with the short term employment on public works, such as irrigation infrastructure, soil conservation, afforestation, road construction and land development. In such a way the programme acts as an income source to poor households especially during slack agricultural seasons or years.

It is quite interesting to realize that, the beautiful words of Mahatma Gandhi that "any effort for the development of India as a whole, should start from the villages of India" and also the important fundamental rights of Indian constitution that "Right to Livelihood" and "equal pay for equal work for both men and women" were fulfilled in this programme.

The MGNREGP was launched in two hundred selected districts on 2nd February 2006 in Phase I and it was extended to 130 more districts in 2007-08 in Phase II. It was further extended to 285 districts from 1st April 2008 onwards, in Phase III. In Kerala, the programme was initiated in February 2006 in the rural areas of two districts viz., Palakkad and Wayanad.

The programme was extended to Kasaragod and Idukki districts by February 2007 and to the remaining districts by January 2009. The Government of Kerala issued detailed guidelines for implementing MGNREGP. The responsibility has been assigned primarily to Local-Self Governments. In Kerala, there are elected Village councils (Gram Panchayats) for an average population of thirty thousand. The agglomeration of a few neighbouring Grama Panchayats is called a Block Panchayat. For each revenue district, there is an elected district council (District Panchayat). Thus there is a three tier system of Local self governments in rural areas, each one with specific functions and responsibilities.

The genesis of the Mahatma Gandhi National Rural Employment Guarantee Act 2005 was passed by Parliament on 23rd August 2005 and it was promulgated on 7th September 2005. Based on the Act the Mahatma Gandhi National Rural Employment Guarantee Programme was ceremoniously launched by the Prime Minister, Dr Manmohan Singh on Feb 2, 2006. It was being implemented in a phased manner. As a first phase it covered 200 of the most backward districts of the country during 2006-07 and in an additional 130 districts have been covered during 2007-08 as second phase. The remaining districts are covered in third phase with the effect from April 2008. It has been envisaged under section-3 of the Act that the state government shall, in such rural areas in the state as may be notified by the Central Government, provide to every household whose adult members volunteer to do unskilled manual work, not less than one hundred days of such work in a financial year in accordance with the programme made under the Act.

The objectives of MGNREGP is to enhance the livelihood security in rural areas by providing at least hundred days of guaranteed wage employment in a financial year to every household whose adult members are volunteer to do unskilled manual work. The Secondary objective is the creation of durable community, social and economic assets and infrastructural development in rural areas.

The features of MGNREGP is provision of time bound wage employment; the act mandates 33 percent participation for women; strengthening of natural resource management through works; strengthening grassroots processes of democracy; wages are paid according to the minimum wages act 1948; infusing transparency and accountability in governance; wages should be paid through bank/post office account; generating employment opportunities in lean season; providing equal wages to both men and woman according to an equal remuneration act 1976; conducting periodical social audit by gram sabha members; dovetailing with other rural development programme.

FUNDING PATTERN AND FUND FLOW

The programme will be implemented as a centrally sponsored scheme on cost sharing basis between the Center and the State 90:10.The Central Government will bear the costs on the following items viz., total cost of wages of unskilled manual workers; seventy five percentage of the cost of material and wages of skilled and semi-skilled workers; administrative expenses as may be determined by the Central Government, which will include salary and allowances of the Programme Officer and his supporting staff and work site facilities; expenses of the National Employment Guarantee Council.

The State Government will bear the costs on the following items viz., twenty five percent of the cost of material and wages of skilled and semi-skilled workers; unemployment allowance payable in case the State Government cannot provide wage employment on time; administrative expenses of the State Employment Guarantee Council.

The Government of India will release its share of funds to District Programme Coordinator. Corresponding State Share to the District will be released by the Commissioner for Rural Development to the District Programme coordinator. The funds shall be utilized by the District Programme Coordinator, Block programme Officer, and the Panchayath Raj Institutions (PRIs) for the implementation of the scheme.

ORGANOGRAM OF MGNREGP

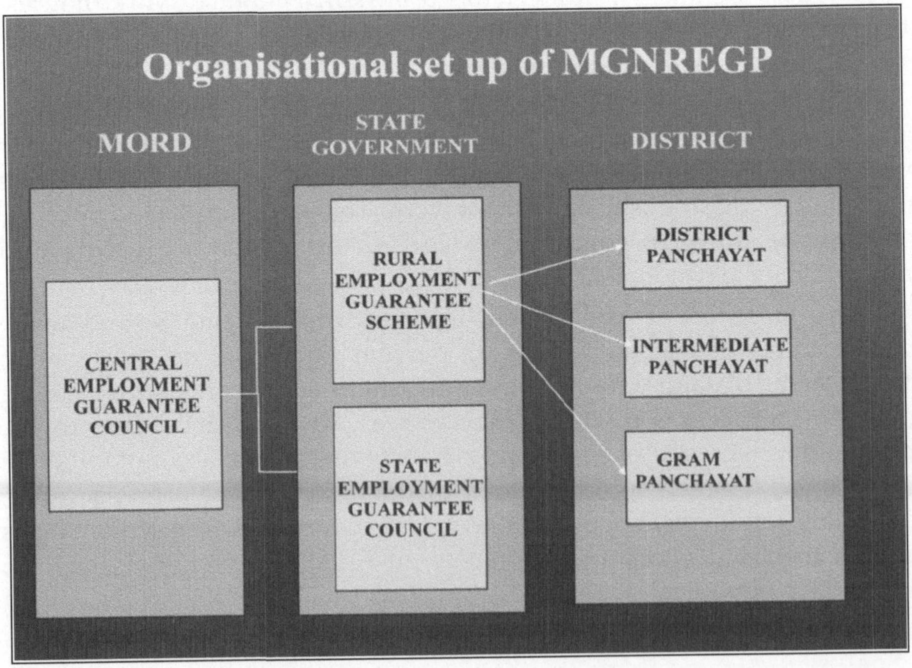

FUNCTIONS OF VARIOUS AGENCIES AT DIFFERENT LEVELS

Village Level

At this level Wage seekers are the main stakeholder of the Mahatma Gandhi National Rural Employment Guarantee Act 2005. The rights of the wage seekers as per the Act are, application for registration; obtaining job card; application for work; choice of time and work within fifteen days of the work applied; right to get unemployment allowance in case employment is not provided within fifteen days of submitting the application or form from the date of when work sought.

Gram Sabha Level

The gram sabha has been given following rights and responsibilities under the Act. It will recommend works to be taken up under MGNREGP. It will conduct social audits on implementation of the programme. In addition, it is suggested that the Garm Sabha be used extensively as a forum for sharing information about the programme.

Gram Panchayat Level

It is the pivotal body for the implementation of the programme at the village level. It responsible for the following activities viz., planning of work; receiving application for registration; verifying registration registering application; registering households; issuing job cards; receiving application for employment; issuing dated receipts; allotting employment within fifteen days from the date of application for job; executing works; maintaining records; convening the Gram Sabha for social auditing; monitoring and implementing work at the village level.

Block Level

It operates at intermediate Panchayat/block Panchayat level. It will be responsible for the consolidation of the Gram Panchayat plans at the block level in to a block plan and for monitoring and supervision. The programme officer essentially acts as a coordinator for MGNREGP at the block level. The chief responsibility of the programme officer is to ensure that anyone who applies for work gets employment within 15 days. A Programme Officer's other important functions are scrutinizing the annual development plan opposed by gram panchayat; consolidating all proposal of in to the block plan and submitting it to the intermediate panchayat; matching employment opportunities with the demand for work at the block level; monitoring and supervising implementation; disposal of the complaints; ensuring that social audits are conducted by the gram sabhas and following up on them; payment of employment allowance in case employment is not provided on time.

District Level

District Panchayat will be responsible for finalising the district plans and labour budget and for monitoring and supervising the Employment

Guarantee Programme in the District. The state government will designate a District Programme Coordinator, who can be either the Chief Executive Officer of the District Panchayat, or The District Collector, or any other District level officer of appropriate rank. The overall responsibility for ensuring that the programme is implemented according to the Act belongs to the District Programme Coordinator (DPC) at the District level. A District Programme Coordinator (DPC) will be responsible for information dissemination; consolidating Block Plans in to district plan; ensuring administrative and technical approvals, Muster Roll verification; submission of monthly progress report.

State Government Level

State Employment Guarantee Council (SEGC) is to be set up by every State Government under section 12 of MGNREGA. The State Employment Guarantee Council shall advise the state government on the implementation of the programme and evaluate and monitor it. Other roles of the State Employment Guarantee Council include deciding on the preferred works to be implemented under MGNREGP and recommending the proposals of works to be submitted to the Central Government under Schedule I Section 1 (ix) of the Act. The state Council will prepare an Annual Report on the implementation of the MGNREGS in the State to be presented to the State Legislature.

The state government will be responsible for wide communication of the Programme; setting up State Employment Guarantee Council; establishing State Employment Guarantee Fund; ensuring that the State share of the MGNREGP budget is released on time; delegation of financial and administrative powers to the District Programme Coordinator and the Programme Officer as is deemed necessary for the effective implementation of the Programme; establishing a network of professional agencies for technical support and for quality control measures; regular review, monitoring and evaluation of MGNREGP process and outcomes; ensuring accountability and transparency in the programme at levels.

Central Government Level

Central Employment Guarantee Council (CEGC) has been set up under the chairmanship of the Minister of Rural Development. The Central council is responsible for advising the Central Government on MGNREGP related matters and monitoring and implementation of the programme for submission to Parliament. Ministry of Rural Development (MORD) is the nodal ministry for the implementation of MGNREP. It is responsible for ensuring adequate resource support to the State and Central Council. It has to undertake regular review, monitoring and evaluation of processes and outcomes.

IMPLEMENTATION OF THE MGNREGP

The Mahatma Gandhi National Rural Employment Guarantee Pogramme was implemented in a phased manner as three phases during 2006 to 2008. At Phase I it was implemented in 200 of the most backward districts of the country during 2006-07. As a Phase II it was extended to an additional 130 districts during 2007-08. In Phase III the remaining districts were covered under the programme.

MODE OF IMPLEMENTATION AND IMPLEMENTING AGENCY

The sole responsibility of implementing the programme at grass root level done through Panchayat Raj Institutions. The Gram Panchayat is the single most important agency for executing works as the Act mandates earmarking a minimum of 50 per cent of the works in terms of costs to be executed by the Gram Panchayat. The other implementing agencies can be Intermediate and District Panchayat, line departments of the Governments, Cooperative Societies with a majority shareholding by the Central and State Governments, and reputed NGO,s having a proven track record of performance. Self-Help Groups, kudumbasree may also be considered as possible implementing Agencies.

KEY PROCESSES OF IMPLEMENTATION

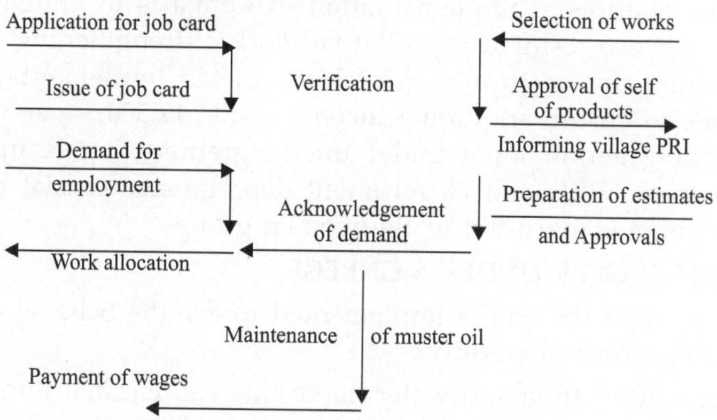

Stakeholders of MGNREGP

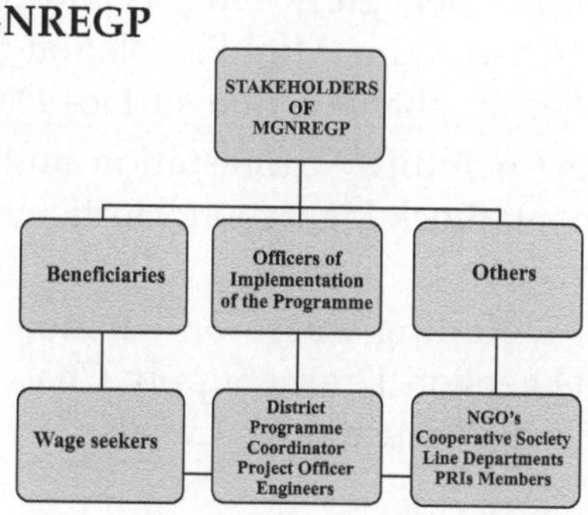

MGNREGP IN KERALA

Kerala has one of the highest unemployment rates in the country. But most of the unemployed are educated. Thus MGNREGP has only limited application in tackling the problem of unemployment among the poor of Kerala. Yet it has a niche ideal for about 4 to 5 lakh people who are willing to do physical labour and for whom an additional annual income of Rs. 12,500/- obtained from the Employment Guarantee Programme would be a substantial boost in income and purchasing power.

Implementation of MGNREGP in Kerala, programme is being implemented in phased manner. In first phase Palakkad and Wayanad districts were covered. In second phase in an additional two districts Idukki and Kasaragode were covered. As third phase it has extended to remaining districts Alappuzha, Ernakulam, Kannur, Kollam, Kottayam, Kozhikode, Malappuram, Pathanamthitta, Thiruvananthapuram, Thrissur.

Mode of implementation of programme is, Panchayati Raj Institutions given central role in implementation of Mahatma Gandhi National Rural Employment Guarantee Programme whereas the most radical feature of implementation of the programme in Kerala is the central role given to Kudumbashree mission to the effective implementation of the programme.

Special features of implementation in Kerala is to mitigate agrarian crisis through eco-restoration initiative works; strengthening Panchayati Raj Institution by the provision of lead role in implementation of the programme; to ensure additional income of Rs. 12,500/- per year to any family seeking employment under the programme; create new kind of relation between PRIs and Government departments; crucial roles under this programme is entrusted to the women groups.

PERMISSIBLE WORKS UNDER MGNREGP

The types of the works implemented under the Scheme shall be on the following order of priority:

1. Water conservation and water harvesting e.g. Earthen Bunding, Stone Bund, Continuous Contour Trench, Water Absorption Trench, Loose Boulder Structure, Earthen gully Plug, Gabions, Farm pond, sunken Pond, Check wall. Check dam, Mini Percolation tank, Percolation tank, Diversion Drain, Feeder channel, Sub surface Dam, Staggered Trench.
2. Drought proofing (including afforestation and tree plantation) e.g. Pasture Development, Block Plantation, Horticulture plantation, Barren Hill Plantation, Avenue Plantation.
3. Irrigation canals, including micro and minor irrigation works e.g. Feeder Channel, Diversion Drain, Supply Channel, Open wells, Field Channels, Main canal, Distributory Canals, Lift Irrigation.

4. Provision of irrigation facility to land owned by households belonging to the Scheduled Castes and Scheduled Tribes or to land of beneficiaries of land reforms or that of the beneficiaries of Indira Awas Yojana programme.
5. Renovation of traditional water bodies e.g. Desilting of tanks, Repairs to tanks, Rehabilitation of micro irrigation source.
6. Land development e.g. earthern Bunding, Stone Bund, Loose Bolder Structure, earthen gully plugging, Land leveling, stone terracing, Boulder removal, Pebble Bunding.
7. Flood control and protection works, including drainage in water-logged areas e.g. Drains in the open field, filling the low lying areas, revetment to bunds.
8. Rural connectivity to provide all-weather access. Roads can be taken up as last priority not exceeding 10% value of all types of works taken up.

PROBLEMS OF MGNREGP

There are number of the problems have been encountered by the various studies on Mahatma Gandhi National Rural Employment Guarantee Programme. They are given as follows;

Limited public land: There is more priority given to public land to undertake MGNREGP work than private land. In context of Kerala the public land limited, so it has been decided to take up eco-restoration works in degraded forest lands.

Identification work: It is well-nigh impossible to identify works especially in the coastal region and plantation areas under this programme. It has been decided to seek the expert support from Government of India to come out with a shelf of projects which can be taken up in such geographical areas.

Unemployment &Education: Kerala has one of the highest unemployment rates in the country. But most of the unemployed are educated. Thus the MGNREGP has limited application in tackling the problem of unemployment among the poor of Kerala. Yet it has a niche ideal for about 4to 5 lakh people who are willing to do physical labour work. Vijayanand and Jithendran,(2008).

Lack of technical staffs: Paucity of the technical staffs delay in wage payment and other MGNREGP activities. The majority cases of panchayats in Kerala have reported this kind of problems. Chathukulam and Gireesan, (2007), Vijayanand and Jithendran, (2008)

Publicity: As per the MGNREG Act the officers are asked to give sufficient publicity to the people about the works. But most of the government officers do not give publicity to the scheme as they want to show that labour is not easily available. (Vendan and Murugavel, 2010).

Durability of assets: More number of workers under this programme are belongs to semiskilled and unskilled category those people involving all types of work such as creation of irrigation canals, feeder channel, laying roads etc., which are needed skilled labour in this case it leads to less perfection on works which is created through this programme. Sharma, 2009 reported that roads built by the workers under MGNREG Programme is washed away during heavy downpour thus the entire programme has no lasting value other than providing employment.

Discrimination: There is degree of discrimination in allotting works under this programme. The study reported that favouring and discriminating against people in allotting type and location of work. Vendan and Murugavel, (2010).

Clashing with agricultural works: Vijayanand,(2008) reported that there is clashing with agricultural season during implementation of the programme.

Administration: There are much hand works such as clerical work, data entry, muster roll maintenance, preparation of annual plan etc., should be done by the administration it leads to the more consumption time and fund. Banerjee, (2009) reported that more funds are expending for administrative works and maintenance than scheme benefits.

Quality of works: There is much focus on quantum of works than quality of works which is created through this programme. A study reported that there is no much focus on guaranteeing a minimum quality of assets that are created through this Programme. (Vendan, and Murugavel, 2010). More emphasis on providing work opportunities to unskilled labour and no attempt is being made to upgrade the skill of labours. (Sharma, 2009)

PROSPECTS OF MGNREGP AND AGRICULTURE IN KERALA

There is greater emphasis given on natural resource management through eco-restoration work and also Government of Kerala is planning for spending more than 2/3rd of the investment in agriculture and allied sectors, 40 percent of Development Fund of PRIs (Rs. 627.31 Crores) to be earmarked for the productive sector.

Integration with other activities: A strong natural resource management focus has been given to MGNREGP. Bharathapuzha River rejuvenation with action plans emanating from the Village Panchayat as building blocks was taken up as a mega project under the scheme. Attempt is on to integrate MGNREGP and People's Plan.

Women Participation: There is enthusiastic women participation under this programme. The study reveals that Kerala stands leading in women involvement in various activities of the programme. It has been reported that MGNREGP has contributed very high level of women involvement nearly 80% of workers have been women. (Vijayanand and Jithendran, (2008). Among the fourteen districts of Kerala Thrissur stands first position in women participation with the average of 95.91 percentages. Thus the impressive participation of women under the programme is a harbinger of social change.

Women Empowerment: The MGNREGP has become a beacon of light in empowerment of rural women, and contributed substantially for the increased living and economic condition by generating employment and also proving equal wages to both male and female workers.(Ramesh, and Kumar,2009). The implementation of MGNREGP has contributed to very high levels of women empowerment, particularly in the following aspects viz., as the work is organized by women's groups, the gender perspective gets built in automatically; as women are comfortable working along with their neighbors, nearly 80% of the workers have been women. (Vijayanand and Jithendran, 2008); for the first time equal wages are really paid and this has boosted the earnings of women.

Kudumbasree and their involvement towards MGNREGP: Kudumbasree is given in the implementation of the programme. Under Kudumbasree every family below poverty line is organzied into a Neighbourhood Group (NHG) at the local level consisting of 15 to 40 families with each family being represented only by a woman. The NHGs are federated into an Area Development Society (ADS) at the level of the Ward of the Village Panchayat. The ADS in a Village Panchayat are federated into a registered body called the Community Development Society (CDS). Each NHG, ADS and CDS has five volunteers carrying out different functional roles.

Kudumbasree has been entrusted with the task of organising public works under MGNREGP are Muster Rolls and other records are maintained by the ADS, implements are provided to labourers by them and the transparency and monitoring requirements are also carried out by them. The welfare amenities to the workers are also provided by the ADS. Since ADS is an organization of the poor and is basically a woman's group, there has been greater sensitivity and community participation in the implementation process. The wages are paid into Bank accounts the habit of thrift which was already inculcated through the Kudumbashree experiment has further been strengthened. The Bank deposits are increasing, the intra-household status of the woman has also been improving commensurately as she controls substantial cash resources and withdrawal can be only on her decision.

Empowerment of PRIs: Panchayati Raj institutions especially Gram Panchayat is the most formal democratic institution under the directive principle of Indian constitution. The Mahatma Gandhi National Rural

Employment Guarantee programme empowers and strengthens the democratic decentralisation process at the grass root level by incorporating Gram Sabha and Panchayat in entire planning and decision making process viz., a lead role has been entrusted to PRIs in order for smooth implementation of the programme at grass root level. According to the MGNREG Act 2005 at least 50 percentage of the cost work should be allotted to Gram Panchayat.

Employment growth: With the inception of the programme there is more employment opportunities are generated in rural areas and also it arrests some sort of migration from rural areas to urban areas for seeking job. Kanmony, 2010 reported that India experiencing employment growth after the phase of jobless growth during 1990s only because of MGNREGP. The MGNREGP has suddenly increased purchasing power of poor and there is visible local economic development. Vijayanand and Jithendran, (2008).

Right to employment: This programme provides right based law that is getting employment opportunities under this programme is a right of an individual. Singh and Choudhary, (2008) opined that it provides Right to Work. But practically it is the manifestation of Right to Life.

Mobilisation of resources: The programme has become a significant vehicle for regeneration of India's depleting natural resource base. (Harza,2009). It also plays a vital role to mobilize and strengthened the untapped natural resources (physical, natural and human) for the development of village economy (Patel, 2006).

Livelihood security: This programme lays the foundation for the livelihood security through guaranteed augmented wage employment. Vijayanand and Jithendran, (2008) reported that there is increased purchasing power of poor and also there is visible local economic development.

MGNREGP: A PARADIGM SHIFT

There have been a series of wage Employment Programmes (WEPs) for the poor but the Mahatma Gandhi National Rural Employment Guarantee Programme represents a paradigm shift and it is different from earlier wage Employment Programmes in several aspects such as concept, planning and organization. (Vijayanand, S.M. 2008)

CONCEPT

Sl.No.	MGNREGP	WEPs
1.	Legal guarantee of right to employment	No grand vision, based on executive decisions and instruction
2.	No-exclusive and total coverage	Limited in coverage
3.	Self targeting	Patronage based
4.	Focus on employment	Focus on assets
5.	Focus on productive sector-for sustainable development	Focus on public work, predominantly in roads.
6.	Gender sensitive	Male dominated
7.	Central role for PRIs	Marginal role for PRIs

PLANNING

Long preparatory plan	Hurried quick-fix plans
Real planning from below covering who, what, where, when and how.	Hotch-potch list of workers
Integrated with varied development works	Limited to schematic works
Multidimensional action plans covering time, space, manpower and resources.	Two dimensional action plan covering resource and works

ORGANISATION

Panchayat central place	Middlemen-contractors central place
All activity done in house	Most of the activity carried out by the middlemen and contractors

NEW INITIATIVES

The right beginning of the political decision was taken to converging Anti-poverty sub plan with Mahatma Gandhi National Rural Employment Guarantee Programme. A convergent of Anti-Poverty Sub-Plan is to be prepared using the Kudumbashree network.

The components of the Anti-Poverty Sub-Plan would include:

MGNREGP - for wage employment

SGSY and Kudumbashree programmes – for skill development and self employment

SSA (Sarva Siksha Abyan)
NRHM (National Rural Health Mission)
ICDS (Integrated Child Development Programme) } for HRD

Annapoorna and Anthyodaya Anna Yojana for food security

IGNOAPS (Indira Gandhi National old Age Pension Scheme)
Health Insurance } Social security

IAY (Indira Awas Yojana)
People's Plan } Minimum needs infrastructure

NEED FOR THE HOUR

The MGNREGP is the first ever law internationally, that guarantees wage employment at an unprecedented scale. It is the flagship programme of the Government of India. It aims at enhancing livelihood security of households in rural areas of the country by providing hundred days wage employment in a financial year whose adult members volunteer to do unskilled manual work. Unemployment is a major problem in rural areas. This programme is to assess the performance of MGNREGP on employment generation, public and private asset creation and empowerment of rural people economically, politically and socially.

POLICY PRESCRIPTION FOR EFFECTIVE IMPLEMENTATION OF MGNREGP

The programme has important flaws, which need to be corrected to make it more efficient and fulfill the needs of the poor along with achievement of targets envisaged under the Mahatma Gandhi National Rural Employment Guarantee Act 2005.

1. Identification of works in public, private and government institute farms and prioritization of works. The works should be identified in public, private and government institute farms and prioritized based on the productivity and benefits to be gained by the rural people from the works.
2. A proper and more systematic work calendar should be prepared at Gram Panchayat level. The absence of the systematic work calendar can lead to clashes between agriculture and MGNREGP works thereby agricultural sectors could be adversely affected as well as results in people losing their livelihood either in agriculture or MGNREGP.
3. Proper training and technical support should be given to MGNREGP staff. Providing proper training and technical support to MGNREGP staff (Data Entry Operators, ADS member, Overseer etc.,) can help to avoid working mechanically and make them more voluntary in working, thereby work efficiency improved.
4. It is suggested to give wage details of beneficiary workers to bank in English. In this study 'delay in wage payment' was noticed as a major constraint, because the bank officials do not know Malayalam thereby further banking procedure for disbursing wages get delayed. If the wage details of beneficiary workers are given in English all the bank officials can understand, though they belong to other states.

5. MGNREGP cell should be strengthened by providing sufficient and well trained staff. The lack of sufficient and well trained staff at Gram Panchayat level affect the smooth implementation of programme at field level.
6. Proper computer and internet facility should be provided to MGNREGP cell at Gram Panchayat. Since in MGNREGP monitoring, recording, maintaining transparency and transferring all the details of the activities of this programme is through computerized manner, so there is necessary for the proper internet and server facility at the Gram Panchayat level for effective functioning and speeding communication with higher ups.
7. Grama Sabha meeting should be convened at right time. In MGNREGP Grama Sabha meeting is an important component and it plays crucial role in discussing various activities of this programme and also acts as a decision making unit, therefore the meeting of Grama Sabha should be informed to people through Grama panchayat notice board, Panchayat president and members thereby it become more participatory in nature and a good plat-form for decision making.
8. Vehicle or transport facility should be arranged to officers. Many of the worksites are in interior places of villages where there is lack of transport facility. If proper transport facility is arranged, it will be helpful for having frequent contact to worksite and good rapport with people thereby efficiency of works can be improved and also grievances heard in time.
9. MGNREGP should be integrated with some other scheme for which money is available at local level. It was perceived that, local body rely on only MGNREGP fund for all the developmental activities of rural areas rather than spending available money in their hand, therefore it is suggested that there is a need for integration of MGNREGP and other schemes of local body for up-lifting the rural areas as a whole.

There should be provision to upgrade the skill of workers. If there is provision under this mega programme for upgrading the skill of unskilled, semi-skilled labourers, this may help them to seek livelihood in other sectors where skilled labourers are required.

CONCLUSION

The programme provides right based employment and also creating rural assets in a sustainable manner. It enhances the livelihood security in rural areas by providing hundred days guaranteed wage employment. Majority of works are organised and done by the women group which leads to gender perspective gets built automatically. The provision of disbursing wages through bank inculcates the habit of thrift which in turn increases the household cash reserve. It act as a tool for efficient mobilization of physical, natural, human resources lead to the development of village economy. Even though there are some teething problems with the implementation of the programme it perceived as millennium development goal and also it is so clear that it strives hard to wipe out the tears of rural poor by means of generating employment opportunities. It makes difference in living standard of rural poor slowly and smoothly.

REFERENCES

Adhikari, A. and Bhatia, K. (2010): NREGA wage payments: Can we Bank on the Banks? *Econ. & Polit. Weekly*, XIV.(1): 37.

Banerjee, H. (2009): NREGA: A Case Study in Andaman & Nicobar Islands, *Kurukshetra*, 58(2): 27- 28.

Banerjee, K and Saha, P. (2010): The NREGA, The Maoists and the Developmental Woes of Indian States, *Econ & Polit. Weekly*, XLV.(28): 42-47.

Chathukulam, J and Greesan, K. (2007): Impact Assessment of NREGS in Kerala Evaluation of System and Processes, *The Gazette of India*, MoRD. 48: 174-176.

Devadas, R.P. (1999): Empowerment of Women through Self-help Group. An Indian Experience in Empowering Women: Key to World Development, *M.P Publication Ltd.*, New Delhi, pp: 22.

Dutta. S. (2009): NREGA in West Bengal: Success and Challenges, *Krukshetra*, 58(2): 31-33.

Economic Review. (2007): National Rural Employment Act. Government of Kerala - 2007, State Planning Board, Thiruvananthapuram, pp: 336-340.

Govind, B. (2010): Perambra Panchayat Innovated to Revive Paddy Farming, *The Hindu*, July 12, 2010, pp: 4.

Harza, A. (2009): Transforming Rural India, *Kurukshetra*, 58 (2): 7-10.

Kanmony, C.J. (2010): Livelihood for the Marginelised, *Yojana*, 54: 54-56.

Mallika,V. (2010): National Rural Employment Scheme: The Millennium Development Goal, *Kisan World*, (2): 45-46.

Maulick, B. (2009): Implications of NREGA- District Barabanki, Uttar pradesh: A Case Study, *Kurukshetra*, (2): 5-37.

Ministry of Rural Development. (2006): National Rural Employment Guarantee Act (NREGA) Report from the Field Study, Available at Online http//www.nrega.nic.in/best_pre_doc.pdf.

Ministry of Labour and Employment. (2010): Report on Employment and Unemployment Survey, Ministry of Labour and Employment, *Labour Bureau*, pp: 151.

Nair, K.N, Sreedharan,T.P and Anoopkumar, M. (2009): A Study of National Rural Employment Guarantee Programme in Three Gram Panchayats of Kasaragod District, Online at http//cds.edu.accessed on 2/10/09.

Patel, A. (2006): Role of PRI's in Implementing Rural Employment Guarantee Scheme, *Kurukshetra*, (12): 24-29.

Puri, M. (2006): The NREGA: Rural People to Grow with the Nation, *Kurukshetra*, (4): 17-19.

Ramesh, G and Krishnakumar,T. (2009): NREGA: Facet of Rural Women Empowerment, A Case Study in Karimnagar District in Andra Pradesh, *Kurukshetra*, 58(2): 29-30.

Rao, M. (2008): Employment Guarantee Scheme is a Lifeline for the Vulnerable Sections, *Kurukshetra*,(6): 46-48.

Roy, A and Dey, N. (2010): NREGA: Breaking New Ground, *The Hindu*, Jan.12, pp: 3.

Roy, S. (2009): NREGA: Impact on the Villager in Tripura- Field Study, *Krukshetra*, 58(2): 27-28.

Sankari,V. and Murugan, S.C. (2009): Impact in Udangudi Panchayat Union. Tamilnadu - A Case Study, *Krukshetra*, 58(2): 39-41.

Sharma, J. (2009): NREGA Potential and Challenges, *Krukshetra*, 58.(2): 3-6.

Singh, D.K. and Mishra, A. (2006): Backward Linkages of Rural Employment Guarantee Scheme, *Kurukshetra*, (8): 30-34.

Singh, J.N. and Mishra, A. (2006): Backward Linkages of Rural Employment Guarantee Scheme, *Krukshetra*,(8): 30-34.

Singh, R.P. (1998): Impact Assessment of WEPs (JRY & EAS) in Selected States of India, Online at http//www.nird.ap.nic.in/clic/resingh10-1998.html.

Srinivasan, G. (1992): Reforms Agenda for NREGS, *Krukshetra*, 58(3): 31-33.

Srivastava, N and Srivastava, R. (2010): Women, Work and Employment outcomes in Rural India, *Econ.& Polit. Weekly*, XLV(28): 49-60.

Subramanium,V. (2009): Social and Political Dividends from NREGA, *The Hindu*, Oct.19/ 2009, pp: 13.

Tomor, M.S. And Yadav, B.S. (2009): Need to Sharpen NREGA, *Krukshetra*, 58(2): 3-6.

Vendan, M. and Murugavel. (2009): NREGA – Driver of Rural Economy, *Krukshetra*, 58(2): 15-18.

Vendan, M. and Murugavel. (2010): NREGS: Key Issues, *Agrl. Finance*, 42(1): 26-29.

Vijayanand, S.M. and Jithendran, V.N. (2008): Implementation of NREGA- Experience of Kerala, *The Gazette of India*, MoRD, 48: 174-176.

Vijayanand,S.M. (2008): National Rural Employment Guarantee Scheme and Earlier Wage Employment Programmes – A Comparison, *The Gazette of India*, MoRD, 48:179-184.

Vijayanand, S.M. (2008): NREGA and Panchayati Raj Institutions Learning from Kerala, Online at http// www.crd.kerala.gov.in/pdfs/dec/nrg10_12_08.pdf.

Pages: 46-58

Rural Development and Techno-Innovations
Edited by: **Dr. Alka Chauhan; Er. Chhavi Kumar 'Bharti' & Dr. Pawan Kumar 'Bharti'**
ISBN: 978-93-88854-07-8
Edition: **2019**
Published by: **Discovery Publishing House Pvt. Ltd., New Delhi (India)**

4 Initiatives on Business Development in Fishery and Aquaculture Sectors and Seed Production of Indigenous Magur at Farmers' Field in West Bengal

Subrato Ghosh

ABSTRACT

There exist several opportunities in sustainable inland aquaculture in India. Fisheries and aquaculture are the two most profitable businesses in Andhra Pradesh, West Bengal and other states. Fishery scientists have stressed the need for strengthening entrepreneurship initiatives in aquaculture sector to improve the health of blue economy in the country. Small scale entrepreneurs, especially women SHGs can play an important role in boosting the domestic aquaculture production. Small-scale businesses in agriculture and aquaculture sectors can get benefit from modification of their business models based on best practice dissemination, which is developed by researchers based on case studies. In this communication, some steps have been presented, which have been taken to facilitate growth and development of aquaculture-based industry in India. ICAR has started a technology management and business incubation drive, intended for the Indian agricultural sector to promote agribusiness. An example of successful entrepreneurial venture on breeding and seed production of high-priced and cultivable freshwater catfish magur *Clarius batrachus* on a commercial scale has also been presented. Conversation was made with professional magur breeder Sri Dipankar Bera at his hatchery site to note his set-up and method of magur seed production.

INTRODUCTION

Aquaculture in India is a very important economic activity and booming sector with a wide range of emerging potential. An unparalleled average

Formerly Guest Lecturer, Master of Fishery Science Division, Utkal University, Bhubaneswar - 751 002 Odisha (India)

annual growth rate of over 4.5% over the years has placed India in the forefront of global fish production, only after China. In 2015-2016, total fish production in India was 10.79 million tonnes; our country is the second largest aquaculture producer (world share 46%), combing capture and culture fisheries and the third largest global fish producer (world share 46%). In 2016-2017, export of fish and fishery products from India had a worth of Rs 37,870 crore (US$ 5.78 billion) and the quantity was 11,34,948 tonnes. Appropriate technologies, financial investments and entrepreneurial enthusiasm primarily account for this situation. Indian aquaculture industry contributes to food and nutritional security and employment, supports livelihoods and raises the socio-economic status of poor fishing communities. Role of fisheries and aquaculture in increasing protein food supply and earning foreign exchange have been important – both are sunrise sectors in Indian economy. In 2009-2010, Indian seafood exports business crossed the $2-billion mark (US$ 2.1 billion) by exporting about 663,603 tonnes of seafood.

IMPORTANCE OF PUBLIC-PRIVATE PARTNERSHIP

In February 2013, a Seminar/Congress was organized at ICAR-Central Inland Fisheries Research Institute, Barrackpore, West Bengal (WB) on the public-private partnership (PPP) in aquaculture and culture-based fisheries. Delegates including researchers, private companies, NGOs, government agencies and other participants agreed that the integration and promotion of public private partnership mechanisms in government policy and programmes for aquaculture and culture-based fisheries is essential for the growth of the sector and calls on state/central governments to take concrete further steps to establish, accelerate and strengthen public-private partnerships for the benefits of all the stakeholders.

According to Prof. M.S. Swaminathan, renowned agriculture scientist and Former DG, ICAR: 'It is now time to explore a new approach to investing in aquaculture research and development, an approach which involves all types of financial capital - from philanthropic to public to private. Each can play an important role and through coordination and integration, different types of capital can work together to finance the sector to bring the desired result for aquaculture development in 21st century and beyond'. In crop sector, excellent partnerships exist between public and private sector institutions, especially in the seed industry. Such collaboration in fisheries and aquaculture sector needs to be encouraged by the Governments.

Amongst others, three recommendations of this programme at ICAR-CIFRI were: (a) Development of a deeper understanding among practitioners of the aquaculture R&D as well as of academia, of necessity, philosophy and ethics of transparent public-private partnerships for the accelerated development of the sector, through exposure to national and international best practices in PPPs in aquaculture and other food related sector; (b) Creation of an enabling environment including necessary incentives to encourage the Foreign Direct Investment (FDI), the entry of financial companies, insurance firms and partnerships between private companies, the government and communities in the construction of physical infrastructure essential for additional aquaculture resources, better water quality and ensuring ready access to quality fish seed, feed and breed, hi-tech facilities for product development, quality control, trading and marketing facilities; (c) Provide necessary backing and guarantees to financial institutions and private insurance firms to extend their services at reasonable market rates to small farmers, as well as medium and large-scale farmers in aquaculture and culture-based fisheries (Sinha *et al.*, 2013).

FISHERIES IN ANDHRA PRADESH AND WEST BENGAL

In recent years, there has been a significant expansion in commercial pond carp culture in India. While much of this development has focused on Andhra Pradesh (AP) and Punjab, there are other states such as Orissa, Karnataka, West Bengal and Tamil Nadu where commercial carp culture is gaining momentum. Aquaculture of Indian major carps, rohu (*Labeo rohita*), catla (*Catla catla*) and mrigal (*Cirrhinus mrigala*) has become an established and sustainable vocation in AP particularly in four districts Kolleru, Krishna, West Godavari, and Nellore. Kolleru and the surrounding districts of Krishna and West Godavari are the primary culture areas. In Nellore, Indian major carp culture is practiced at a lower intensity to that practiced in Kolleru. In East Godavari, Indian major carps are primarily cultured in polyculture systems with either black tiger shrimp (*Penaeus monodon*) or giant freshwater prawn (*Macrobrachium rosenbergii*).

In AP, pond culture was initiated in the Kolleru lake region in 1976. Initially, 133 fish ponds were constructed by the State Government. The initial successes that were achieved by a few private farmers encouraged large numbers of people in Krishna and West Godavari districts to take up commercial fish farming in and around Kolleru lake. By 1981, several fish farms ranging from 2-100ha were operating in the region. Most of the carp culture in AP is located in and around Kolleru Lake. By 1985, fish culture had expanded to other irrigated areas in Krishna and Godavari districts, and on a smaller scale to Nellore, Guntur, Prakasam and East Godavari districts. Kolleru Lake and the surrounding areas of West Godavari and Krishna districts are currently the centre of Indian major carp and striped catfish (*Pangasianodon hypophthalmus*) production. Much of the production is traded, mainly by road transport to 19 Indian states. During 2016-2017, inland fish production in AP and WB had been 2352000 tonnes and 1671000 tonnes respectively.

In AP, the semi-intensive carp culture system, popularly known as 'Kolleru carp culture', operates at production levels of between 7000 to 10000 kg/ha/year. In the Kolleru region, an estimated 700000 tonnes of carp is produced per year. The pond systems are based on two culture species, *viz.* rohu and catla. These fishes are stocked at ratios of 80 to 90 : 10 to 20 (rohu : catla) with the occasional addition of mrigal. The Kolleru carp culture system has become the dominant production model for Indian major carp culture. Important components and activities in Indian major carp culture in AP are the fish farmers, pond management, supplementary feeds, chemical fertilizers, organic manures, fish seed and yearling production, harvest, ice manufacture, packing materials, short and long distance transport and harvested table-size fishes.

Fisheries and aquaculture in WB are the two most profitable businesses. No other Indian state is topographically blessed with as diversified fishery resources as in WB. It is the only state in India where fish and shellfish are cultured in freshwater, brackishwater, sewage-fed water bodies and in coastal marine waters. The congenial climatic condition coupled with human resources traditionally rich in fishery knowledge has aided the state in securing the leading position in fish seed (hatchery-produced spawn and fry) production for several years. In addition to the conventional cultivable and economically-important fishes like Indian major carps, exotic carps, indigenous catfish Magur and giant freshwater prawn, thrust has been given in commercial seed production and culture of *Ompak pabda*, Vietnam koi, *Pangasius pangasius*, marine fishes *Rachycentron canadum* (cobia) and *Trachinotus blochii* (pompano), Amur carp, *Chanos chanos* (milkfish), *Litopenaeus vannamei* and others. In WB, 1.74 million tonnes of fish was produced in 2016-2017, which includes inland and marine fishes. In 2016, contribution of WB to country's fish production (inland and marine) had been 14.9%, of which, WB contributed 33.1% of country's inland fish production. WB ranks second in table size fish production in India, only after Andhra Pradesh. It is the gateway of seven north-eastern and three eastern states, thereby providing ample scope for business promotion.

INVESTMENT PROMOTION UNIT OF DEPARTMENT OF FISHERIES, WB

Under the recommendation of the task force and kind interest shown by Hon'ble Chief Minister, Department of Fisheries, Government of West Bengal started dialogue with the private investors and subsequently the Investment Promotion Unit (IPU) was set up under the Department of Fisheries, which is Mission Mode Project to facilitate growth and development of aquaculture-based industry in WB. The Business Portal of IPU is an exclusive portal that aims to cater to all business-related information needs of the end users. The content of the portal has been complied with objectives to render all relevant industry-related information to the prospective entrepreneurs. At IPU, the promotion of trade is an exacting mission, translating into a search for new frontiers and new horizons in the national of commercial interactions, both at macro and micro levels. Apart from organizing successful trade exhibitions in the state, IPU organizes buyer-seller meets promotion through department stores, contact promotion and product development programmes, disseminates information on products and markets. IPU aims to promote, encourage and endorse aquaculture business ventures in WB, facilitate private investors in fisheries sector, increase state's fish productivity through commercial venture (Source: http://coopwb.in/investment), aims to unlock Fisheries Investment Potentials and providing all out assistance to the investors for hassle-free investment.

The main activities and services of IPU are: (a) Organising various trade fairs and exhibitions for promotion of trade in fisheries and aquaculture; (b) Identifying and nurturing specific export products with long range growth prospects; (c) Cultivating overseas buyers through timely and efficient services; (d) Assisting companies in product development and adaptation to meet buyers requirements; (e) Organising 'Buyer-Seller Meets' and other exclusive shows in order to bring buyers and sellers together; (f) Arranging product displays; (g) Inviting buyers and organising the meetings with Indian suppliers; (h) Providing assistance in locating suitable collaborators for transfer of technology, joint ventures, marketing tie-ups and investment promotion; (i) Organising seminars/conferences/workshops; (j) Encouraging and involving small and medium scale units in export promotion efforts.

The Business Information Centre (BIC) of IPU focuses on: (a) Make information available in interactive mode; (b) Provide useful linkages to trade and trade-related institutions; (c) Provide access to current market information and specialized online data bases; (d) Ensure information is easily retrievable and deliverable online; (e) Identify global trading opportunities; (f) Facilitate use of existing data and ease of updating content by various users in multiple locations; (g) Support development of active information networks at regional and national level. The 'Business Portal of IPU' is a single window access to all possible business related information vital for an entrepreneur, particularly for those of small and medium firms. The information is provided in the form of a well-developed content framework supported by hyper links, online services, frequently asked questions, economic news and latest updates in the national and global business scenario. Thus, it provides an easy access to diverse aspects of business in a user-friendly manner. In a nutshell, the Business Portal of IPU endows the readers with a step-by-step guide for starting, developing and sustaining an aquaculture-based business in WB.

AGRI-BUSINESS INCUBATION CENTRE AT ICAR-CIFA, BHUBANESWAR

Incubator is an organization that 'seeks to give form and substance' – that is, structure and credibility – to start up emerging ventures. Consequently, a new business incubator is a facility for the maintenance of controlled conditions to assist in the cultivation of new companies. Commonly classified by ownership and capital sourcing, incubators may be: (a) public, (b) private, (c) academia/University. Entrepreneur (or the incubatees of business incubator) is an innovator who introduces new technological process or products. Entrepreneurs alter technological possibilities and alter convention through innovative activity. The gap between the present realities of agriculture and future vision is wide which calls for the reform, which would be much deeper than the present efforts being done. The reform that needs to involve from changing incentive structure of agriculture which emphasize on food production to income, from subsidy-based interventions to empowerment, from schemes of wealth transfer to investment, from inputs support to technology support. The central focus of such reform is entrepreneurship development in agriculture and agri-business. The entrepreneurs are the actors in the growing agri-business, which is more remunerative and profitable then agriculture practiced in a traditional way.

Starting in 2006, the advocacy and implementation of a national Intellectual Property and Technology Commercialization Policy through the Indian Council of Agricultural Research (ICAR), New Delhi has gradually led to the evolution of National Agriculture Research and Education System from a knowledge generator to a technology or demand-driven and market-led agricultural research and development system. This transition has been supported by funded programmes and projects leading to initialization of technology commercialization and agri-incubation processes across the country. These incubation centres are slowly emerging as vibrant hubs for technology transfer to industry and for attracting entrepreneurs into this sector. Under NAIF (National Agriculture Innovative Fund) programme, the 'incubation fund' has been earmarked to further strengthen and expand the agri-business incubators' network and address the critical gaps observed for successful commercialization of technologies through business incubation for making them an attractive proposition to any commercial entity.

Fisheries is one of the major research mandates of ICAR, where planning, promotion and coordination of research and education activities is executed through its eight fishery-related research institutes to fulfil its vision 'Fish for all'. Within agriculture, the growth of sectors like poultry and fisheries have been faster than the cereals like rice, wheat or pulse in last six decades. With the aim of utilizing the vast research and development facilities and knowledge available with its institutions, ICAR has started a technology management and business incubation drive, intended for the Indian agricultural sector to promote agribusiness. The Agri-Business incubation centre has been set up at ICAR-CIFA, Bhubaneswar, which is an ongoing Project of ICAR implemented at the institute that started in May 2016. ICAR-Central Institute of Freshwater Aquaculture is the premier research institute in India on freshwater fish and shellfish farming, which has the Mission: 'Excellence in research for developing sustainable and diversified freshwater aquaculture practices for enhanced productivity, quality, water use efficiency and farm income'. It conducts basic and strategic research for the development of sustainable culture systems for freshwater finfish and shellfish, and aims at diversification of culture practices. The role of business incubation and steps taken by Governments in developing start up policy are well-appreciated, where the budding entrepreneurs, start-ups will be encouraged. Agri-business Incubation Centre of ICAR-CIFA has expressed interest in technology transfer/commercialization on non-exclusive basis through industries/entrepreneurs in respect of certain technology/design developed by the institute (Source: http://www.cifa.nic.in/sites/default/files/Commercialisation of Technology.pdf). Scientists of the Institute had been 'inventor scientists' of the technologies.

BUSINESS INCUBATION CENTRE AT ICAR-CIFT, KOCHI

This was sanctioned at ICAR-CIFT under the NAIF scheme in January 2016. The Business Incubation Centre (BIC) under the Zonal Technology Management and Business Planning and Development platform at ICAR-Central Institute of Fisheries Technology, Kochi is a unique example of success for technology commercialization, which support operations on business projects as a measure of enhancing the foundation for new technology-based commercial enterprises and establishing a knowledge-based economy. It focuses on finding new ways of doing business in fisheries and allied agricultural fields by finding doors to unexplored markets. Agri Businesses Incubation Centres are envisaged to provide the necessary support for validation and up-scaling of technologies and encourage their reach to the user as an attractive business proposition. Such centres are expected to facilitate innovator and researchers to turn their ideas into commercial venture. The centre will focus on incubation and business development programme, including entrepreneurship skill development and Grassroot Innovators activities.

The ABI Centre at ICAR-CIFT focuses on finding new ways of doing business in fisheries by finding doors to unexplored markets. The Centre helps prospective entrepreneurs, by providing pro-active and value-added business support in terms of technical consultancy, infrastructure facility, experts' guidance and training to develop technology-based business ideas and establish sustainable enterprises. It acts as a platform for the speedy commercialization of the ICAR technologies, through an interfacing and networking mechanism between research institutions, industries and financial institutions.

CREDIT IN AQUACULTURE SECTOR AND IMPROVING FINANCIAL SERVICES

The lack of access to credit remains a problem for many small-scale enterprises. Those operating in the fisheries and aquaculture sector are no exception. Rural banks are perhaps the most likely institutions for microcredit start-up support to entrepreneurs wishing to develop fishery and aquaculture enterprises. Government-backed credit and risk guarantees for rural banks are important public interventions for rural microfinance initiatives. A good example of a PPP arrangement in financial services is the Global Commercial Microfinance Consortium, which promotes private sector investments in developing countries. The National Bank for Agriculture and Rural Development as a refinance agency for commercial banks, co-operative banks and regional rural banks, has been the major facilitator of credit to the fisheries sector. In view of the brackishwater shrimp culture boom in 1990s, many financial institutions like Industrial Finance Corporation of India, Industrial Development Bank of India, National Co-operative Development Corporation, State Finance Corporations have also entered into this sector to land credit. Credit support from financial institutes is available for almost all the activities of fisheries and aquaculture and for creation of infrastructure. As has been successfully demonstrated in Bangladesh and elsewhere, easy availability of credit motivates small farmers to take up new technologies and increase production. NGOs in some countries in the region have been playing a major role in bringing credit to the doorsteps of the needy rural population along with technology transfer, ensuring availability of needed inputs and assistance in marketing.

Aquaculture business may be started in the fields like freshwater aquaculture of economically-important finfishes (major carps, important catfishes, Tilapia, ornamental fishes) in ponds; aquaculture of commercially-important finfishes (sea bass, mullets) in brackishwater ponds; culture of economically-important marine finfishes (groupers, cobia) and molluscs (mussel, oyster) in controlled environment in coastal waters; culture of mud crabs in brackishwater ponds; setting up of large-scale and medium-scale seed production unit (hatchery) of major carps, catfishes and prawn; culture of freshwater prawn; freshwater pearl culture; culture of tiger shrimp in brackishwater ponds; preparation of fish meal as fish feed; pelleted feed production unit for finfishes and prawn/shrimp. Owners of fish farm must prepare a business plan for any aquaculture business before starting it commercially. The market has to be found out and marketing strategy to be fixed (to whom and where to sell the farm produce). Physico-chemical parameters of water and soil of fish culture ponds have to be considered and monitored by fish farmers. Breeding and rearing of ornamental aquarium fishes and seed production of catfish Magur in small land holdings has become successful small-scale aqua-business in India.

Seed Production of Catfish *Clarius batrachus*

Next to major carps, catfishes are considered to be potential cultivable species in India. According to a published article of fishery scientist Dr S. D. Tripathi, techniques of seed production have been standardized in *Clarius batrachus, Heteropneustes fossilis, Wallago attu* and other catfishes, which can be spawned even repeatedly at intervals of 30-40 days. The technology for breeding and seed production of *Ompak pabda* has been developed by scientists of ICAR-CIFA Kalyani RC. Among catfishes, indigenous magur *C. batrachus* is a highly preferred air-breathing fish, possesses medicinal value and fetches a higher market price than major carps. It can be grown in semi-clean small ponds of low water depth after necessary pre-stocking management measures, which involves low cost. Semi-derelict and seasonal village ponds of small size, unsuitable for major carp culture, can be utilized for farming of indigenous magur *Clarius batrachus*, a high-priced fish. Availability of good quality seed (fry/advanced fry) is the basic component and requisite of every successful magur culture programme. In this context, amongst few others, Sri Dipankar Bera at Ramganga GP under Patharpratima Block, South 24 Pgs, WB has taken initiative seriously since 2007. Conversation was made with professional magur breeder Sri Dipankar Bera on 21st and 22nd October, 2018 at his hatchery site to note his set-up and method of magur seed production.

For culture purposes, the potential to obtain *C. batrachus* seed from natural sources has become low due to increasing use of pesticides in the paddy fields which are its main breeding ground. Induced breeding is the only way to obtain quality seeds of economically-important catfishes throughout the year for pond culture. Culture practice of *C. batrachus* will flourish more and will have wider acceptance in rural sector of WB and other states if problems like inadequate supply of seed and proper feed are overcome. Office of the Joint Director of Fisheries (ME & MS Wing), Government of WB has furnished a list/database of 58 indigenous magur hatcheries in WB under private ownership (ten in South 24 Pgs district) which have obtained accreditation and seed certification from Department of Fisheries, GoWB. Recently Sri Dipankar Bera and Sri Animesh Das, Proprietors of Maa Durga Fishery and Hatchery have applied to Office of the ADF, South 24 Pgs on 16/11/2018 for seed certification.

MAGUR BREEDER SRI D. BERA

Sri Dipankar Bera, aged 40 is Proprietor of Maa Durga Fishery and Hatchery located at Vill. Debichak, P.O. Shibgobindapur, Ramganga GP under Patharpratima Block, Dist. South 24 Pgs, WB. Activities like grow-out culture of Jayanti Rohu, monosex Tilapia, culture of milkfish *Chanos chanos* and fattening of mud crab *Scylla serrata* in boxes (both on experimental basis), seed production and culture of bagrid catfish *Mystus gulio* have started here recently, but Sri Bera is doing seed production of *C. batrachus* on a mass scale in captivity since 2007. He obtained basic knowledge on *C. batrachus* seed production while working under Sri Milan Sinha, a renowned magur breeder and Proprietor of Bluetech Dynamics fish farm at Vill. Dakshin Bijaynagar, Joynagar-II Block, South 24 Pgs, WB for three consecutive years. In 2007, Sri Bera obtained 45-days training on fish breeding and culture from Vivekananda Institute of Biotechnology, South 24 Pgs. He also obtained one-week training from Freshwater Fisheries Research and Training Centre, Kalyani under GoWB in 2009 and four-days Block-level training on fisheries at Patharpratima Block in 2008. In the initial period, he visited *C. batrachus* hatcheries at Moyna Block in Purba Medinipur, at Budge Budge-II Block, at two places in North 24 Parganas district and at ICAR-CIFA Bhubaneswar (in 2017) to gain more theoretical and practical knowledge and skill on the subject.

MAGUR HATCHERY SET-UP

Total area of Maa Durga Fishery and Hatchery including ponds is 10 bigha (330 decimal). For magur, Sri Bera has three broodstock ponds of size 40 feet × 20 feet each; 10-15kg brooders of size 150-225gm (8-9 inches) are stocked and maintained in each pond, males and females kept separately. To prepare 1kg brooders' feed, he is using either soyabean dust or fish meal 300gm, mustard oil cake 200gm, wheat flour 200gm and a mixture of pulverized paddy grains and rice bran 300gm, fed @ 3-4% of body weight daily. Here *C. batrachus* breeding season continues from May to mid-September. He has constructed 5 indoor rectangular cement cisterns of size 10 feet × 3 feet × 2.5 feet, where magur brooders are temporarily stocked prior to induced breeding operation. Sri Bera uses Ova-FH or Ovaprim as inducing agent, stripping is done after 16-18 hours of injection. About 4000nos eggs obtained from a single female. Circular concrete cemented structures of 3 feet diameter with 6 inches water level are used as egg incubation-cum-hatching chambers. Sri Bera has four such structures, each costs Rs 500/-. He has observed hatching out of larvae from 24th-25th hour of egg fertilization. Fine meshed net with net frame is placed in the upper water column in egg incubation chambers so that sufficient water column exists between the net and the bottom of chamber. Fertilized eggs are placed over net. Hatchlings are kept here for 72 hours till yolk sac is observed.

Sri Bera has 25nos of rectangular glass aquaria of size 3 feet × 2 feet × 1 foot; each costs Rs 1500/-. For the first 22-26 days after absorption of yolk sac, *C. batrachus* larvae are reared in glass aquaria, 500-700 pieces in each aquarium. Boiled egg yolk, zooplankton *Daphnia* sp and *Moina* sp are fed to growing larvae in aquaria, chopped tubifex worm is used (15gm/glass tank) from 7th day in addition to zooplankton. It attains 24mm from an initial size of 5mm in aquaria. Faecal/waste matter is siphoned out and water exchange is done twice daily in every glass tank. After 26 days, the one-inch stage are stocked in outdoor earthen cisterns/ponds of size 40 feet × 20 feet (water level 1.5-2.0 feet), 5000 pieces in each and Sri Bera has constructed six such cisterns. Growing *C. batrachus* fry are fed a mixture of fish meal or soyabean meal, wheat flour, Vit-Mineral mixture, mustard oil cake and seven-seas cod liver oil in dough ball form during late evening @ 10% of body weight daily, 200gm each time in each earthen cistern in earthen bowls. These are reared for 35-40 days and attain 2.5-3.0 inches (6-8gm) advanced fry stage, which are sold by Sri Bera @ Rs 6/-/piece.

HIS OPINION

Sri Bera has opined that if farm-made supplementary fish feed (with 22% protein) is prepared either in pellet or dough ball form using wheat flour that costs Rs 8-10/-/kg, the feed will cost Rs 20/-/kg. Similar kind of commercial pelleted feed will cost Rs 30/-/kg. About 1.5-1.8kg feed is required to produce 1 kg table-sized fish; Rs 10/- may be saved in per kg produce. Hand pelletizer can be used to produce farm-made pelleted feed using meat meal (Rs 40/-/kg), wheat flour (Rs 8-10/-/kg), soyabean dust (Rs 40/-/kg), fish meal (Rs 30/-/kg) and pulverized paddy grains (Rs 10/-/kg). Mustard oil cake cannot be pulverized properly during rainy season, so it must be stored in pulverized form. During winter, its price is lessened as production becomes more. Sri Bera is using Pasupati Brand pelleted fish feed (22% protein); each 25kg sack costs Rs 700/-.

He stated that Patharpratima and Kakdwip Blocks are such places in WB where freshwater, brackishwater and marine resources are available, fish farmers can have provision of those. Different kinds of commercially-important inland fishes can be cultured in freshwater and brackishwater ponds. Many people from these regions go to distant places like Kolkata and Sealdah, stay for weeklong for a job of only Rs 6000/-/month, but they can gain more income from fish farming (Indian major carps, brackishwater finfishes, catfishes, crabs, giant prawn) in proper manner in 33 decimal water area, utilizing the resources. Sri Bera is planning for fattening of *S. serrata* in submerged-type boxes in shallow region near bank of local tidal river namely Borchura-Gobodia. Sri Bera has received technical guidance from scientists of ICAR-CIBA Kakdwip RC in breeding and seed production of *M. gulio* on a commercial scale. He has started it from 2016.

Kakdwip Research Centre of ICAR-CIBA has developed a complete package comprising of homestead/backyard hatchery technique and grow-out culture of *Mystus gulio* in brackishwater system (Source: www.uniindia.com). Dr P. K. Mukhopadhyay, Retd. Principal Scientist, ICAR-CIFA and scientists of ICAR-CIBA, Kakdwip have visited Maa Durga Fishery and Hatchery.

END NOTE

Sri Bera explained the concept of preparation of 'organic juice', which enhances zooplankton production in *C. batrachus* broodstock ponds and culture ponds. A mixture comprising pulverized paddy grains 7kg, yeast 500gm and date palm molasses 4kg is required for every single use in 33 decimal pond. About 4-5lit water is added to the mixture in a large earthen bowl and kept undisturbed for 72 hours in a covered state. The semi-thick liquid produced is applied in ponds once in every 15-20 days, that leads to zooplankton growth within three days. Expert magur breeder Sri Milan Sinha, who is also influential teacher of Sri Bera, has installed a flow-through system coupled with bio-filter, which helps to lower ammonia and nitrite concentration in larval rearing tanks below optimum level and maintain dissolved oxygen near to saturation. It resulted in better survivability along with optimum growth of *C. batrachus* larvae. In *C. batrachus* brood fish management, Sri Sinha has developed a modified practice of farm-made supplementary feed, which comprise soyabean whole 35%, fish meal 40%, soyabean oil cake 10%, groundnut oil cake 10%, rice polish 2%, fish oil 2%, Vitamin and minerals 1% fortified with trace elements like cobalt and phosphorus and used @ 3% of body weight three months prior from the breeding season. As larval feed, zooplankton *Brachionus* sp. and *Moina* sp., chopped tubifex filtered through nylon net, adequately washed in freshwater and disinfected with Dimethyldidecylammonium chloride, was used (Sinha *et al.*, 2014).

Attempt has been made to produce *C. batrachus* seeds using a low-cost village-level hatchery technique (Das, 2002). Participatory magur breeding technology (low-cost) developed by Dakshin Dinajpur Krishi Vigyan Kendra, WB is expected to open the vistas of income generation of rural youth as well as it may help to provide magur seed to the fish farmers to enable them to take magur culture as an alternative means of self employment (Source: http://www.ddkvk.in). Skilled and technologically-sound entrepreneurs like Sri Sinha, Sri Bera and others in WB have come up with new ideas in seed production of C. batrachus, that has high consumer preference, with modifications and improvement made over conventional method. It has led to production of healthy and high quality fry/advanced fry on a large scale in village conditions. This practice will definitely encourage economically-viable *C. batrachus* grow-out culture and production systems for livelihood and nutritional security. Government of

India has suggested that emerging areas like catfish culture be given the emphasis for diversification of culture practices including identifying catfish farming as a National priority.

Author with Sri Dipankar Bera

Egg incubation-cum-hatching chambers

Magur larval rearing tanks

Sri Bera applying fish feed in ponds

Photographs by: Subrato Ghosh

REFERENCES

Das, S.K. (2002): Seed Production of Magur using a Rural Model Portable Hatchery in Assam – A Farmer Proven Technology, *Aquaculture Asia, VII(2): 19-21.*

Sinha, M., Mahapatra, B.K., Saha, D. and Maitra, N.J. (2014): Mass Scale Seed Production of Magur, *Clarias batrachus* at Farm Level through Improvised Modifications, *Int. Jour. of Fisheries and Aquatic Studies*, 2(2): 210-214.

Sinha, V.R.P., Keshavanath, P., Sharma, A.P. and Mohanty, B.P. (2013): PAF Congress on Public Private Partnerships in Aquaculture and Culture-based Fisheries; Proceedings and Recommendations, *ICAR-CIFRI Publication*, Barrackpore, pp: 44.

Pages: 59-77

Rural Development and Techno-Innovations

Edited by: Dr. Alka Chauhan; Er. Chhavi Kumar 'Bharti' & Dr. Pawan Kumar 'Bharti'

ISBN: 978-93-88854-07-8

Edition: **2019**

Published by: **Discovery Publishing House Pvt. Ltd., New Delhi (India)**

5 Life Cycle Assessment for Leather Products using Software GABI 6.0

Dr. Ashok K. Rathoure

INTRODUCTION

The Earth is experiencing challenging situations due to the increasing greed and need of humanity. The actions of man have not only caused immense pollution but also degradedrich assets of environment. This resulted in some notable changes which in turn areaffecting back humans only and therefore this means that unfortunately we act both asproblem progenitors and victims.The environment is under increasing pressure from solid and liquid wastes emanating from the leather industry. These are inevitable by-products of the leather manufacturing process and cause significant pollution unless treated in some way prior to discharge.Tanning is the chemical process for treating animal skins to produce leather. The process for tanning leather was invented in 1858 at a manufacturing scale, but has been seen in history as early as 7000 B.C. There are many steps that are performed when tanning leather. In the course of our research, we reviewed books on this topic and watched videos of the tanning process. While older methods of tanning used vegetable tanning and mineral tanning systems, modern tanning methods involve the extensive use of chemicals.

The aim of LCA is to analyze and reduce the environmental impacts of leather products. In order to achieve the aim, the following objectives are set:

- Investigate what is currently happening during life cycle of the leather (materials used, manufacturing process, treatment and emissions).
- Carry out life cycle inventory based footprints.
- Investigate types of methods to reduce emissions.

Eco Chem Sales & Services New Civil Road, Surat (GJ), (India)

The expansive ecological evaluation that pinpoints the energy, materials and waste flows of a product, and their impact on the environment. The cradle to grave impacts includes the extraction of raw materials; the processing, manufacturing, and fabrication of the product; its distribution to the customer; utility; and the disposal or recovery of the product after use.

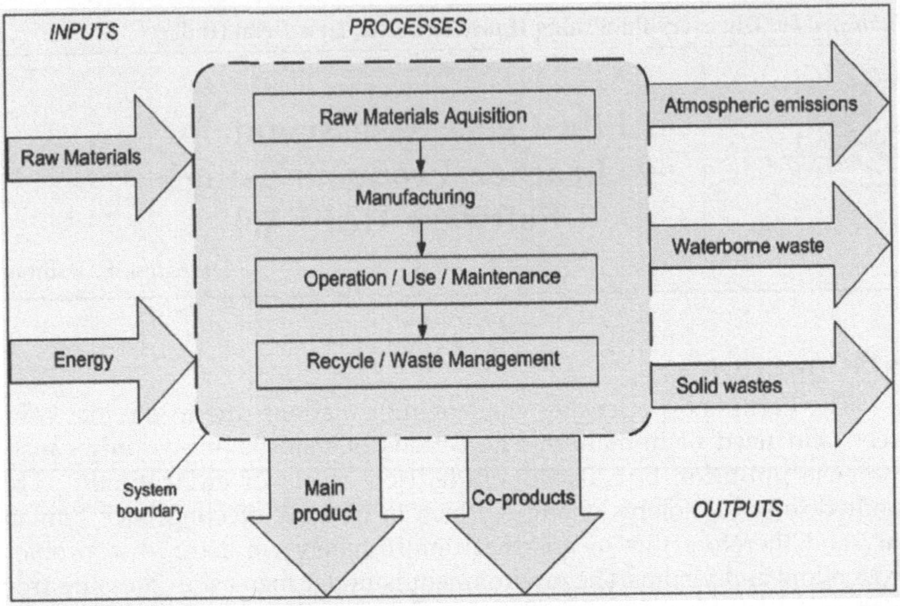

Fig. 5.1: Life Cycle Assessment

The shoe market is very big and complex. It is not easy for the consumer to know or estimate the true value of a product´s features and the environmental impact it has. The aim of this study is to analyze and improve a pair of leather shoes, including materials selection and end of life strategies to lower environmental pressure due to water and energy use and CO_2 equivalent emissions. Life Cycle based footprints for carbon dioxide equivalents; water and energy were calculated and related to a functional unit.The ever increasing attention to the environmental impact of the process industry imposes an obligation to constantly improve the global sustainability of the tanning process. Among the numerous phases of the tanning process, the beam house accounts for most of the total polluting charge, due to the use of sodium sulfide and lime during the manufacturing process of hides. Hence, the authors have recently developed an alternative unhairing process that eliminates the use of sulfides. The actual reduction of the environmental impact of this process, in relation with the traditional one, was evaluatedperforming. The leather industry generates large amounts of a Cr-containing solid waste (wet blue leather). This material is classified by the Brazilian Environmental Council as a category-one waste, requiring a special disposal. The patented process Br n. PI 001538 is a technique to remove chromium from wet blue leather, with the recovery of a solid collagenic material (collagen), containing high nitrogen levels. This work aimed to evaluate the residual effect of soil application of collagen on the production of dry matter, content and accumulation of N in common bean plants, after the previous growth of elephantgrass cv. napier, as well as to quantify the mineralization rate of N in the soil.

PATENTS ON LCA

Patent 1:

Title: Lifecycle product Analysis

Authors: Tao Wang, Sridhar Srinivasan, PiyushAgrawal

Patent number: US 20140279823 A1

A life-cycle environmental impact assessment method for a building, usingmain materials, according to one embodiment of the present invention, comprises the stepsof: extracting a main material inventory comprising materials of which the degree ofimpact on an environmental impact assessment of the building exceeds a predeterminedvalue, and cement having a relatively high greenhouse gas basic unit; calculating, on thebasis of the extracted main material inventory, a quantity associated with environmentalimpact assessment from the whole quantity inputted into the building; and conducting anenvironmental impact assessment with respect to multiple environmental impact categorieson the basis of the calculated quantity, through a database of environmental impactcharacterized according to building materials.

Patent 2:

Title: Method for assessing environmental impact of manufacture and disposal of product

Authors: Shigeyuki Miyamoto, RyosukeUgo

Patent number: US5652708A

Publication Year: 1997

Abstract: A system for conducting an LCA for a device includes a configuration engine that assists users to configure the scope of the device for the LCA study. The configuration engine is operably coupled to an LCA engine that is able to obtain information according to a standard of LCA for the device from the material content under the scope of the device for the LCA to compute one or more LCA measures for the device.

Moreover, the system also includes a server storage operably coupled to the LCA engine that stores the material content under the scope of the device for the LCA.

Tools and Methodology

'GaBi 6', developed by PE International, is used as the modeling software for LCA. The end outcome of the LCA will be a database and a set of models describing the inputs and outputs of the absolute product life cycle. Diverse processes or flows can be placed in the models to allow experimentation with diverse technologies and functional units. One of the complications in preparing the LCA model is to assure flexibility. This aspect has been kept in mind from early stage assuring that model can be used widely.LCA is an analytical approach that helps to calculate the harmfulness of the whole production process for environment and human life. There are various software products available for performing LCA like SimaPro 7.3.2, GaBi-6, etc. A parallel approach to LCA has emerged naming Well-To-Wheels (WTW) study. WTW are specific for transport application, unlike LCA, which can be applied to product system.

International Organization for Standardization

The International Organization for Standardization (ISO) within its series 14040 and 14044 gives appropriate direction for carrying out the Life Cycle Assessment. ISO is a universal private establishment which includes national bodies from industrialized as well as developing countries aiming to regulate and standardize different products and services. These ISO activities started in 1994 and aim to produce the first complete series of LCA standards. The 14040 series of ISO comprises LCA and hence it pertains both technical and organizational aspects.The organizational phase, apart from covering the subjects like stakeholders involvement, also primarily involves the formation of vital review methods keeping in mind the virtual allegations disclosed to the public. The LCA framework helps to get a profound knowledge of complicated issues and provides a reliable LCA procedure. Four general standards and technical reports have been generated by ISO under 14040 series (Environmental management - Life cycle assessment). ISO standards are given below in table 5.1.

Table 5.1: ISO Standards

Standard	Subject
ISO 14040	Principles and Framework
ISO 14041	Goal and Scope Definition and Inventory Analysis
ISO 14042	Life Cycle Impact Assessment
ISO 14043	Life Cycle Interpretation

ISO has played a key role in fetching together various schools of LCA, by involving conformity on every single point mentioned in above stated standards. The international standards and additional technical reports have also significantly improved the recognition of LCA as a prime tool for decision support by all government and non-government bodies. At last, it is expected that after the formation of the first full LCA series, a second, revised series will be accumulated, taking in account the new advancement in LCA methodology.

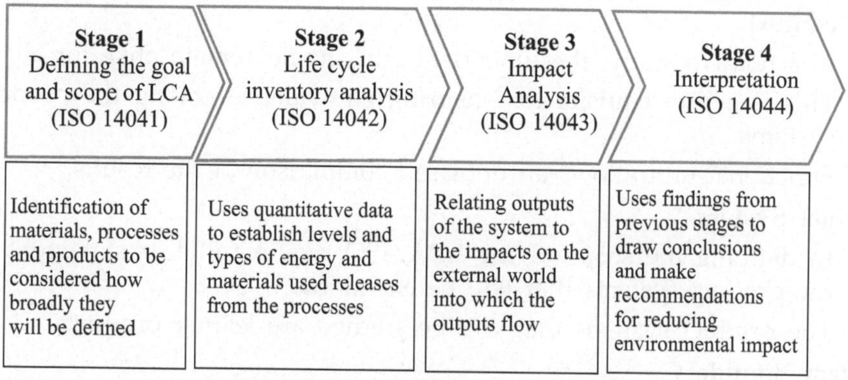

Fig. 5.2: ISO defined LCA stages

Life Cycle Assessment is conducted in four different phases as defined in ISO:

1. **Goal definition and scoping**: The purpose of LCA is identified, study of the products is conducted and boundaries are determined.
2. **Life-cycle inventory**: The energy and raw material inputs are quantified and LCA associated environmental releases are computed.
3. **Impact analysis**: The impacts on human health and environment are reviewed.
4. **Report Results**: The prospects to reduce energy, material inputs and environmental impacts are evaluated at each phase of product life cycle.

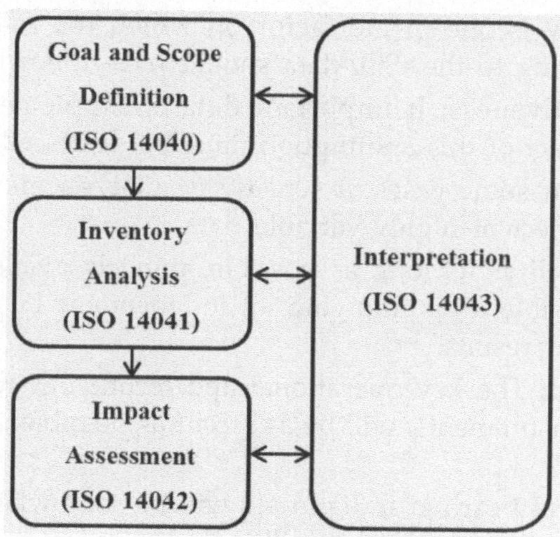

Fig. 5.3: Goal and Scope

Functional Unit

- The performance distinctiveness of the different processes of LCA can be examined by defining a unit, which scales the flows to a familiar context.
- In a relative study, the functional unit should remain alike for all.
- This is a pre-requisite for ensuring equivalence among the product systems.
- Functional unit allows an unbiased comparison of the results.

Product System

- In defining the scope of the LCA, ISO requires a clear statement of the product systems that will be examined.
- The product systems that will be studied are leather products.

System Boundary

The system boundary for LCA links the technological system and nature. Ideally, all the inputs and outputs which are fundamental to the function of a product should be followed upstream and downstream to flows of energy or matter; however the compilation of such a broad data set requires vast resources. The system boundaries are made to define the exterior interfaces of the product system. Hence, the prime motive for determining the system boundary must be to include in the system the activities relevant to the purpose of the study and is related to the goal definition. Defining the system boundary at an early stage prevents over allocation of resources to the areas that have an insignificant impact on the final results.

Data Quality

Data quality is one prime factor on which the reliability of study depends. According to the ISO, data should have following parameters:

Representativeness: If important data is supplemented from other sources, the impact of this assumption must be discussed properly

Accuracy: In some cases, a sensitivity analysis may be required to determine the effect of highly-variable data.

Reproducibility: As long as possible, publicly available data will be used where possible, thus allowing an independent LCA practitioner to reproduce similar results.

Age desired: The key operational and technology-related data, such as emissions measurements, will be as recent as possible, and typically less than 5 years old.

Geographical bearing: Indian data will be used wherever possible. If Indian data cannot be obtained it will be supplemented with international data.

Technology: The most recent available technological data will be used to determine LCA balance. Future technology developments will also be examined in the scenario analysis

Completeness: The data input to the study will be 100% complete

Uniformity: The same methodology must be applied to all components of data collection and analysis for consistent results.

Life Cycle Inventory

The quantification of inputs and outputs of a system, i.e. its material and energy flows, is called life cycle inventory (LCI). When the production processes of more than one product are analyzed, the problem of allocation is experienced in LCI. It is used to measure data and define the baseline metrics of life-cycle processes. The assemblage of the Life Cycle Inventory (LCI) is a massive task. It is highly data demanding. It requires very thorough study and enumeration of total energy and material flows for each part of the system to be examined and a systematic understanding of the critical parameters which can affect each process of system. Process flow diagrams are used to outline the relationships between unit processes and flows across the system boundaries. Each unit process must be qualitatively described to avoid any overlap.

Data Collection

Data is collected from various sources such as company publications, annual reports, articles, books, academic publications, and interviews with industry experts. Along with these, a variety of research papers are also studied for getting reliable data. In all cases references of chosen sources are listed and any data quality issues are noted. Existing data source must be used as long as possible. Calculation methods are used to correlate the raw data collected to the functional units within the models. All such calculations should use the same calculation technique.

Data Validation

The results of the Data Inventory compilation and calculations are checked using mass and energy balance. Any discrepancies must be addressed, and data gaps must be filled. This process is steady with the ever repeating nature of LCA, usually requiring a return to the data collection phase in an attempt to resolve the data gap.

Allocation

In an ideal LCA model, the inputs and outputs will be mathematically linked by a proportional linear relationship. However, this process is not as easy in real world and has multiple inputs and outputs, along with, a wide range of intermediate products as well. It would be incorrect to attribute all the environmental impacts of a complex process to the single output of interest for the current LCA. In such cases allocation is necessary to precisely relate the various data. Allocation is necessary to find a more appropriate scaling of the environmental impact for plastic and paper bag production, but the basis for allocation must also be decided. A mass basis would yield a different allocation than an energy basis, and in some cases an economical basis may be more appropriate. The ISO 14041 standard advises that allocation should be avoided wherever possible by dividing the process into sub-processes with elementary flows, or can be done by expanding the system boundary to go for the additional flows. In many cases, these approaches are not feasible asset as it greatly increases the data collection workload which tends to be beyond the scope of the project. Each approach must be carefully examined in allocation so as to finally determine the most suitable approach.

Life Cycle Impact Assessment

The key objective of LCA is to determine the outputs to the environment by studying the material and energy balance. Outputs with similar environmental impacts can be grouped and classified to cluster their environmental impact. This classification quantifies the potential environmental impact of the product system and simplifies the result to a single parameter, such that global warming, smog creation etc. The group classifications are referred to as Impact Categories, and the standard ISO 14042 sets out the guidelines for Life Cycle Impact Assessment (LCIA).

Classification

LCA is assigned to one or more impact categories for the output substances. Each impact category is an independent indicator, so that an output substance may be accounted for in several different impact categories.

Selection of Impact Categories

To select impact categories, goals and intended use of results are mandatory. As stated, if relative assertions from Life Cycle Impact Assessment (LCIA) are disclosed to the public, they should be accepted throughout the world impact categories, and be environmentally relevant to the spatial and temporal context. The overall energy demand of each product system will be evaluated as this can be directly related to the consumption of energy resources along with impact categories. Hence it can be seen that life cycle impact assessment basically transforms the life cycle inventory into the observed impact categories or end points which effectively gives detail about the human health and environmental effects.

Interpretation

This is the concluding phase of Life Cycle Assessment study, which evaluates the data collected and calculated. It provides opinion for changes to the other phases of LCA.

According to the ISO 14043 standard, the basic three elements must be satisfied in interpretation phase:

- Recognition of significant issues based on the results of the Life Cycle Inventory and Life Cycle Impact Assessment.
- Estimation which results in completeness followed by uniformity checks.
- Conclusions, recommendations and reporting.

The first element stated above, involves the findings obtained from the LCA which should be reported along with statements on data quality and uncertainty. The results drafted should reflect the prime motives which are defined in the goal and scope of the LCA study. Major issues can be drawn from the LCI for substances that are not listed in the impact categories. Essential contributions of the study such as energy production can also be reported as a significant finding.

The second factor comprises the evaluation element which is to increase assurance in the reliability. The techniques required for evaluation of completeness, sensitivity, and consistency is significant. Checking the completeness requires the LCA practitioner to evaluate the models so as to search for data gaps. Checks for sensitivity quantify how uncertainty in the data can influence the final results. A consistency checklist reviews that whether the constant application of the goal and scope, the product systems, data quality requirements, spatial/temporal considerations, allocation rules, and impact assessment methods are there or not.

The third and final part in interpretation is reporting, in which conclusions and suggestions for the target audience is taken care of. If the conclusions drawn are not consistent or reliable with the goal and scope of the study, additional study through the LCA phases will be required till the required consistency is achieved. Recommendations given must be based on the final conclusions of the study, and be valid to the intended application. The final report produced should be unbiased with transparent conversation of the assumptions and judgment decisions.

AEIOU Framework

This canvas sheet helps to interpret the observations by studying distinct components such as:

Activities: This heading includes all the project related activities that were carried out by us during this semester. Till now, we have done-

(a) Research

(b) Study

(c) Group Discussion

(d) Analysis v. Stipulation

(e) Brain Storming

(f) Project Report
(g) Presentation
(h) Project report
(i) Data collection

Environment: This component gives detail about the work background in which the project work is carried out. For our project research we worked in:

(a) Library
(b) College
(c) Computer Laboratory
(d) Cyber café
(e) Household

Interactions: This heading gives information about the class of people with whom communications regarding the project work are done. This helped to get a profound understanding as well as doubt clearance and hence a clear objective of project work is decided on its basis. We interacted with:

(a) Faculty
(b) Senior colleagues or student
(c) Technical Experts
(d) Environmental Engineers
(e) Supermarket manager
(f) Consumer
(g) Company manager

Objects: This comprises the stuff or items which are brought in use while doing our project work. We used:

(a) GaBi 6 Software
(b) Laptop
(c) Reference Books
(d) Review Papers

Users: This heading provides details about the field or area where the prime motive of our project work can be applied. Hence, this includes the chief consumers or people who can actually apply LCA in their day to day working. When arranged in descending hierarchy, our project can be used by:

(a) Leather industry
(b) Bag making industry
(c) Footwear making
(d) Supermarket
(e) Technical textile industry
(f) Household
(g) Shoes production industry like Bata

Empathy Canvas

Users

(a) Footwear Industry
(b) Supermarket
(c) Leather or Tanning Industry
(d) Technical Textile Industry

Stakeholders

(a) People
(b) LCA Consultant

Activities

(a) Research
(b) Patent search
(c) Data collection
(d) Analysis
(e) Presentation

Ideation Canvas

This is one kind of idea funnel canvas in which all the ideas related to the project work are compiled and stipulated. Following components are a part of ideation canvas:

People: This simply give details about different persons having different scope of knowledge, with which all the requisite discussions regarding the project work is done. We seek advice from-

(a) LCA Consultants
(b) Teachers
(c) Environmental Engineers
(d) GaBi 6 Users
(e) External Faculty
(f) Senior Students

Activities: All the tasks performed during the project research are included in this section of canvas. Hence, it comprises the entire activities carried out in project work. We performed:

(a) Research
(b) Data collection
(c) Study
(d) Analysis
(e) Group discussion
(f) Brain storming

(g) Project report
(h) Presentation

Situation/Context/Location: This comprises the prime areas where the project's main idea is applied or used. Our project mainly includes:

(a) Leather industry
(b) Malls
(c) Supermarkets
(d) Footwear industry
(e) Bag making industry

Props: This section of canvas is crucial because it clearly defines the possible solutions, which the project provides. A major question, How this project is salubrious? is answered in here. The potential solutions that our project research gives are-

(a) Pollution reduction
(b) Cost effective
(c) User-friendly
(d) Treatment efficiency
(e) Water conservation
(f) Energy conservation
(g) Product durability
(h) Proper knowledge
(i) Product design
(j) Environmental impact

Product Development Canvas

This canvas sheet provides us with the purpose of project along with views of customers when they experienced the product / idea developed in the project study. This has components such as:

Purpose: This section gives information regarding the key intentions of the project work. We are trying to achieve below stated purposes-

(a) Product durability
(b) Load reduction
(c) User-friendly
(d) Pollution reduction
(e) Product design
(f) Proper knowledge
(g) Water conservation
(h) Product design

People: This heading provide details about the group of people with whom, interaction is done so as to carry out the project related activities. We talked with:

(a) Environmental Engineers
(b) Teachers
(c) LCA Consultants
(d) GaBi 6 Users
(e) College Faculty
(f) Students

Product Experience: This section of canvas basically states the expected or predicted advantages after experiencing the product or implementing the core idea of the project work. Our project research includes product experience such as:

(a) Easier Selection
(b) User-friendly
(c) Comfort
(d) Availability of Data
(e) Reliable Information

Product Functions: It enlists all the tasks which were done during the project work. Hence, in other words, it gives us the idea about various functions which were performed during the research. We did functions like:

(a) Goal and Scope
(b) Enlist Energy Requirements
(c) Boundary determination
(d) Data Interpretation
(e) Result computation

Product Features: This column includes the fundamental features or factors which influenced the project research and hence helped to draw the observations efficiently. Our project has features such as:

(a) GaBi 6 Software
(b) Browsing
(c) Input Quantification
(d) Process Flowchart
(e) ISO Guidelines

Components: All the important apparatus which are used during the entire project study are included in this category of canvas. The major components for our project work are:

(a) Laptop
(b) GaBi 6 Software
(c) Review Papers
(d) Reference Books

Customer Revalidation: This section of canvas sheet is one of the important part which tells us about the reactions of customers when, experienced the project work. The communication with consumers gives us the reviews and hence helps in deciding whether the idea presented in project work is practically advantageous or not. We get diverse views like:

(a) Ease in Software Operation
(b) Dependable Study
(c) Insufficient Data Accuracy
(d) User Favorable

Reject, Redesign, Retain: This section converge the above cited categories and hence directly states whether the study rejects a prior art, redesigns it with improvement or retain it as it is giving a more reliable data followed by research. Our project is all about:

(a) Retain

IMPLEMENTATION

Leather products: Leather is a material that comes from the hide (skin) of an animal. The most common domestic animal sources are livestock animals, including cows, pigs, sheep, and goats. Exotic leather is formed from the hides of wild animals, including crocodiles and snakes. The use of leather for clothing and shelter dates back to prehistoric times. In modern times, leather is widely used for a variety of products, from clothes and shoes to car seats and furniture. The advocacy group People for the Ethical Treatment of Animals (PETA) launched a public campaign in 2012 to urge consumers not to purchase leather, and attempts to focus attention on the cruel treatment of animals farmed for their skins. Most leather comes from developing countries such as India and China, where animal welfare laws are either non-existent or not enforced (PETA).

Raw Materials

Worldwide leather production derives from the processing of mainly three animal typologies:

- Bovine
- sheep and Lambs
- Goats

Fat contents and hides are given in table 5.2 below.

Table 5.2: Fat content of animal hides/skins

Cattle hides	approx. 0.5 - 2%
Pig hides	approx. 5 - 30%
Goatskins	approx. 3 - 10%
Sheepskins	approx. 10 - 40%

FAO publishes yearly World statistical compendium for raw hides and skins leather and leather footwear with estimates on worldwide raw hides and skins production. Data covering last 20 years are represented in the following figure:

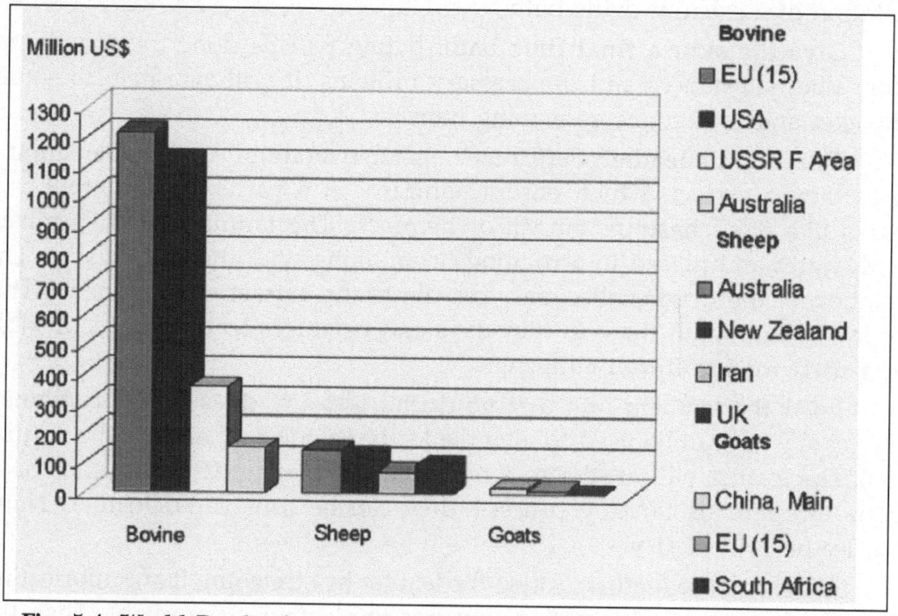

Fig. 5.4: World Production of Raw Hides and Skins (Bovine, Sheep, Goats)

Manufacturing Process:

(a) Prepping the hide
(b) Tanning the Leather
(c) Finishing the Leather

Prepping the Hide

Remove the Skin from the Flesh of an Animal

Skin the animal by setting it on its back, on an incline when possible. Use a good hunting knife for skinning, and a gut the animal.

Pull the Flesh off the Hide

Use a mechanical fleshing machine to remove the flesh from the inside of the skin. Running the inside of the skin over the steel roller of the machine will eliminate any excess flesh.

Salt the Skin

Apply salt to the skin or create brine and soak the skin. This will act as a preservative to keep the hide from decomposing. Fold the hide in a half so the flesh sides are together. Leave for 24 hr. scrap away any remaining salt and repeat.

Soak the Skin in Water

Soaking will help to remove any dirt or other materials from the skin. The longer the hide soaks, the easier it may make the hair removal process.

Remove the hair from the skin: This can be done chemically with a solution of a calcium oxide bath.

Give the skin a final lime bath: Bating will be done to remove any inter fiber substances and unnecessary proteins. It will also help to soften the skin and loosen any remaining hairs.

Tanning the leather: Perform a vegetable tanning. A vegetable tanning uses tannin extract, which occurs naturally in a variety of different tree barks like oak, chestnut, tanoak or hemlock. The tannin extract is mixed with water and placed in a rotating drum along with the animal skin. The rotation of the drum will evenly distribute the extract over the skin. This process takes about three to four days and produces leather that is flexible and used for furniture or luggage.

Load the leathers into a large drum.Add any dyes to the container. Dyes are what can be used to give the leather a color other than the natural look.The leather will need through rinse after tanning.After the skins have gone through the tanning process, they can be considered leather. Hang the leather out to dry.

Finishing the leather: Soften the leather by stretching it and lubricating it with natural oils. This process ensures the leather stays pliable.Then the leather can be buffed or polished.

Pollution: The production processes of leather a high environmental impact, most notably due to:

- The heavy use of chemicals in tanning process.
- Air pollution due to transformation process (hydrogen sulfide during de-hairingammonia during de-liming, solvent vapors).

One ton of hide or skin generally leads to the production of 20 to 80 m^3 of turbid and foul-smelling wastewater, including chromium levels of 100-400 mg/L, sulfide levels of 200-800 mg/L and high levels of fat and other solid wastes, as well as notable pathogen contamination. Pesticides are also often added for hide conservation during transport.

GaBi 6 SOFTWARE

GaBi is the next generation product sustainability solution with a powerful Life Cycle Assessment engine to support the following business applications:

- **Life Cycle Assessment**
- **Design for Environment:** developing products that meet environmental regulations.
- **Eco-efficiency:** reducing material, energy and resource use in the most cost-effective way.
- **Eco-design:** developing products with smaller environmental footprints such as fewer GHG emissions, reduced water consumption and waste.
- **Efficient value chains:** enhancing efficiency of value chains e.g. R&D, design, production, suppliers and distribution.
- **Life Cycle Costing:**

  Cost reduction: designing and optimizing products and processes for cost reduction.
- **Life Cycle Reporting:**

  Sustainable Product Marketing: product sustainability labels and claims, Environmental Product Declarations (EPDs).

  Sustainability Reporting: environmental communication and product sustainability reporting

LCA knowledge sharing: reporting and analysis for internal departments, management and supply chain.

- **Life Cycle Working Environment**

  Responsible manufacturing: developing manufacturing process that addresses social responsibilities.
- It also provides an easily accessible and constantly refreshed content database that details the costs, energy and environmental impact of sourcing and refining every raw material or processed component of a manufactured item. In addition, it looks at the impact on the environment presenting alternative options for manufacturing, distribution, recyclability, pollution and sustainability.

Life Cycle Assessments - Made Easy

GaBi makes it easy for businesses to carry out Life Cycle Assessments (LCA) in order to protect their most precious asset; their brand. It also enables them to deliver more sustainable yet cot efficient products that better satisfy consumer expectations.

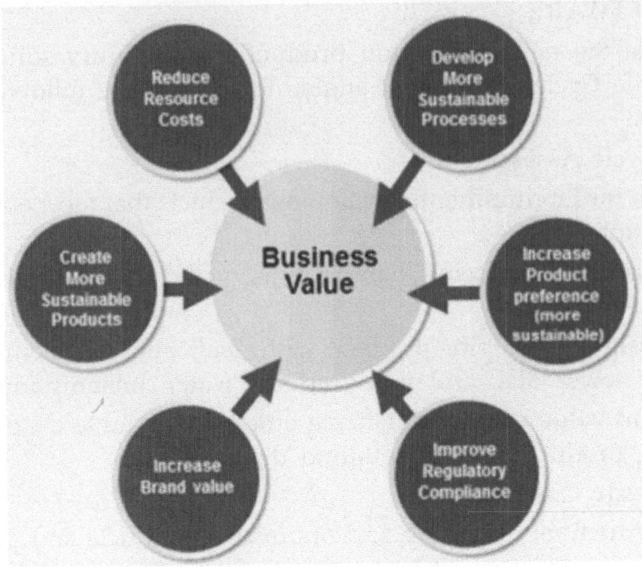

Fig. 5.5: GaBi 6 Software

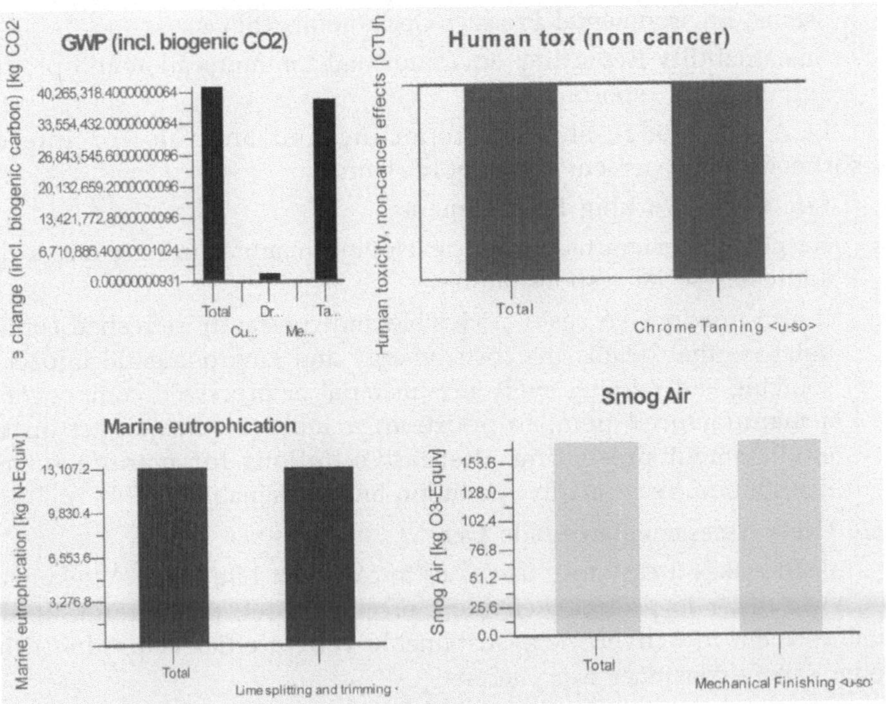

Fig. 5.6: Outpout of GaBi 6.0

CONCLUSION

Thistechnical review provides the information about the entire life cycle of plastic bags and paper bags. This information can be used for suggesting ways to reduce environmental impacts, identify improving opportunities for environment.One ton of hide or skin generally leads to the production of 20 to 80 m^3 of turbid and foul smelling wastewater, including chromium levels of 100-400 mg/L, sulfide levels of 200-800 mg/L and high levels of fat and other solid wastes, as well as notable pathogen contamination.

REFERENCES

Anonymous (2014). Leather - Design Life Cycle. Available online at http://www.designlife-cycle.com/leather/

Anonymous (2018). Life Cycle Assessment, Carbon Footprint in Leather Processing (Review of Methodologies and Recommendations for Harmonization) Online at http://leatherpanel.org/content/life-cycle-assessment-carbon-footprint-leather-processing-review-methodologies-and

Federico Brugnoli. (2012). Life Cycle Assessment - Carbon Footprint in Leather Processing, Eighteenth Session of the Leather and Leather Products Industry Panel Shanghai, China, 01 – 05 September 2012. Online at http://leatherpanel.org/sites/default/files/publications-attachments/lca_carbonfootprint_lpm2012.pdf

Kurian Joseph and N. Nithya (2009). Material Flows in the Life Cycle of Leather. Journal of Cleaner Production 17(7):676-682 DOI: 10.1016/j.jclepro.2008.11.018.

Kyle Albers, Peter Canepa, Jennifer Miller (2008). Analyzing the Environmental Impacts of Simple Shoes A Life Cycle Assessment of the Supply Chain and Evaluation of End-of-Life Management Options. Thesis of Master of Environmental Science and Management from the Donald Bren School of Environmental Science and Management, University of Santa Barbara, California. Online at https://www.bren.ucsb.edu/research/documents/SimpleShoesFinalReport.pdf

Lima D.Q., Oliveira L.C.A., Bastos A.R.R., Carvalho G.S., Marques J.G.S.M., Carvalho J.G., and de Souza G.A. (2010). Leather Industry Solid Waste as Nitrogen Source for Growth of Common Bean Plants. Applied and Environmental Soil Science. http://dx.doi.org/10.1155/2010/703842

Llorenç Milà, Xavier Domènech, Joan Rieradevall, Pere Fullana, Rita Puig (1998). Application of Life Cycle Assessment to Footwear. The International Journal of Life Cycle Assessment. 3(4): 200-208

Marcello Braglia.DomenicoCastiello, Monica Puccini, Sandra Vitolo, Francesco Zammori. (2009). Life Cycle Assessment (LCA) of the Oxidative Unhairing Process by Hydrogen Peroxide. Available online at http://www.polotecnologico.com/file/lca_tanningprocess_final.pdf

Notarnicola Bruno, Puig Rita, Raggi Andrea. (2011). LCA of Italian and Spanish Bovine Leather Production Systems. Afinidad -Barcelona- 68(553): 167-180.

Pages: 78-94

Rural Development and Techno-Innovations
Edited by: Dr. Alka Chauhan; Er. Chhavi Kumar 'Bharti' & Dr. Pawan Kumar 'Bharti'
ISBN: 978-93-88854-07-8
Edition: 2019
Published by: Discovery Publishing House Pvt. Ltd., New Delhi (India)

6

Sericulture

An Agrobased Industry for the Upliftment of Tribal People of Uttarakhand, India

Priyanka B.upadhyay[1]
Nitin H. Thodsare[2]
R.P. Srivastava[3]

ABSTRACT

The technique of silk production is known as sericulture. Silk is produced in more than 40 countries of the world, Asian countries contributing approximately 95% to the global silk production. India is the second largest producer of silk in the world after China and has the distinction of producing all the five types of silk namely mulberry, tropical tasar, oak tasar, eri and muga. Sericulture is an agro industry and is playing an important role in the economic development of silk rearing pockets of rural India. One hectare of mulberry plantations generates employment of about 12 man years and family members of all age groups can engage themselves in various sericulture activities, such as, cultivation of food plants (mulberry, castor etc.), silkworm rearing, egg production, silk reeling, weaving etc. Sericulture has an enormous potential in India provided the inputs are made available to rural people, especially women. Its marketing is organized by Central Silk Board/State Sericulture Departments/Co-operative Federations etc..In India, Uttarakhand is the only state which produces all the five varieties of silk. The total silk production (including vanya silk) in the state was 0.10 per cent of the national silk production during 2009-10. In Uttarakhand, out of 21MT of raw silk produced during

1 Doon (PG) College of Agriculture Science & Technology, Camp Road, Selaqui Dehradun - 248 011, Uttarakhand (India)
2 Regional Plant Quarantine Station, Haji Bunder Road, Sewri (East), Mumbai - 400 015 (India)
3 Bioactive Plant Natural Product Laboratory, Department of Entomology, College of Agriculture, G.B. Pant University of Agriculture & Technology, Pantnagar (U.S. Nagar) 263 145 Uttarakhand (India)

the year 2010-11, 20MT was mulberry, 0.1MT tasar and 0.5MT eri silk. Oak tasar is generally practised in the hilly areas viz. Nainital, Bageshwar, Almora, Pithoragarh, Garwhal, Uttarkashi and Rudraprayag and mulberry sericulture in Dehradun and Nainital districts. During the year 2012 employment generation through Swarn Jayanti Gramin Swarojgar Yojna in Nainital and Udham Singh Nagar districts was 6530 man days/year. In India, the employment generation in 2011-12 was raised to 7.56 million persons compared to 7.25 million persons in 2010-11, indicating a growth of 4.3 per cent.

INTRODUCTION

Sericulture is an agrobased, labour intensive, foreign exchange earning sector of Indian economy.It has been successful in eradication of poverty, resulting in social and as well as economic development especially in rural areas. It can be practised even with very low land holding requiring little capital investment. Sericulture is an integral par of tribal life practised by 1.5lakh tribal population in the states of Jharkhand, Chhattishgarh, Odhisa, Madhya Pradesh, Uttar Pradesh, West Bengal, Bihar, Maharastra and Andhra Pradesh. Sericulture provides tremendous oppurtinities to women in rural areas particularly in silkworm rearing and reeling activities with reference to income and about 60 per cent women are involved in sericulture related activities in India (Roy, 2012). Sericulture is practised round the year in southern and eastern parts of India with four to five crops a year. It is a powerful tool for rural employment, for example one hectare of mulberry can provide full time employment to about 16 persons and also furnishes export-earnings of about 300 crore per year.

SERICIGENOUS INSECT SPECIES

India occupies a unique position among the silk producing countries of the world by producing all the five commercially exploited silks namely (1) Mulberry silk produced by mulberry silk worm *Bombyx mori* Linn feeding exclusively on the mulberry leaves (*Morus* spp.) (2) Eri silk produced by *Samia Cynthia ricini* (= *Philosamia ricini* Hutt) feeding on the leaves of castor (*Ricinus communis*), Kessuru (*Heteropanax fragrans*) etc. (3) Indian tasar Silk/Tropical tasar silk produced by *Antheraea mylitta* Durry feeding on the leaves of Arjun (*Terminalia arjuna*) and Asan (*T.tomentosa*) (4) Oak tasar/Temperate tasar silkworm *A. proylei* J. feeding on the leaves of oak (*Quercus* sp.) and (5) Muga silkworm produced by *A.assamensis* (=*A.assama*) feeding on som (*Persea bombycina*) and saolu (*Litsea monopetala*) leaves.The mulberry silkworm is completely domesticated species.Tropical tasar, temperate tasar and muga silkworms are semidomesticated while eri is domesticated species.Tropical, temperate tasar, muga and eri silkworm are collectively called as "Vanya Silk".

Silkworm species, their food plants and distribution

Silkworm Species	Host Plants	Distribution Area
Mulberry silkworm, *Bombyx mori*	*Morus alba, M.indica, M.multicaulis, M. bombycis*	Karnataka, Andhra Pradesh, Uttar Pradesh, Uttarakhand, Himachal Pradesh, Kerela, Madhya Pradesh, Chhattisgarh, Odhisa, Jharkhand, Bihar, Jammu & Kashmir
Tropical Tasar silkworm, *Antheraea mylitta*	*Terminalia arjuna, T.tomentosa, Shorea robusta, Zizyphus jujube, Lagestroemia purviflora*	Jharkhand, Bihar, Chattisgarh, Madhya Pradesh, Odhisa, West Bengal, U.P, Andhra Pradesh, Maharastra and Karnataka
Oak Tasar silkworm, *Antheraea proylei*	*Quercus serrata, Q.incana, Q.himalayana, Q.leucotricophora, Q.semicarpifolia, Q.grifithi, Q.dealbata*	Arunachal Pradesh, Mizoram, Nagaland, Manipur, Assam, Meghalaya, Uttarakhand, Himachal Pradesh, Jammu & Kashmir
Eri silkworm, *Philosamia ricini*	*Ricinus communis, Manihot utilitissima, Evodea fragrance, Heteropanax fragrans*	Assam, Manipur, Bihar, Jharkhand, West Bengal, Andhra Pradesh, Odhisa
Muga silkworm, *Antheraea assamensis*	*Machilus bombycina, Litsea polyanthus, L.salicifolia*	Assam, Meghalaya, Borders of West Bengal

Source: Bhatia *et al.*, 2010

GLOBAL RAW SILK PRODUCTION

There are more than 40 countries practising sericulture in the world. The leading producers of raw silk are China, India, Uzbekistan, Thialand, Vietnam, Brazil etc. The total world raw silk production during 2011-12 was about 1,13,479 Metric Tons (MT). China leads with a total silk production of 1,40,000 MT (79.10%) while India with 23,060MT (17.54%) ranks second in global silk production.

Trends in World Raw Silk Production (MT)

Country	2006	2007	2008	2009	2010	2011
China	1,30,00	108, 420	98,620	104,000	115,000	104,000
India	18,475	18, 320	18,370	19690	20,410	23,060
Japan	150	105	95	90	53	44
Brazil	1,387	1,220	1.177	811	770	558
Korea	150	150	135	135	135	135
Uzbekistan	950	950	865	750	2,448	2,448
Thialand	1,080	760	1,100	665	655	655
Vietnam	750	750	680	550	550	550
Others	1,000	500	350	30	30	29
Total	153,942	131,175	121,392	140,051	140,051	131,479

Source: Central Silk Board, 2013

All the countries except China and India are witnessing a declining trend in raw silk production in the last two decades.

BRIEF OUTLOOK OF INDIAN AND CHINESE SERICULTURE INDUSTRY

China with 8,07, 053 ha of area under mulberry cultivation has a silk economy almost five times greater than India. The area under mulberry grew in China from 7,21,013ha in 2001 to 9,22,60 ha in 2007 but declined to 8,07,052 ha in 2010. The mulberry area in India declined from 2,32,076 ha in 2001-02 to 1,70,314 ha in 2010-2011due to urbanization and industrialization and increase in labour cost in the major cocoon producing areas of South India. China also experienced the same problem but with the efforts of the government sericulture developed rapidly and the cocoon output increased from 16.33% to 51.35% in 2010. As a result both mulberry area and cocoon production experienced a positive growth between 2001 and 2010.The cocoon production per 100dfls was 78.21 kg in 2010 in China which was much higher than that of India (55.23Kg).The dfl consumption/ ha and cocoon productivity in India were higher than those in China in recent years due to predominant production in tropical and sub tropical climatic conditions of India. The profit earned by Indian farmers in cocoon production was higher than Chinese farmers for most of the years. However, both the countries experienced positive growth rate in cocoon production due to technology development (Kumaresan, 2013).

INDIAN SERICULTURE INDUSTRY AT A GLANCE

India is the second largest producer and largest consumer of raw silk in the world. Currently, the demand of raw silk in the country is about 29, 000MT of which 23060 MT(2011-12) is produced in the country and the rest about 6000MT is imported from China. Sericulture has better prospects for growth in developing countries rather than in the advanced countries thus India has tremendous opportunities in increasing mulberry silk production in its tropical belt i.e Karnataka, Andhra Pradesh and Tamil Nadu.

Mulberry sericulture dominates in India and is practised as a full time avocation in Karnataka, Andhra Pradesh, Tamil Nadu and West Bengal and as a seasonal activity in Jammu & Kashmir, Uttarakhand, etc. where it is restricted to one or few seasons. Karnataka is the largest producer of mulberry silk followed by Andhra Pradesh. Production of raw silk was 23,060 MT in 2011-12, of which, mulberry silk output aggregated to 18,272 (79.24%). The remaining 4, 788MT (20.76%) was vanya silk. An increase of 25% was recorded at the end of the XI five year`plan and the employment rate also increased from 6 million persons to 7.5 million persons during this period.

Raw Silk Production in India

Year	Mulberry Raw Silk Production (MT)	Vanya Raw Silk Production (MT)	Total Raw Silk Production (MT)
2007-2008	16245	2075	18320
2008-2009	15610	2760	18370
2009-2010	16322	3368	19690
2010-2011	16360	4050	20410
2011-2012	18272	4788	23060
2012-2013	18755	4924	23679

Source: Central Silk Board, 2013

Schemes/Initiatives by Government to Promote Sericulture Industry

- To promote silk industry, the Indian government has approved the continuation of Catalytic Development Programme (CDP) in the XII plan period (2012-2017).The scheme will generate direct and indirect employment for 9.24 million people by 2017.
- An outlay of RS. 899 crore has been earmarked for central, state and beneficiary in special states status such as North East states as well as Jammu& Kashmir, Himachal Pradesh, Uttarakhand, Chhattisgarh and Jharkhand.

- The core objective of the scheme is to scale up production particularly production of quality, bivoltine and improved cross-breed silk cocoons in the country through cluster approach.
- The government targets to achieve 39% growth in silk and a special initiative involving flexi funds have also been proposed implementing sericultural projects.
- The government has enhanced the basic custom duty on import of raw silk from 5 to 15%. This enhancement will definitely attract the farmers to take up sericulture on a large scale across the country.
- The Central Silk Board (CSB) has proposed to increase the raw silk production from 23,060MT to 32, 000MT by the end of XII five year plan period, out of which 5,000MT will be bivoltine raw silk and 9,000MT will be vanya silk. It is proposed to increase the employment generation level from 75lakh persons to 92.42 lakh persons.
- Silk Mark Organization of India (SMOI): The silk mark scheme, a quality assurance label was introduced in 2004 by SMOI to protect the interests of consumers, manufacturers and traders who deal in pure silk. It also aims generic promotion of silk industry which faces stiff challenge from other fibres.

MULBERRY SERICULTURE

It is practically classified into three components (1) Cultivation of host plant (Moriculture) (2) Rearing of silkworms (3) Post cocoon technology. Mulberry is a fast growing deciduous plant occurring in tropical, sub-tropical and temperate regions.Its adaptability under various climatic conditions is a distinct advantage for developing mulberry sericulture in different parts of the country (Srivastava, 2005).

MULBERRY VARIETIES

The CSB has authorized mulberry varieties Victory-1 (V1) and Anantha for south zone and Vishala for all over the country during the XI five year plan. Other important hybrid varieties of mulberry include Mysore local, Kanava-2, S-13, S-34, S-36, S-54, Vishwa etc.

SILKWORM HYBRIDS

A detailed list of bivoltine, multivoltine x bivoltine and multivoltine hybrids authorized by CSB during XI plan and their cocoon yield potential have been presented

(A) Bivoltine

Hybrid	States/Zones/Regions	Yield/100dfls(kg)
Dun17×Dun18	HP, Karnataka, West Bengal (hills), Assam	68-70
CSR46×CSR47	Uttarakhand, HP, UP, Karnataka, AP, TN, Orissa, WB (hills), Assam, Mizoram	65-70

(Contd...)

Gen3×Gen2	AP, TN, WB (hills), Assam, Kashmir valley	65-70
SLD4×SLD8	Karnataka, AP,TN hills, West Bengal hills, Assam, Mizoram, Kashmir valley	65-70
APS45×APS12	TN hills, Jammu region	64-70
APS105×APS126	AP, TN hills, WB hills	60-70
KSO1×NP4	Karnataka, HP,Jammu region	60-70
NK2×NP4	Assam, Jammu region	60-70

(B) Multi x Bivoltine

Hybrid	States/Zones/Regions	Yield/100dfls(kg)
PM×CSR2(SL)	UP, AP, Karnataka, TN (plains)WB (plains), Assam, Jharkhand, Manipur	55-60
Mcon1×Bcon4	Karnataka, AP, WB (plains), TN(plains), Jharkhand	45
Mcon4×Bcon4	WB(plains), Orrisa, Jharkhand, Assam	50
APN3×APS12	UP, Karnataka, WB, Jharkhand	66-70
APM2×APDR105	UP, Karnataka, WB, Jharkhand	66-70
APDR15×APDR115	Karnataka, WB plains, Jharkhand	60-65
MH1×CSR2	UP, Karnataka,AP, TN (plains), WB, Orrisa, Assam	60-65

(C) Multivoltine

Hybrid	States/Zones/Regions	Yield/100dfls(kg)
Mcon1×Mcon4	AP, Karnataka, TN, WB	35-40
N×Mcon4	AP, TN (plains), WB	35-40
PM×C110	WB	40-45

Source: (CSB, 2013)

BY-PRODUCTS OF MULBERRY SERICULTURE

In sericulture, nothing is wasted. Every part of mulberry plant from root to fruit is utilized. The silkworms, their pupae and silk waste are as important as mulberry plants and silk in generating value added products.

CLASSIFICATION OF BY-PRODUCTS IN MULBERRY SERICULTURE

- **Mulberry plant:**
  - **Twigs/stem/shoots**: They are used in wound healing, as dermal ointment, manufacture of fibre board, sports, ornaments and in furniture industry, fuel, artificial cotton, substratum for mushroom cultivation, degradable plastics, natural colouring etc. Recently carboxy methyl cellulose have been extracted from mulberry stem which is finding wide use in detergents and cosmetics.
  - **Leaves/ unused leaves:** Utilized as fodder for poultry, fishes and also fed to cattle to increase milk production, artificial diet for silkworm, herbal organic tea called as "Kuwacha" is also prepared from leaves.

- **Roots:** Roots are antihelmintic, used for the production of anti AIDS drugs.
- **Bark:** Bark is used for the manufacture of paper
- **Diseased old plants/weeds/intercrops:** Production of biogas, biofuels: Mulberry crop residues (approax. 2500kg/ha/annum, calorific value 46,000cal/g) are good source of fuel wood, almost parallel to *Eucalyptus* and *Arjuna* in calorific value, better than other agricultural crop residues viz. cotton, bajara sticks. It reduces dependence on forest tree for fire wood. The crop residues are also utilized for producing vermi compost fertilizers.
- **Fruits:** Used in the preparation of jam, jelly, juice etc., reduces high fever, endemic malaria, prevents diarrhoea and cold. Wine made from fruits is helpful in the treatment of cancer, arthritis, urinary disorders, lower cholesterol and have antioxidant property.

Mulberry plant is further utilized in pharmaceuticals, detergents, leather industry, starch processing industry, biosensor research, textile processing industry, biotransformation and phytoremediation. The use of high protein mulberry tree fodder should be encouraged to provide supplementation of crop residues and natural pastures thereby increasing productivity and overall use of available on-farm biomass (Ramesh *et al.*, 2003).

– **Silkworm**

(i) Silkworm as food:

- The larvae and pupae are rich in proteins. Healthy larvae are sterlized, vacuum dried and sold as commercial food in China, Korea and Japan. Vitamin E and K are extracted from phytol, a compound present in silkworm faeces.
- In powder form, the pupae are used as a common source of animal protein in soups and sauce preparations. They are also used as food additives for chicken, fishes, and pigs. Pelade layer obtained from reeled cocoons is easily digestible and forms a valuable ingredient of food.
- Eri silkworm pupae are a great source of nutrition for the tribal people in North East India. They contain high amount of proteins (55-60%), total lipids (26%) and free amino acids (5-8%). One hundred grams of dried pupae provide 75% of the average individuals daily protein requirement. The pupae contain high amount of lipids and unsaturated fatty acids than common animal protein.

(ii) Silkworm in medicine

- Moth wine prepared from adult silkworms is used to cure ailments and also revert from trauma.
- A medicine named "Guanxuebao" developed from silkworm excreta is effective against cancer. Chlorophyll, pectin, phytol, tricontanal etc. extracted from silkworm faeces is used to treat hepatitis, pancreatitis, nephritis, stomach and gastric disorders.
- Silk threads obtained from silkworms are used in surgical and ophthalmologic operations due to its fine structure, soft fibres, good tensile strength, easy to tie and difficult to untie. It is used in the preparation of anti-hay fever masks, gauze pads and bandages for dermatological disorders.
- Silk is used as artificial skin due to its wound healing properties.
- *B.mori* is used as a bioreactor in the production of enzymes and also to lower blood glucose level due to the presence of deoxynojirimycin, a nitrogenous compound more effective than insulin.
- Silkworm pupae are rich in lecithin and can be used as a matrix for bone and ligament regeneration, wound healing, vascularization of implants. Silkworm pupal extract is used to cure impotency. In Korea "Nuegra", a natural alternative to Viagra has been developed using silkworms.
- Serripeptidase, an anti- inflammatory proteolytic enzyme produced in the intestine of silkworm larvae to break down cocoon walls is used to treat rheumatoid arthritis, osteoarthritis, chronic sinusitis and post operative inflammation.
- A fungus "*Dongchunghacho*" living inside silkworm larvae is reported to be effective against cancer, strengthens immune system, cures fatigue and cardiac ailments (Dandin and Kumar, 2007).
- Recently, the Indian tropical tasar silkworm *A.mylitta* has been studied as a scaffold for engineering a cardiac patch in vitro. Damaged human heart muscle cannot be regenerated. Scar tissue grows in place of damaged muscle cells. To develop a treatment for the repair of cardiac tissue, scientists are attempting growing replacement tissue which would be used to repair damage cardiac muscle. *A.myliita* is proving a potential substrate for this research (Iyengar, 2012).

(iii) Silkworms in cosmetics: Silk fibroin and sericin find their use in cosmetics due to their unique gloss, flexibility, elasticity, coating power, spreading capacity, adhesion and formidability.

(iv) Miscellaneous uses of silkworms

- Pupae oil is used in the manufacture of sodium and potassium soaps, varnishes, dyes etc.
- The residue obtained during chrysalis oil extraction is used as a natural organic fertilizer.
- Silkworm moth oil is used to obtain textile dyes and superior soaps and candles.
- Pupae oil (25%) mixed with linseed oil (75%) is used in manufacture of paints and varnishes.

– **Silk waste:**

- These include the unreelable portion of silk shell, like floss and pelade layer utilized in manufacture of spun silk, pure silk. Defective cocoons for example: double cocoons, immature cocoons etc are all unreelable and are utilized in manufacture of spun silk yarn.
- Seri farm residues: Compost and vermicompost: The silkworm litter, rearing bed refuse, left over mulberry leaves, soft twigs, farm weeds serve as rich source of manure releasing 280-300kg nitrogen, 90-100kg phosphorus. Recycling of farm yard residues help farmers to bring down dependency and expenditure on farm yard manure and chemical fertilizer. A sericultural farm of 1ha can generate approximately 12-15MT of organic residue (Chavancy, 2005).

NEW SILKWORM SPECIES

Cricula trifenestrata is a unique species that produces golden silk floss. It was identified in India during 2002 in Assam, Arunachal Pradesh, Meghalaya, Sikkim, North Bihar, West Bengal and Anadaman island and is popularly known as Amroli due to its feeding on mango leaves. The other host plants are cashew nut and som. The species is not traditionally commercialized in India.

Use

- Accessories and crafts are made from wild cocoons of *Attacus* and *C.trifenestrata.* The fibre is soft, fine porus, heat resistant, antibacterial and non-allergic.
- Products made from *Cricula* sp. are more water absorbent than other silks
- They can be utilized in controlling blood cholesterol, resistance to large intestinal cancer.

SERICULTURE IN UTTARAKHAND

Uttarakhand is traditionally a non sericulture state and at present rural tribes are inhabiting in 12 districts of Uttarakhand.The Doon valley in Dehradun has suitable climatic conditions for the cultivation of host plants viz. mulberry, sal, arjun, asan, oak, soalu etc. and rearing of various species of silkworms viz. mulberry, oak tasar and muga silkworm. Dehradun alone contributes 90% to the Uttarakhand state silk production.

INFRASTRUCTURE

Sericulture was first introduced by Captain Hutton in 1858 at Mussorie. In 1881 Lister and Company introduced sericulture at Majra village situated at Dehradun-Haridwar National Highway. After independence, the Government took steps to promote sericulture and Regional Sericultural Research Station (RSRS) was established in the year 1986 at Dehradun by upgrading univoltine sub station, Majra. The station was later shifted to Sahaspur in the year 1993 which is about 25 kms from Dehradun on main Chakrata road. The station since then is working to carry out adaptive trials in demonstration of sericultural farms and with selected farmers besides taking part in transfer of technologies to field and extension communication programmes. The station has 12 Researches Extension Centers (REC) responsible for demonstration and transfer of technology to the state seri departments and farmers viz.: REC, Bageshwar in Uttarakhand, REC, Una, Nadaun and Ghumarwin in Himachal Pradesh, REC, Gonda, Gorakhapur, Chutmalpur and Sub REC, Bhadrasi,(Varanasi) in U.P., REC, Fatehnagar in Rajasthan and Sub REC, Panchkula in Haryana. REC CUM CDC, Haldwani in Uttarakhand under Swarnjayanti Gramin Swarazgar Yojana (SGSY) project & Community Development Centre, Kalsi-Vikasnagar in Dehradun.The total area under RSRS, Sahaspur is 15.62acres, out of which 8.49 acre area is under mulberry cultivation. Approximately 2000 acres mulberry plantation is available in Govt. farms as well as in private holdings. There are 72 mulberry farms in the sector and 11 Central Silk board units are established in the state to provide technical support for the development of sericulture in Uttarakhand.

Sericulture infrastructure in Uttarakhand

Sericultural Districts	12
No. of Blocks	34
Sericultural Villages	521
Sericultural rearers Mulberry Vanya Total	 4223 377 4600
Departmental farms	72
Chawki rearing centres	54
Mulberry nurseries	33
Grainages Oak tasar	 2

(Contd...)

Eri Muga	2 1
Cocoon market	5
Growth centre	1
Sericulture training school	1
Rearing unit	7
Silk handlooms Certified Upgraded	 103 94
Silk park	1
CFC yarn Dyeing unit Fabric processing unit	 1 1

Source: Directorate of Sericulture, Uttarakhand

The Uttarakhand Cooperative Resham Federation is promoting oak tasar. In Dehradun alone, 18-20 weavers are active to maintain quality. Two weaving units are active at Timli and Munsiyari under the active collaboration of the federation. Bhimtal (Nainital) based Regional Oak Tasar Research station (RTRS, CSB) is exploring tremendous potentials of oak tasar culture in Uttarakhand and has created a world record in the field of silkworm egg laying during 2009. The average eggs per moth were 240-260 as compared to China's 160-200 eggs. Appropriate Technology India (ATI) and Garhwal Aromatics have done considerable work in promoting oak tasar sericulture in Chamoli district and nearby areas.

RAW SILK PRODUCTION

In Uttarakhand, out of 21MT of raw silk produced during the year 2010-11, 20MT was mulberry, 0.1MT tasar and 0.5MT eri silk and during 2012-2013, the bivoltine silk production increased to 23MT (Central Silk Board, 2013). At present 12 districts of the state are identified and annually about 100MT mulberry cocoons are produced by around 4000 beneficiaries.In a bid to enter the world market, the state government has also collaborated with a Chinese company to produce world class silk.The company would provide technical know-how for cocoon rearing.

Raw Silk Production in Uttarakhand

Raw Silk Production (MT)	2009-10	2010-2011
Mulberry	14	20
Tasar	0.50	0.1
Eri	2.0	0.5
Total	16.50	20.6

Source: Pandey and Srivastava, 2012, CSB, 2013

Estimated mulberry sericulture status in Uttarakhand by end of 2012-13

Mulberry Sericulture	2012-13
Mulberry plantation (Acre)	400
Dfls intake (Lac)	4.08
Cocoon production(MT)	127.0
Raw silk production (MT)	17.0

Source: Directorate of sericulture, Uttarakhand

PROSPECTS OF SERICULTURE IN UTTARAKHAND

Uttarakhand produces all the species of silkworm which are commercially exploited in India:

- **Mulberry sericulture:** Mulberry sericulture is generally practised in the plains. Consistent efforts are being made by the government to establish mulberry sericulture in the hilly areas but with little success. Rearing of two crops i.e spring (March- April) and autumn (September-October) is preferred for commercial cocoon production and about 95-115MT cocoons are produced annually. Summer (May- June) and late autumn (Oct- November) rearing is also conducted for increased production. Cocoon productivity/100dfl is 27-40kg in spring crop and 21.17-30.03kg in autumn crop.
- **Oak Tasar sericulture:** Oak tasar culture is generally practised in hilly areas of Uttarakhand.It was established in 1970, its subdivision was established at Bhimtal in 1972. Oak tasar was popularized covering wider areas of Garhwal and Kumaun regions by Appropriate Technology India (NGO) in 1996 when it launched it as an oak tasar project for the upliftments of the weaker sections of the society. Oak plant species generally *Quercus leucotricophora*, *Q.floribunda* and *Q.semicarpifolia* are used as host plants for the oak tasar silk worm *A.proylei*. Spring cropping pattern is generally practised.At present, only Uttarakhand and Manipur produce approximately 3-4MT oak tasar raw silk, while all the other sub-himalayan state produce only about 1MT.
- **Muga sericulture:** Muga sericulture was introduced in Uttarakhand in Dehradun at the end of the VII five year plan during 1991.It is practised in Doon valley (Dehradun), Haldwani (Nainital) and Bageshwar during June-September.The climatic conditions of Nainital district as a whole and Haldwani sub-division in particular is quite favourable for muga silkworm rearing during these seasons. Nainital and Dehradun districts also provide immense possibility to rear it as a summer crop too. About eight plant species have been identified as muga silkworm host plants, the major are som (*Persea bombycina*), soalu (*Litsea polyantha*) distributed in Ramnagar, Bhimtal, Almora, Pithoragarh

regions of Kumaun and Mussorie, Askot, Tehri and Pauri Garhwal regions of Garhwal.The raw muga silk production during 2004 was around 0.25MT.The department of sericulture, Govt. of Uttarakhand, Dehradun has taken up the systematic plantation of muga host plants.The feasibility of four crops system of muga rearing during May-October has been established against six crops in Assam. Efforts are also being initiated through WGO's to stablize the seed crops and ensure strong base for commercial muga culture in the state.

- **Eri culture:** Eri silkworm is a polyphagous insect species. The primary host plants are castor (*Ricinus communis*) and Kesseru (*Heteropanax fragrans*). Beside these plants eri silk worm feeds on *Jatropha* species, tapioca (*Manihot utilissima*), Payam (*Evodia fraxinifolia*), Barkerseru (*Alianthus excelsa*) to list a few. Eri silkworm rearing could be achieved in the state as it has vast forests cover and castor plant is abundant in the tarai areas. Initiatives from the government should be more strengthened for its production in the state.

Initiatives/Support from Uttarakhand Government to develop Uttarakhand as bivoltine silk belt

- The government aims to develop Uttarakhand as the "Bowl of Bivolitne Silk". This sector has the prospect of emerging as a major unique selling point for the state in the years to come.
- The state has taken measures to promote Oak tasar, Eri and Muga silk. Uttarakhand is poised to emerge as a leading producer of Oak tasar cocoon. Silk is being exported to USA and Spain.
- Muga cocoon produced in the state is comparable in quality to the best of it in Assam. Three cocoon markets have been established to ensure competitive price to the rearers through open auction.
- A revolving fund of $0.46 million has been allocated for silkworm breeders. To ensure the local consumption of silk yarn, the Directorate of Sericulture and Uttarakhand Co-operative Resham Federation have introduced silk fabric production.
- A revolving fund of Rs. 2 crores with 50% share from CSB, has been created for spot payment to sericulture farmers at Nainital, Dehradun and Haridwar.The funds are controlled by Uttarakhand Co-operative Resham Federation.
- The details of every rearer such as Dfls reared, deductions etc. are computerized before market operation to ensure spot payment.
- Floor price of cocoon lots are maintained on the basis of Kakame cost (It is the cost of quantity of cocoons required o produce one kg raw silk)
- Swarn Jayani Gramin Swarojgar Yojna was initiated during 2007 to benefit farmers, tribesmen of Nainital and Udham Singh Nagar. By

the end of 2012, the yojna benefited about 3090 people residing below poverty line and generated 6530 man days/year income.

- The cocoon costs are paid on the same day to the farmers
- To ensure local consumption of silkyarn and value addition, silk weaving is introduced in Kashipur, Bhimtal, Rampur and Dehradun The Govt. has also opened auction house in Dehradun to help farmers get better prices for their produce.A weaving unit has been established at Kalsi block of Dehradun district by Uttarakhand Cooperative Resham Federation to benefit the jaunsari tribesmen and women.

Jaunsari tribe is the largest tribe of Uttarakhand with more than 38.78% population. Other tribes include Bhotiyas, Buksa, Tharu and Raji. The project, 'Integrated farming system and human resource planning and management for livelihood, security and capacity building of tribal community in Uttarakhand' sub component sericulture has been started by ICAR during the year 2012-13, under Tribal Sub Plan (TSP) in Kalsi and Chakrata blocks of district Dehradun to make them self dependent. The project has given training on different aspects of mulberry sericulture and also distributed high yielding mulberry varieties and fertilizers in Vyas Bhund, Sahia and Dhanpoo villages of block Kalsi and Sawara and Mohna villages of Block Chakrata of district Dehradun. Nearly 228 farmers will be benefited. The project aims to:

- Improve socioeconomic development of tribals
- Human resource development- skill development and exposure to the concept of economic utilization of natural resources
- Employment generation in their own habitat as sericulture is labour intensive
- Intercropping and utilization of 'byproducts of sericulture' makes it more sustainable (eg. twigs for thatch making and sericultural waste for vermicomposting)
- Value addition: Training the tribals on cocoon stifling, storage of cocoons and reeling/spinning, makes their produce more valuable and enhances the profit
- Pupal waste: Dead pupae are a rich source of protein and oil. They are utilized in feed making for fishes, poultry and pigs. The tribals could start the fish, poultry and pig culture.It is another step to value addition.

COCOON MARKETING IN UTTARAKHAND

The cocoons cannot be stored by the farmers due to their poor economic condition as well as impairment of cocoon quality, therefore the Uttarakhand government has set up marketing system for cocoons.The main cocoon market is situated at Selakui, 20Km from Dehradun.Price for the produce is given through open auction system. The floor price is fixed after kakame cost evaluation is carried out at Demonstration-Cum Technical Service Centre, Dehradun. Marketing of cocoons is facilitated by Uttarakhand Cooperative Resham Federation. The 60% cost of cocoon is provided as loan to reelers and to take part in the bidding. The Uttarakhand Cooperative Resham Federation oversees the transaction to ensure that sericulture farmers are not exploited due to low silk price or due to over production.

Seed Cocoon marketing: Silkworm seed production centre, Dehradun purchases seed cocoons for producing hybrid seeds. In this system Rs 150/ kg is fixed for seed cocoons having 80% pupation rate. Rs 3/per cent increase is accrued to Rs 150 and above 90 per cent pupation rate Rs 50 are accrued/ percentage. In this way farmers get a good price for their produce.

FUTURE PROSPECTS AND CONSTRAINTS

The raw silk production by the end of 2012-13 is estimated to 17MT while cocoon production is estimated to 127MT. Directorae of Sericulture, Uttarakhand aims to enhance raw silk production to 42MT by the end of XII five year plan (2012-2017) and is likely to benefit approx. 6383 rearers/ farmers. The mulberry plantation area will be increased from 400acre in 2012-13 to 2500 acre by end of 2016-17.

In Northern India, sericulture is a subsidiary occupation, the farmers are largely marginal and landless, increase in their income will enhance sustenance on sericulture besides checking migration. Unlike South India, mulberry in North India is grown mainly as road side border plantation. The production and quality of cocoons is directly related to mulberry leaf quality. Despite various efforts by the government, sericulture has not been popular among the tribes of Uttarakhand due to lack of awareness, illiteracy, less desire to work, undesirable weather conditions. The industry can flourish and more employment could be generated through transfer of technology, crop supervision, regular visits and contact with farmers/tribals.

Sericultural practises in rural Uttarakhand, if established well, will definitely increase the living standards of the tribals and poor through higher income and increase in state revenue. Alternative sources of income through mulberry sericulture and its value addition will cause socio-economic upliftment of rural farmers.

CONCLUSION

Adoption of sericulture as a profession by tribal, conserves the environment by non-cutting and felling of trees because sericulture is now their way of life. Interstate migration is checked because sericulture provides additional income at their door level. Regular savings habit has been developed by sericulture practices among the tribes because they earn much more than their standard of living. Sericulture suits the life style of tribes because practice of sericulture is simple and can be done without any cost and skill. Sericulture has been successful in eradication of rural poverty, resulting in social as well as economic development, mainly in rural areas. This industry is capable of generating employment and earning income continuously with low investment. India retains tremendous unexploited potential for silk development. Unlike other countries, where climate-related factors allow not more than a couple of cocoon crops a year, in India even four to six crops are possible. Fortunately, India has the technology to produce bivoltine silk with desired traits but what lacks is investment in new technologies.

REFERENCES

Bhatia, N.K., Bhatt, M.M and Khan, M.A.(2010): Tropical Tasar-utilization and Conservation of Natural Resource for Tribal Development. *The Bioscan*, 1: 187-198.

Central Silk Board. (2013): Note on the Performance of Indian Silk Industry and Functioning of Central Silk Board. 1-8.

Chavancy, G. (2005): Silkworms for Non-textile Industries. The 20th Congress of the International Sericultural Commission, December 15-18, Bangaluru pp: 49-51.

Dandin, S.B and Kumar, N.S. (2007). Biomedical uses of Silk and its Derivatives. *Indian Silk,* January: 5-8.

Iyengar, M.N.S. (2012): Silk from Indian Tasar Silkworm as a Scaffold for Heart Tissue. *Indian Silk*, 2(12): 23.

Kumaresan. (2013): Trends in Cost of Cocoon Production in China and India. *Indian Silk* 4(1-2): 24-26.

Pandey and Srivastava, R.P.(2012): Sericulture in Uttarakhand. *Indian Farmers Digest*, 17-20.

Ramesh, C., K.Ibrahaem Basha, H.Lakshmi, S.V.Seshagiri and K. Pahani Kiran Kumar.(2003): Mulberry - An Ideal Resource for Biotechnological Products. *Indian Silk*. 5-9.

Roy, I. (2012): Sericulture in India. *Indian Silk*. 2(9): 4-6.

Srivastava, R.P. (2005): Sericulture in India: An Overview. *Indian Farmers Digest*, 5-13.

Pages: 95-116

Rural Development and Techno-Innovations
Edited by: Dr. Alka Chauhan; Er. Chhavi Kumar 'Bharti' & Dr. Pawan Kumar 'Bharti'
ISBN: 978-93-88854-07-8
Edition: 2019
Published by: Discovery Publishing House Pvt. Ltd., New Delhi (India)

7 An Empowerment of Farm Women Groups in Agrarian Economy
A Case Study in Tamilnadu

Dr. Esakkimuthu M
Dr. Vennila P

ABSTRACT

India is an agricultural country with over 70 per cent of the country population supported by agriculture. Even while India's industrial and services sectors are growing by leaps and bounds, growth rate of agriculture is below 2 per cent. Farm women are the backbone of agricultural workforce. Women empowerment in rural areas has always been a major challenge, but the active participation of women in the cooperative movement in India, especially in the agriculture and allied sectors with reference to Tamilnadu has shown the way forward for national and state economy of Tamilnadu for women empowerment. Farm women are the backbone of agricultural workforce. Women empowerment in rural areas has always been a major challenge, but the active participation of women in the cooperative movement in India, especially in the agriculture and allied sectors, has shown the way forward for national economy. Research was conducted in Tirunelveli and Madurai districts of Tamilnadu state under the ICAR-All India Coordinated Research Project on Home Science, to study the "Dynamics and performance of women groups in agriculture and allied sectors". In this study, the socio-psychological empowerment of farm women was measured in terms of 34 statements, 11 economic empowerment and 15 legal and political; empowerment statements. In total 60 statements which include positive and negative statements of rural women empowerment. The scale was developed and standardized for the research purpose. The findings revealed that, 51 per cent of the self help group members have

ICAR-AICRPHS (Extension Component), Tamil Nadu Agricultural University, Madurai, Tamil Nadu, (India)

high level of socio-psychological empowerment; 74.33 per cent of self help group members have high level of economic empowerment and 0.66 per cent of them have political and economic empowerment. It could be inferred from the study that, all three dimensions of empowerment plays a pivotal role in development of individual ability and it leads to success of the groups.

Keywords: Measurement, socio-psychological empowerment, agriculture, farm women, Measurement, economic empowerment, dairy sector, economy, development, Networking, financial sustainability, women groups, empowerment.

INTRODUCTION

Agriculture is the backbone of the Indian economy and contributes nearly 50 percent of the total national income. Therefore, the development of the country depends on agricultural development where both men and women shoulder the responsibility of work. Alleviation of poverty and hunger is the major pillar of development (Ganessamurthy, 2007). The role of women becomes the most important guiding factor in this regard. To instrumentalise women for achieving comprehensive socio-economic-ecological-sustainable development, their skill development and empowerment are to be focused. Agriculture in the present scenario is highly competitive and confined to marketability of the agricultural commodity produced (Nair, 2005). Agriculture in India is basically a family enterprise in which women are active participants. Women are a cultivator, co-operator, laborer, and contributor to farm decision making and family income. Women are responsible for at least 50 percent of the total food production of the country. It is known from early civilization that women were the first agriculturists, while men were out for hunting and tending livestock.

India's women empowerment is considered as the phenomenon of nineties and is defined as giving power to creating power within and enabling. Empowerment is a multidimensional social process that helps people to gain control over their own lives. Agriculture is the backbone of the Indian economy and contributes nearly 50 percent of the total national income. Therefore, the development of the country depends on agricultural development where both men and women shoulder the responsibility of work. Agriculture in India is basically a family enterprise in which women are active participants. She is a cultivator, co-operator, labourer, and contributor to farm decision making and family income. Women are responsible for at least 50.00 percent of the total food production of the country (Kapur, 1988). The view point put forth by Surekha and Rajamanamma (1999) described empowerment as an important process through which women are enabled to realize their full identity and power in all spheres of life. According to Sudharani *et al.* (2000) defined empowerment as the process of challenging existing power relations and of gaining greater control over the source of power. Empowerment is a process of awareness and capacity building leading to greater participation, greater decision making power & control and to transformative action.

Indian economy is an agrarian economy. In India, women empowerment is considered as the phenomenon of nineties and is defined as giving power to creating power within and enabling. The word empowerment means multidimensional social process that helps people to gain control over their own lives in different spheres of life. To increase the food production at the rate of at least three per cent per year the efforts of government organizations alone is not sufficient. In this context, appropriate training of practicing farmers, extension personnel and the agricultural teachers and trainers is very crucial in increasing agricultural production. Since ancient times women constitute an important segment of the society. They contributed significantly in shaping the fate of any society and performed a pivotal role in progress of any nation. Even in modern era the women constitute more than 50 per cent of the world's population, one third of the labor force and perform nearly two third of working hours. To keep in mind the above fact, research was conducted in Tirunelveli and Madurai districts of Tamil Nadu state under the ICAR-All India Coordinated Research Project on Home Science, to study the "Dynamics and performance of women groups in agriculture and allied sectors".

Background of the ICAR-AICRPHS Project

The Kondayampatti village of Alanganallur Block (West) Madurai District with a population of 3426 has been selected as the adopted village in view of the availability of all age groups of subjects to carry out the survey, the intervention programs and on account of the better scope for overall development of the village. The village has a Higher Secondary School, Sub centre for Primary Health Centre and *Balwadi* which will facilitate the intervention programs to be implemented for improving the nutritional status of adolescents and preschool children which is one of the mandatory research activities under the All India Coordinated Research Project on Home Science. The mainstay of the villagers is agriculture with paddy, sugarcane, ground nut and banana being the major field crops cultivated in addition to vegetables (ladies finger, cluster bean, tomato, brinjal) and other fruits like lime, sapota and amla. This will provide more opportunities for technology transfer in processing and value addition of the produce. The Government programs which are in operation in the village are Tamil Nadu Women Development Project, Social Welfare and Nutritious Meal Programme, Mahatma Gandhi National Rural Employment Guarantee Scheme, Member of Parliament Local Area Development Scheme etc., Hence the nutrition related intervention programs and income generating activities can be implemented as a harness to these programs so as to bring about empowerment of the villagers and livelihood development of the village. The work plan for carrying out the AICRP research activities pertaining to the different disciplines of Home Science has been charted out based on the AICRP mandate and work has been initiated in the different research projects of the respective Home Science disciplines. The overriding objective of the ICAR-All India Coordinated Research Project on Home Science is "Developing a strong base of research and extension for improving the quality of life of rural farm families through coordinated research activities". The specific objectives is to study the dynamics of women self help groups and their growth pattern and to study the factors contributing to sustainability of women groups.

MATERIALS AND METHODS

In Tamil Nadu there are seven agro-climatic zones. In order to select 25-30% of the districts representing different regions, one district was selected from each agro-climatic zone. Initially Madurai district from South zone and Tirunelveli district from Southern zone were selected for data collection. In Madurai district there are 13 blocks and all the blocks were selected for the survey. From each blocks two villages were selected (12 × 2) and from one block one village were selected. From each village two SHG will be contacted for data collection. Thus, from 25 villages 50 Self Help Groups will be contacted. In Tirunelveli district there are about 19 blocks and 13 blocks were selected randomly. From each blocks two villages were selected (12 × 2) and from one block one village were selected. From each village two SHG were contacted for data collection. Thus, from 25 villages 50 Self Help Groups will be contacted. Totally 100 Self Help Groups were contacted for data collection. In addition 200 members and 300 non-members were contacted to collect data on their empowerment status. Self help groups office bearers, members and non-members were contacted based on simple random sampling method. Pre-tested interview schedule was adopted in the study.

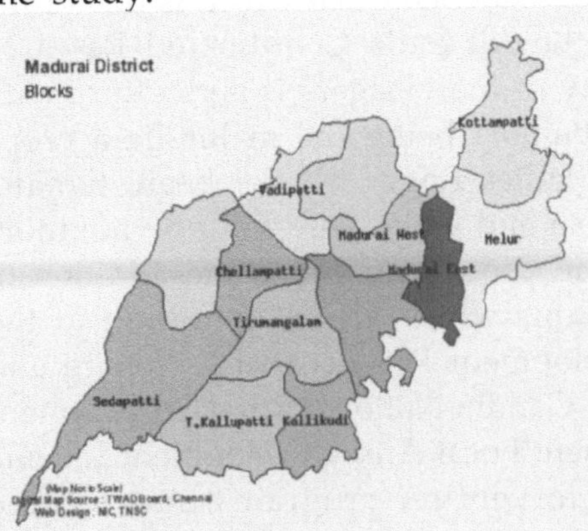

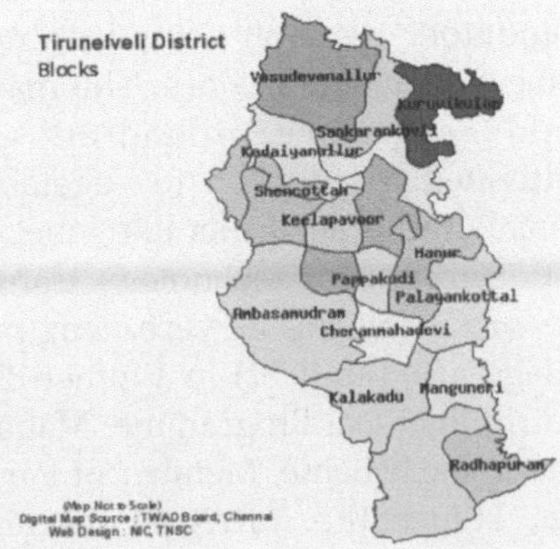

RESULTS AND DISCUSSIONS

Profile of Groups

Table 7.1. Percentage distribution of SHGs according to their present status

Active		Dormant				Discontinued
Group Entrep. & Micro-fin.	Income gen ind. + Micro-Fin	Micro-Fin. +metg/ discussed	Micro-Fin	Money Collection	Token Existence (Money deposit by functionary)	
0	82.0	0	0	0	0	18.0

From the table 7.1 it can be concluded that majority (82.00 %) per cent of the SHG were active and involved in income generation through micro-financing and 18.00 % of the SHGs were discontinued. It also observed from the table, it could be most of SHGs were taken up micro-financing as major activities. It may helpful for upliftment of rural families. The loans were taken to fulfill the needs like children's education, family loan etc.

Table 7.2: Percentage distribution of groups according to gap in formation and registration

Gap in Months					
0	1-3	3-6	6-9	9-12	More than 12
32.00	38.00	29.00	1.00	0	0

It is observed from the table 7.2 that 32.00 % of the SHG's formed the group and registered immediately, 38.00% of the SHG's had a gap of 1-3 month between group formation and registration followed by 29.00% and 1.00% of the SHG's had a gap 3-6 months, 6-9 months gap between group formation and registration respectively. It is revealed from the table, majority of the groups were within three month period registered themselves.

Table 7.3: Average membership of groups at different stages of group sustainability

Membership status (number of members)						
Formation		Registration		Present		
f	Average	f	Average	n=	f	Average
1657	17.00	1582	16.00	82.00	1071	13.00

The table 7.3 indicates that among the total groups (100SHG) on an average there were 17 members in a group at the time of formation and 16 members at the time of registration. Among the sustaining groups (82 SHG) on an average there were 13 members in a group at present. It is clear cut indication that, most often high number of respondents was participated in beginning of the SHGs and drastically it got reduced at present status. In between discontinuation were occurred.

Table 7.4: Monthly collection status by member at different stages of group sustainability

Collection in Rs.						
Formation		Registration		Present		
Total Collection	Average	Total Collection	Average	n= Sustaining Groups	Total Collection	Average
7690	72.7	7865	76.2	1071	14235	173.59

It could be inferred from the above table that at the time of group formation the average monthly collection by the member of the SHG was Rs. 72.7/- per member and it was Rs. 76.2/- per member at the time of registration and at present it has increased to Rs. 173.59 per member. The group sustainability was measured in terms of monthly collection (Rs.) status by SHG members. In the early stage of SHG formation Rs. 72/- was collected, then drastically it was improved upto Rs. 173/- per month. It shows that the women economic empowerment in the Tamil Nadu.

Table 7.5: Percentage distribution of groups according to frequency of deposit

Monthly	Quarterly	Six Monthly	Random/Token Deposit	Discontinued
81.00	1.00	0	0	18.00

The table 7.5 indicates that majority 81.00% of the groups deposited their collection every month in the bank and 1.00% deposited at an interval of 3 months (quarterly) and 18.00% SHG's were discontinued. It exhibit that almost each group office bearers and treasures they used to deposit the money in on monthly basis.

Table 7.6: Percentage distribution of groups according to sustainability

Less than 1 year	1-3 years	3-5 years	5 years & continuing
18.00	2.00	0	80.00

Table 7.6 indicates that 80 self help groups were continuing more than five years, 18 self help groups were continued, less than one year and 2 self help groups were continued upto three years. It exhibits that majority of self help groups had long term sustainability. It leads to empowerment of groups as a whole.

It is understood from the table 7.7 that majority 77.77% have stated that non-cooperation among the members of the group as the main reason for group discontinuation followed by 44.44% expressed that lack of interest, problem in taking the loan, marketing related issues were the reason for group discontinuation and 38.88 % percent opined that lack of knowledge and conflict among members were the reason and 22.22% stated lack of training, 16.66% lack of government support, 11.11% lack of contact with members were the reasons for discontinuance and dormancy.

Table 7.7: Percentage distribution of groups according to reasons for discontinuation and dormancy

Reasons	Per cent
Lack of interest	44.44
Lack of time	38.88
Non cooperation	77.77
Conflict among members	33.33
Lack of contact with members	11.11
Lack of trust	38.88
Lack of trainings	22.22
Lack of govt. support in sale of produce	16.66
Lack of knowledge	33.33
Problem in taking loan	44.44
Marketing related issues	44.44

Table 7.8: Profile of self help groups across states

	Mean of all Groups			Sustaining Groups		Mean of Sustaining Groups		
Total groups F	Status (Range 0-6)	Gap information and registration (Months)	Sustainability (Months)	f	%	Membership status	Collection status	Frequency of deposit (Range 0-4)
100	4.10	2.00	60.00	82	82.00	13.00	173	3.98

From the above table it is clear that mean status of Self Help Group was 4.10and the mean gap between formation and registration was 2 months and these groups sustained for sixty months. Among the 100 SHGs, 82.00 % of the SHG were sustaining and the mean membership status of the sustaining groups were 13, collection status was Rs.173/- and the frequency of deposit was 3.98 for the sustaining groups.

Table 7.9: Percentage distribution of members according to their age

Office Bearer				Members			
F	Young (18-35 yrs.)	Middle age (36-50yrs.)	Old (More than 50 yrs.)	F	Young (18-35 yrs.)	Middle age (36-50yrs.)	Old (More than 50 yrs.)
100	43.00	55.00	2.00	1188	42.42	50.92	6.66

The above table reveals that among the office bearers more than half (55.00 %) percentage of them belonged to middle age and 43.00 per cent of them belonged to young age and 2.00 per cent of them belonged to old age. Among the SHG members half of them (50.92%) belonged to middle age category, 42.42 % belonged to young age and 6.66 % belong to old age category. Table 7.9 explained that more than half of the self help group office bearers belong to middle age group. It shows mostly married women participation is high as a whole.

Table 7.10: Percentage distribution of members according to their education

Office Bearer					Members				
Frequency	Illiterate/ can read & write (0)	Low Upto middle (5)	Medium (Middle to Sr. Sec.) (6-12)	High (Above Sr. Sec.) (Above 12)	Frequency	Illiterate/ can read and write (0)	Low (Upto middle (5)	Medium (Middle to Sr. Sec.) (6-12)	High (Above Sr. Sec.) (Above 12)
100	4.00	10.00	84.00	2.00	1188	54.29	11.36	32.82	1.51

From the above table it is understood that among the office bearers 84.00% of them had medium level of education, 10.00% of the office bearers had low level of education and 4.00% of them were illiterates. Very meager (2.00 %) of the office bearers had high level of education. Among the members, more than half of them (54.29%) were illiterate and 32.82% were medium in their education followed by 11.36 in low level of education and only 1.51 per cent of the members possessed in high level of education.

Table 7.11. Percentage distribution of members according to their organizational status

Office bearer					Members				
Frequency	No membership	Low (1-3)	Medium (3-5)	High (More than 5)	Frequency	No membership	Low (1-3)	Medium (3-5)	High (More than 5)
100	77.00	23.00	0	0	1188	98.48	1.51	0	0

The above table concluded that majority (77.00%) of the office bearers had no membership with any of the organizations and 23.00 % of them had low level of membership with organization. Among the members 98.48% of them had no membership with any of the organization and 1.51 percent of them had low level of membership status with organizations. It shows that most of the self help group members they are no having membership in any other organization.

Table 7.12: Profile of the members

Office bearer			Members		
Age (Mean in years)	Education (Mean in years)	Organizational membership (Mean in No.)	Age (Mean in years)	Education (Mean in years)	Organizational membership (Mean in No.)
37.00	7.00	0	37.00	3.40	0

The above table revealed that office bearer and member was 37 years of age, mean years of education was 7 years for office bearer and 3.40 years for members. Regarding mean organizational membership status for SHG office bearers and members was very poor.

Table 7.13: Percentage distribution of groups according to frequency of meetings

Percentage of groups			Mean value of total groups (Range 1-3) from total groups	Mean value of sustaining groups (Range 1-3)
Regularly	Sometimes	Never		
97.00	2.00	1.00	2.96	2.95

From the table 7.13 it was inferred that majority 97.00% of the groups regularly attended the meeting conducted by the SHG once in a month, about 2.00 % of the groups attended the meeting sometime and 1.00% of them never attended of the meetings. The mean value of total group was 2.96 and the mean value of sustaining group was 2.95.

Table 7.14: Distribution of groups according to activities undertaken and its frequency during meetings of SHG

Activities								
Micro financing		General discussions		Discussion regarding particular issues		Discussing or organizing trainings/lectures/ demo		Overall mean of frequency (Mean Score range 1-3)
% of groups	Frequency (1-3)	% of groups	Frequency (1-3)	% of groups	Frequency (1-3)	% of groups	Frequency (1-3)	
96.00	3.00	44.00	2.00	58.00	1.00	100.00	1.00	1.71

Table 7.14 indicates that 96.00% percent of groups were regularly involved in micro-financing, 44.00% percent of the groups involved occasionally in group discussion and 58.00% percent never discuss about particular issue and cent percent(100.00) they never discussed about training in their meeting.

Table 7.15: Percentage distribution of members /groups involved in income generating

Groups whose members are involved in income generation (n=No of sustaining groups)		Members of groups involved in income generation (n=Total members of sustaining groups)		Members involved in income generation (n=Total members of groups involved in income generation)		Percentage of Members involved in income generation (n= members involved in income generation)			
						Were doing it before membership		Started after becoming member	
f	%	f	%	f	%	f	%	f	%
3	3.65	36	3.36	36	3.03	–	–	36	3.03

The above table indicates that among the total sustaining member(82) three groups (3) were involved in income generation that accounts to 3.65% and only 36 members of the sustaining groups were involved in income generation that accounts to 3.36 % and among the total member (1188) of the groups 36 member were involved in income generation that accounts 3.03 percent.

Table 7.16: Percentage distribution of groups involved in entrepreneurial activities

Groups whose members are involved in entrepreneurial activity			Total members of groups involved in entrepreneurial activity	Members involved in entrepreneurial activity (n=Total members of groups involved in entrepreneurial activity		Entrepreneurial activity with few members (n=Groups whose members are involved in entrepreneurial activity		Entrepreneurial activity involving all members (n=Groups whose members are involved in entrepreneurial activity		Entrepreneurial activity also involving members other than group members (n=Groups whose members are involved entrepreneurial activity			
										Outsider is family member		Outsider is non family members	
F	% (n= total groups)	% (n= sustai-ning groups)	F	f	%	f	%	f	%	f	%	F	%
3	3.65	0	0	3	0	0	0	0	0	0	0	0	0

From the table it is clear that there are three groups whose members are involved in entrepreneurial activities that accounts to 3.65 percentage.

Entrepreneurial groups		Groups with all members involved in entrepreneurial activity (n= Groups whose members are involved in entrepreneurial activity)		Groups with few members involved in Entrepreneurial activity (n= Groups whose members are involved in entrepreneurial activity)		Groups in which outsiders are involved in entrepreneurship (n= Groups whose members are involved in entrepreneurial activity, -given in column 1)			
						Outsider are family member		Outsider are non family members	
f	%	f	%	F	%	f	%	f	%
3	3.65	0	0	3	3.65	0	0	0	0

The above table indicated that only three groups were entrepreneurial groups the accounts to 3.65% and in these three groups few members were involved in entrepreneurial activity that accounts to 3.65%.

Loan

Table 7.17: Use of loan taken by the group members

% of groups who took loan (n= sustaining groups)		% Members distributed among		Amount of total loan taken in rupees	Average loan per group in rupees (n = number of groups who took loan	Percentage balance amount due to be returned in rupees	Average used for the activity for which loan was taken
f	%	f	% (n=no of total members of groups who took loan				
82	82.00	1071	100.00	26,283,500	2,70,963.00	1.41	75.00

The table 7.17 elucidated that in Tamil Nadu all the sustaining groups (82) took loan and the loan amount were distributed among all the members (1071). Total amount of loan accounts to that Rs. 2,62,83,500/- and the average loan per SHG amounts to Rs. 2,70,693/- and the percentage balance amount due to be returned in 1.41% and on an average 75.00 % used the loan for the activity for which it was taken.

Table 7.18: Source of investment for entrepreneurial activities by groups

No. of entrepreneurial groups	Amount invested (Rs.)	Source wise % of amount invested (% to be calculated from the total amount invested)			
		From personal savings of members	Group saving of SHG	Bank loan	Any other
0	0	0	0	0	0

The table 7.18 indicates that in among the 82 sustaining groups, none of the groups were invested the amount into entrepreneurial activities. It shows that women in rural areas started micro-finance among the self help groups for the household needs.

Income

Table 7.19: Annual income of members from income generating activity/ entrepreneurial activities

Average income per member from Income generating activities (Rs.) (n= total members engaged in income generating)	Average income per member from entrepreneurial activity (n= total members engaged entrepreneurial activity)
0	0

From the table 7.19 reveals that annual income of the self help groups from income generating activities and entrepreneurial activities is nil. It shows that most of the self help groups lies the concept of microfinance.

Trainings

Table 7.20: Percentage distribution of members according to training undertaken and its usefulness

Total members who took training (n=members of sustain groups)		Percentage of members who took training related to group formation (n=total members who took training)		Percentage of members who took training related to income generating/entrepreneurial (n=total members who took training)		Usefulness of training (Mean score 1-3)
F	%	F	%	f	%	
350	32.67	0	0	350	32.67	3.00

Table 7.20 elucidates among the sustaining groups more than 32 percent of members alone took training related to income generation activities, nearly 32 percent of SHG members were undergone training related to income generating and entrepreneurial activities and none of the respondents who took training related to group formation.

Empowerment of SHG Members

Empowerment Status

Table 7.21: Distribution of SHG members according to socio-psychological empowerment

Percentage of office bearers			Percentage of members			Overall percentage		
Low (1-2.33)	Medium (2.34-3.66)	High (3.67-5.0)	Low (1-2.33)	Medium (2.34- 3.66)	High (3.67 -5.0)	Low (1-2.33)	Medium (2.34- 3.66)	High (3.67 -5.0)
0.5	48.00	51.00	0	48.00	52.00	0.3	48.00	51.66

Data on socio-psychological empowerment status of office bearers and group members of SHGs present in the form of data in the table 21 revealed that approximately 51.66 per cent respondents belongs to high category, followed by 48 per cent in medium category and 0.3 per cent were low category of socio- psychological empowerment.

The comparison of socio-psychological empowerment of office bearers and members of SHGs in Tamil Nadu found that 51 per cent of office bearers and 52 per cent of the members of SHGs fall in high level of empowerment. Further, equal per cent (48%) of the office bearer and members of SHGs were fall under the category of medium level of empowerment. And least amount (0.5% of office bearers and none of them from SHGs members) were also fall under the low category of socio-psychological empowerment. Thus it can be interpreted from the results that by becoming office bearers the women tend to become more socio-psychological empowered in overall office bearer category.

Table 7.22: Comparison of distribution of SHG members and non-members according to socio-psychological empowerment

Percentage of office bearers and members			Percentage of Non members		
Low (1-2.33)	Medium (2.34- 3.66)	High (3.66 -5.0)	Low (1-2.33)	Medium (2.34-3.66)	High (3.67- 5.0)
0.30	48.00	51.66	0	55.33	44.66

An empowerment of women is because of associating themselves with SHGs or otherwise, the socio psychological scale, economic and legal empowerment was administered over those women also who were not member of any SHG.

Data on comparison of socio-psychological empowerment of members and non-members of SHG is given in table 7.22. It can be observed the data that more than fifty five percent (55.33 %) non members were in the medium category and 44.66 percent in high category. On the other hand, office bearers of SHGs were 51.66 per cent were in high category and 48 percent were in the medium category. Thus, it can be concluded from the table that women after becoming the member of SHG become more socio-psychological empowered.

Table 7.23: Distribution of SHG members according to economic empowerment

Percentage of office bearers			Percentage of member			Overall percentage		
Low (1-2.33)	Medium (2.34- 3.66)	High (3.67-5.0)	Low (1-2.33)	Medium (2.34-3.66)	High (3.67-5.0)	Low (1-2.33)	Medium (2.34-3.66)	High (3.67-5.0)
0	28.00	72.00	0	24.50	75.50	0	25.66	74.33

Results in table 7.23 discussed distribution of SHG members according to their economic empowerment of office bearers and SHG members. The overall percentage of SHG members revealed that 74.33 per cent women (both office bearers and members) fall in high level of economic empowerment, 25.66 per cent of women fall in medium level of economic empowerment and none of them had low level of economic empowerment. It shows that, idea of microfinance play a huge impact in rural women empowerment. It was evident from the table 7.23, one-fourth of women fall under medium level of economic empowerment.

Table 7.24: Comparison of distribution of members and nonmembers according to economic empowerment

Percentage of office bearers and members			Percentage of Non members		
Low (1-2.33)	Medium (2.34- 3.66)	High (3.67- 5.0)	Low (1-2.33)	Medium (2.34-3.66)	High (3.67- 5.0)
0	25.66	74.33	0	22.66	77.33

Data in table 7.24 depicts comparison distribution of members (office bearers and members) of SHGs and non members according to their economic empowerment.

The perusal of data revealed that three fourth of the SHG members (74.33%) are high level of economic empowerment and one forth of SHG members (25.66 %) reported that they are medium level of empowerment attained economically. On the other hand 77.33 percent non members and 22.66 percent members reported to fall in medium category of economic empowerment. And both groups are depicting that, none of them from the low level of economic empowerment. It shows that women in rural areas attained the status of economically empowered.

Table 7.25: Distribution of SHG members according legal/political empowerment

Percentage of office bearers			Percentage of member			Overall percentage		
Low (1-2.33)	Medium (2.34-3.66)	High (3.67-5.0)	Low (1-2.33)	Medium (2.34-3.66)	High (3.67-5.0)	Low (1-2.33)	Medium (2.34-3.66)	High (3.67-5.0)
24.00	75.00	1.00	18.50	81.00	0.5	20.33	79.00	0.66

Distribution of SHG members according legal/political empowerment of members and office bearer is given in table 7.25. The overall percentage of members (Office bearers and members) revealed that approximately 79 per cent women reported to fall in medium category and 20.33 percent fall in low category of legal/political empowerment and merely 0.66 percent of the respondents fall under high category.

The comparison of legal/political empowerment of office bearers and members of SHGs revealed that more number of office bearers (75%) fall under the medium category of legal/political empowerment as compared to its members (81%). On the other hand, reverse trend was found in high category of legal and political empowerment where 0.5 percent members and one percent office bearers fall in this category.

The SHG members were already expose to various group meetings, bank and other social activities make them empowered. Office bearers also equally empowered in terms of their level of political empowerment. Generally, one universal fact is that all the office bearers were empowered in terms of their political empowerment. Most of them desire is to become an Panchayat President or some administrative post in village.

Table 7.26: Comparison of distribution of members and non-members according to legal/political empowerment

Percentage of members (office bearers and members)			Percentage of Non members		
Low (1 to 2.33)	Medium (2.34 to 3.66)	High (3.67 to 5.0)	Low (1 to 2.33)	Medium (2.34 to 3.66)	High (3.67 to 5.0)
20.33	79.00	0.66	34.33	64.00	1.66

The Comparison of distribution of members and non-members according to legal/political empowerment is given in table 7.26. The scrutiny of the data revealed that sixty four per cent non members fall in medium category of legal/political empowerment. In case of members of SHGs (Office bearers and members), 79 percent fall in medium category, 20.33 percent in low category and 0.66 percent in high category of legal and political empowerment, respectively.

Table 7.27: Comparison of distribution of members and non-members according to level of empowerment

Percentage of members (off. Bearers & Members of sustaining groups)			Percentage of non-members		
Low (1-2.33)	Medium (2.34-3.66)	High (3.67-5.0)	Low (1-2.33)	Medium (2.34-3.66)	High (3.67 to 5.0)
0	81.43	18.56	0	52.33	47.66

Perusal data of overall comparison in distribution of members and non-members according to their level of empowerment (socio- psychological + economic + legal/ political empowerment) reveals that 18.56 percent members and 47.66 percent non-members of SHGs reported to be highly empowered (Table 7.27). It indicate that medium level of empowerment is prevailing in among the SHG members due to the concept of microfinance was adopted by most of the sustaining self help groups in the study area.

Table 7.28: Comparison of level of empowerment of members and non-members

Mean score							
Members (off. Bearers & members of sustaining groups)				Non members			
Psycho-social	Economic	Legal	Overall	Psycho-social	Economic	Legal	Overall
3.69	3.90	2.55	3.45	2.10	2.75	3.13	2.66

Further, 3.45 percent members of SHGs and 2.66 percent non-members reported to be in overall empowerment category. Thus, it can be interpreted from the findings that majority of women of SHG members in Tamil Nadu are empowered. Obviously, result indicates that SHGs members were extremely empowered in terms of their level of empowerment. On the other hand, non-members overall level of empowerment was very poor than SHGs members. It explained that concept of SHGs definitely had some needful empowerment in terms of their livelihood security.

Extent of change in empowerment status

Table 7.29: Distribution of SHG members according to perceived change in socio-psychological empowerment

Percentage of office bearers			Percentage of Member			Overall percentage		
No change (0-1)	Some change (1-2)	To a large extent (2-3)	No change (0-1)	Some change (1-2)	To a large extent (2-3)	No change (0-1)	Some change (1-2)	To a large extent (2-3)
0	87.00	13.00	4.50	85.5	10.00	2.25	86.25	11.5

From the Table 7.29 shows that, SHGs office bearers had change about 87 percent of them had some change in terms of their socio-psychological empowerment, rest of 13 percent of the respondents had a large extent of change and none of them had no change. SHGs members had 85.50 percent had some change, 10 percent had change at large extent and 4.50 percent had no change in their socio-psychological empowerment. In overall figure shows that majority (86.25 percent) had some change, 11.5 percent had large extent of change and 2.25 per cent had no change.

Table 7.30: Distribution of SHG members according to change in economic empowerment

Percentage of office bearers			Percentage of members			Overall percentage		
No change (0-1)	Some change (1-2)	To a large extent (2-3)	No change (0-1)	Some change (1-2)	To a large extent (2-3)	No change (0-1)	Some change (1-2)	To a large extent (2-3)
0	85.00	15.00	0	91.00	9.00	0	89.00	11.00

It shows that 85 percent office bearers and fifteen per cent office bearers reported ' Some Change' followed by 'Change to a large extent', by 91% members had some change and 9 % members had large extent change in their economic empowerment after joining the group. From the result it can be mostly women in SHGs were attained the level of some change. It seems that, women in rural area were mostly poor economic status. Their status was changed after becoming the member of SHGs. The concept of self help prevails in rural Tamil Nadu.

Table 7.31: Distribution of SHG members according to change in legal/political empowerment

Percentage of office bearers			Percentage of Member			Overall percentage		
No change (0-1)	Some change (1-2)	To a large extent (2-3)	No change (0-1)	Some change (1-2)	To a large extent (2-3)	No change (0-1)	Some change (1-2)	To a large extent (2-3)
70.00	30.00	0	79.00	21.00	0	76.00	24.00	0

Perusal of data on change in perception of SHG member regarding legal/political empowerment (Table 7.31) exhibits that approximately 70 percent office bearers and 43 percent members perceived that there is change to a large extent, in their legal/political empowerment. Data further revealed that 79 percent members and 21 percent office bearers reported 'Some Change' in their political/legal empowerment after linking themselves with SHGs. It shows that members in SHGs were they do not have any change, after joining in SHGs in terms of their political/legal empowerment. Now, it clearly indicates that people in SHGs also they never involved in any of the political activities. It indicates that politics is meant for only men's.

Table 7.32: Comparison of change in empowerment of office bearers and members

Mean score								
Off. Bearers				Members			Overall change	
Psycho-social	Economic	Legal-political	Overall	Psycho-social	Economic	Legal-political	Overall	Overall change
2.13	2.15	1.3	5.58	2.1	2.09	1.21	5.4	10.98

Comparison of change in empowerment of office bearers in table 7.32 reveals that overall empowerment was 5.58. It was a summated value of (Psycho- social+ economic + legal -political). On the other hand, overall change for member was 5.4, (Psycho- social+ economic + legal -political). In total SHG members had overall change was 10.98. It shows that women in SHGs were having more amount of change in empowerment. It also observed from the rural situation was that socio-psychological and economic empowerment was higher than legal/political empowerment. Women in rural area thinking that, politics is only for men world. They were aware of it, but not able to participate in the activities, because of family responsibility and social norms.

Summary

- Most of SHGs were taken up micro-financing as major activities. It may helpful for upliftment of rural families. The loans were taken to fulfill the needs like children's education, family loan etc.
- Most often high number of respondents was participated in beginning of the SHGs and drastically it got reduced at present status. In between discontinuation were occurred.
- The group sustainability was measured in terms of monthly collection (Rs.) status by SHG members. In the early stage of SHG formation Rs.72/- was collected, then drastically it was improved upto Rs. 173/- per month. It shows that the women economic empowerment in the Tamil Nadu.
- More than half of the self help group office bearers belong to middle age group. It shows mostly married women participation is high as a whole.

- Most of the self help group members they are not having membership in any other organization.
- Organizational membership status for SHG office bearers and members was very poor.
- The comparison of socio- psychological empowerment of office bearers and members of SHGs in Tamil Nadu found that 51 per cent of office bearers and 52 per cent of the members of SHGs fall in high level of empowerment. Further, equal per cent (48%) of the office bearer and members of SHGs were fall under the category of medium level of empowerment. The least amount - 0.5% of office bearers and none of them from SHGs members were also fall under the low category of socio-psychological empowerment. Thus it can be interpreted from the results that by becoming office bearers the women tend to become more socio-psychological empowered in overall office bearer category.
- Comparison of socio-psychological empowerment of members and non-members of SHGs shows that more than fifty five percent (55.33 %) non members were in the medium category and 44.66 percent in high category. On the other hand, office bearers of SHGs 51.66 per cent were in high category and 48 percent were in the medium category. Thus, it can be concluded from the table that women after becoming the member of SHG become more socio-psychological empowered.
- The result of the economic empowerment of office bearers and SHG members, showed that The overall percentage of SHG members revealed that 74.33 per cent women (both office bearers and members) fall in high level of economic empowerment, 25.66 per cent of women fall in medium level of economic empowerment and none of them had low level of economic empowerment. It shows that, idea of microfinance play a huge impact in rural women empowerment.
- The SHG members were already exposed to various group meetings, bank and other social activities make them empowered. Office bearers also equally empowered in terms of their level of political empowerment. Generally, one universal fact was that all the office bearers were empowered in terms of their political empowerment. Most of them desire to become an Panchayat President or some administrative post in village, in the future.

PRACTICAL AND SCIENTIFIC UTILITY

1. Minimization of number of self help groups members to maintain group cohesiveness.
2. Sustainability of self help groups through up scaling of enterprise.
3. Self help groups leadership efficiency of office bearers could be improved through capacity building

4. Dormant groups could be up-scaled by starting up on micro-finance and regular group meetings.
5. Government buildings could be used as a common platform for group meetings and discussion of the social issues.
6. Capacity building to self help groups leaders to promote efficiency.
7. Linkage of self help groups with stakeholders for marketing of produce.

ACTION FIELD PHOTOGRAPHS

Fig. 7.1: Income generation activities on dairy enterprise

Fig. 7.2: SHG women on cattle management

Fig. 7.3: Interview with SHG office bearer

Fig. 7.4: Interview with small scale entrepreneur

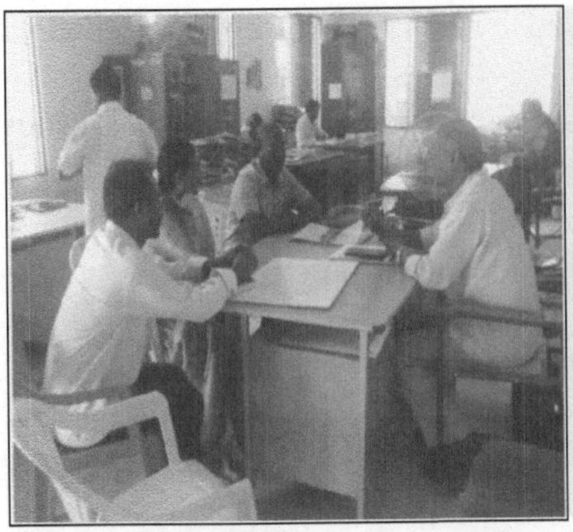

Fig. 7.5: Discussion with project officer for women empowerment

Fig. 7.6: Focused group discussion with self help groups

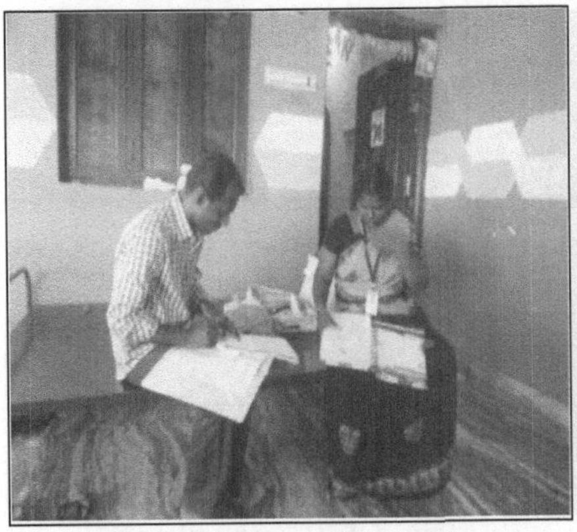

Fig. 7.7: Interview with secretary of self help group

Fig. 7.8: Interview with non-member

Case study: Success Story of Innovative Farm Women

Sl.No.			Personal Information
1.	Name of the farm women	:	Mrs. R.Sathya
2.	Age	:	47
3.	Education	:	High school
4.	Occupation	:	Business (Farm based entrepreneurial unit)
5.	Detail Address	:	No. 38 Max Spring Apartment, Kondayampatti, Madurai, Tamilnadu
6.	Family information	:	Family Size: 4Monthly income: Rs. 4,000/- Land holding (Acre): Nil
7.	Family Assets	:	Own House

(Contd...)

Sl.No.			Personal Information
8.	Background information before initiation of the innovation/Success Stories	:	Mrs. R Sathya, 49 years old women entrepreneur who lives in Kondayampatti village of Madurai district, Tamilnadu. She has completed her primary schoolings from the same village itself. She got married at the age of 22 with a military man. She had 3 girl children's. After few years her husband expired, she went through a bad economic crisis with her daughters.
9.	Practical utility of the innovation/Success stories	:	She attended ICAR-AICRP on Home Science free training program on "Value added products from millets" at Entrepreneurial Development Centre, Home Science Extension, Home Science College and Research Institute, Madurai during the month of January 2016. During training program she was actively involved in all the activities, she made good networking among the peer groups. Initially, she prepared small amount of Adai mix, Kali mix and she sold to neighbors. She had good opinion from neighbors and started a small scale unit. She directly procuring raw materials (Black Gram, Millets, Sorghum, Ragi and Maize) from Allanganallur, Pallemedu farmers with paying of ready cash. All the grains were properly cleaned, soaked and sun dried then powdered in the form of flour mix. She has own brand name called SWASAM NATURALS (Natural breath) with attractive labels pasted in the stand pouch cover. Based on the market value she used to fix the rates for the products. The quantity of the products varies from 150g to 300g. She has also tried with new evolving novel products such as Maize dosa mix fetching good demand in local market. She has also done good amount of marketing strategy for the products. Issuing Pamphlet to the public is one of the ways of promoting brand name. She has exhibited her products in KVK fair, Agri-Science fair, Food festival etc.

(Contd...)

Sl.No.		Personal Information
		Impact of technological empowerment: SHG women entrepreneur technically empowered to prepare the products and to explain the same to their peer groups meetings, mass media, agri-expo, traditional food fest mela etc. Under the AICRP on Home Science project, by the technical support of this team nearly 50 Self Help Group women have been trained and sold the millet based products in their home. They acted as master farmer under Tamil Nadu state *Mahalir Thittam* scheme at Madurai district. **Economic impact per month:** Gross Expenditure = Rs. 22,000/- Gross Income = Rs. 11,500/-Net profit = Rs. 10,500/-
10.	Income before initiation	Nil
11.	Income after initiation	Rs. 10,500/-

CONCLUSION

The study reveals that most of the self help groups in Tamilnadu were taken up microfinance is the major activity for the empowerment of women. Among the self help groups, very few women groups were involved in income generating activities like dairy enterprise, goat rearing and crop husbandry. It shows that women's are socio-economically sound well beings in the Tamilnadu society. It may be conclude that the overall empowerment extent of rural women was observed of medium level which can be considered good. Hence, there is a strong need of awareness with various agricultural innovations and direct motivation, so that the tribal women can get desired empowerment for their self reliance. The agricultural universities, research stations play a main role by executing different developmental programme for women empowerment in the study area.

REFERENCES

Ganessamurthy, V.S. (2007). India: Economic Empowerment of Women, New Century Publications, New Delhi, pp: 32.

Nair, P.R. (2005). Alleviating Poverty: Case Studies of Local – Level Linkages and Processes in the Developing World, Rainbow publishers, Utter Pradesh, pp: 233-251.

Kapur, K. (1988): Women the Co-partner in Agriculture Production, *Maharashtra Journal of Extension Education*, 7(6): 177-185.

Surekha Rao, K. and Rajamanamma, J. (1999): Empowerment of Rural Women through DWCRA Programme, National Conference on Empowerment of Women for National Development, Dhule, pp: 101-107.

Sudharani, K., Sreelatha Kishori, K. and Surendra, G. (2000): Empowerment of Rural Areas, *Rural India*, 14 (2): 195-198.

Pages: 117-138

Rural Development and Techno-Innovations
Edited by: Dr. Alka Chauhan; Er. Chhavi Kumar 'Bharti' & Dr. Pawan Kumar 'Bharti'
ISBN: 978-93-88854-07-8
Edition: 2019
Published by: Discovery Publishing House Pvt. Ltd., New Delhi (India)

8 Vegetable Seed Industry in India
Current Status and Future Strategies for Growth of Industry

Basavaraj Makanur[1]
Esakkimuthu M[2*]
Shilaja Punetha[3]

ABSTRACT

India is home to a very strong and vibrant seed industry. Globally, India stands at the 3rd place in the size of seed market in terms of quantity, next to USA and china. The Indian seed market has shown a consistent growth from 1970s. The last two decades have been very dynamic, with major contribution from private seed industry. The current Indian seed market size is estimated to be approximately Rs. 8000 Crores. The Indian seed industry is undergoing wide ranging transformations – which include an increasing role of private sector seed companies, rising presence of multinational seed companies with focus on biotechnology, and wide ranging changes in regulatory frameworks, which would affect seed research, marketing, and trade in coming years. The lack of organized statistics in the vegetable sector has masked the contribution of the private seed industry. The hybrid vegetable seed market in India is estimated to be around Rs. 1500 Crores. It is reckoned that the Indian vegetable seed market is growing at a rate more than 10-15% per year. Among the different crops vegetables are the fastest growing sector in the world. The National Seed Replacement Ratio (SRR) in vegetables which was only 20% in 1980's is today considered to be above 70% and growing with each year. India's seed industry has grown in size and level of performance over the past four decades. Both private and public sector companies/corporations are involved with the production of seed. The public sector component comprises two central corporations, viz. National Seed Corporation (NSC) and State Farm

[1,3] G.B. Pant University of Agriculture and Technology, Pantnagar, Uttarakhand (India)
[2] Kerala Agricultural University, RARS, Pilicode, Kerala (India)

Corporation of India (SFCI) and 16 State Seed Corporations. The private sector comprises around 200 seed companies, which include national and multinational companies and other seed producing/selling companies. Presently Indian seed industry is governed by the following Acts: Seed Act 1966, Seed Rules 1968, Seed Control Order 1983, Essential Commodities Act 1955, Plants, Fruits and Seeds (Regulation of import into India) Order 1989, New Policy on Seed Development 1988, National Seed Policy 2002, Protection of Plant Varieties and Farmers' Rights Act 2001 and Seed Bill 2004). Another factor attracting international seed companies to India is the country's varied agro climatic conditions and abundant skilled and unskilled labour, as seed production, particularly hybrid seed production, is highly labour intensive. Private seed production is largely centered around Bangalore for vegetable crops and Hyderabad for field crops. The emergence of these two seed production centers is due to ideal climatic conditions, better infrastructure, the technology and research leadership, and the expertise of the two regions' seed farmers in manipulating crops for perfectly synchronized flowering. The speedy implementation of the Enactment of the Protection of Plant Varieties and Farmers' Rights Act is urged. There is a need for promoting joint venture collaborations between industry and national and international institutions. The need for creation of awareness among farmers and general public on the benefits and risks associated with transgenic crops is also very important. The private vegetable seed industry in India has set the ball rolling to arrive into an era of matching the world standard of productivity, nutritional security, year round availability.

INTRODUCTION

India is home to a very strong and vibrant seed industry. Globally, India stands at the 3rd place in the size of seed market in terms of quantity, next to USA and china. The Indian seed market has shown a consistent growth from 1970s. The last two decades have been very dynamic, with major contribution from private seed industry. The current Indian seed market size is estimated to be approximately Rs.8000 Crores (1.8 Bil USD). There have been two important phases of growth in Indian agriculture. The first one was ushered through the introduction of high yielding Rice and Wheat varieties in late 1960's; this green revolution has helped India to attain food security. However, this phenomenon was generally restricted to the irrigated regions of the Country. The second phase of growth, the last two decades; has been silently led by the Indian private seed industry. The growth in this phase has been more wide spread across India in raising the farmers' income and in turn the rural livelihood phenomenally. The major contribution made by the private seed industry in launching hybrids in rainfed crops like cotton (65% rainfed), Bajra (65% rainfed) and Maize (50% rainfed) has made this growth more equitable. This has been primarily driven by increased productivity achieved through introduction of high yielding hybrids from the private industry and improved varieties from public sector in all segments of crops like cereals (Rice, Wheat, Maize, Jowar, Bajra), oil seeds (Sunflower, Soybean etc.), fiber crops (Cotton and Jute) and vegetable crops (Tomato, Okra etc.).

Thanks to the adaptation of recent advances in biotechnology and plant breeding, India has made important progress in productivity and production of many crops. Today, India is not only food secure but also progressing towards nutritional security because of better genetics developed by Public and Private sector. We are now self sufficient in crops like rice and wheat and net exporter in crops like cotton and maize. Challenges still exist in producing oil Seeds and Pulses. Advances in crop genetics and adaptation of advanced agronomic practices in vegetables have increased the Indian food production and have helped to keep pace with the growing population. The world population is expected to grow to 8 billion by the year 2025 making the food and nutritional security the most important social issue. Horticultural crops have been greatly expanded due to reasons of economical, social and nutritional security in the country. It is estimated that in this decade we will be having surplus vegetable production and will become a net exporter of vegetables also. The improvement in vegetable genetics has been a contribution of private seed industry. Vegetables and fruits contribute to health security that is of paramount importance for the general well being of the population while grain crops provide the much needed nutritional security.

India has taken a bold step towards self sufficiency in food. However, self sufficiency in the true sense can be achieved only when each individual in the country is assured of balanced diet. This created an urgent need for providing health security to our population by supplying nutrition through balanced diet. Indians are predominantly vegetarians and depend on vegetables for bulk of their nutrients and minerals. More recently, the role and usefulness of anti-oxidants present in vegetables in human health has been demonstrated, adding value to this set of crops. Vegetables cultivation has been known to stimulate development because it is labour intensive, earns higher returns and involve extra skills. Development in vegetable production will therefore contribute not only to food and nutritional security but also to poverty alleviation and income generation.

Vegetables form the most important component of a balanced diet. India is the second largest producer of vegetables in the world next only to China with an estimated production of about 146 million tonnes from an area of 8.0 million hectares at an average yield of 16.7 tonnes per hectare. India shares about 15% of the world output of vegetables from about 2.8% of croppped area in the country. However our per capita consumption is quite low. We can grow variety of vegetables all the year round. Varied agro-climatic conditions in India make it possible to grow a wide variety of vegetable crops all the year round in one part of the country or another. India can claim to grow the largest number of vegetable crops compared to any other country of the world and as many as 61 annual and 4 perennial vegetable crops are commercially cultivated.

In the post partition period a good infrastructure for vegetable research has been created. At present vegetable research is being carried out at four central institutes, one National Research Centre and 26 State Agricultural Universities. The All India Coordinated Research Programme of the Project Directoreate of Vegetable Research provides facilities for multidisciplinary, area specific research on 23 vegetable crops and provides a national grid for multilocation testing of technologies developed by various institutions. As a result research on various aspects of major vegetable crops is being undertaken in order to improve existing varieties and standardize production techniques.

Vegetables are one of the cheapest source of nutrition and have important role in fighting hunger in this over populated country. More than 50 indigenous and exotic vegetables of temperate and tropical origin are native to India. The history of domestication, adaptation and assimilation of such a large inventory of kinds and varieties point to their interesting link with the waves after waves of early people, natives and even those who migrated from central Asia to make India their home.

INDIAN SEED INDUSTRY: A HISTORICAL PERSPECTIVE

From a public sector dominated industry during 1960's, the Indian seed sector has evolved into a multi faceted industry with large private sector participation and an increasing emphasis on R & D. The foundation of organized field crop seed production program in the country was laid with the establishment of National Seeds Corporation. However, over the past four decades there have been several changes and improvisations in the system, by the private seed industry in order to bring it in tune with requirements that are unique to Indian agriculture.

The history of vegetables is also a welcome reminder that India received so much more from the world than it could possibly give back. The excavations of pre-historic and proto- historic sites provide an authentic historical evidence of cultivation of vegetables such as peas, melons and beans by the people of major civilization that flourished along Indus River Valley, as far back as 2500 BC. The excavations at Maheshwara and Navadatoli in Madhya Pradesh have further established peoples' knowledge of vegetables in vedic period (around 1200 BC). Rigveda and Atharva Veda, written during that period, cite medicinal properties of onions and garlic. Jain works, Budhist Sutras and Jatakas exhorted usage of eggplant, cucumber, bottlegourd etc. for general well being.

Indian National Science Academy (1980) has brought out relevant botanical names of plants mentioned in medical treatise like "Charaka Samhita" dated to be around 600 BC and in the "Sasruta Samhita" of 3rd to 4th Century AD (Ray *et al.*, 1980). Invaders, travellers and traders all contributed in introduction and spread of large number of vegetables used by Indian since long time. Mughals, who invaded in 15th century and ruled until British took over and who were gourmets of good food, included liberal doses of onion and garlic in the recipes for flavouring their culinary delicacies, especially the meat dishes. Colonising traders from Portugal, France, Netherlands, Denmark and Britain brought crops like cabbage and cauliflower, hot pepper, potato, etc. between 14th-17th centuries.

Interestingly, the ubiquitous Tomato which claims today the largest production came just about 200 years ago. Similarly cauliflower which was introduced by Europeans, not only claims substantial area today but is one crop that has undergone major genetic upheaval within a short period- thanks to voluntary selection by local cultivators, mostly during early part of this century itself. The evolution of a new and distinct class: Indian Cauliflower is a fascinating story of unlocking its hidden genetic potential by people who did not know much about the intricacies of plant breeding.

The present prominent status of vegetables in overall nutritional security of the country can thus be attributed to centuries of domestication of indigenous genetic diversity, large number of introductions from far off lands followed by their adaptation, and more recently, value addition through genetic advances. Today, India prides itself as the second largest producer of vegetables in the world. It has maintained a measured growth in production for meeting the growing demands at home and abroad. The projections of requirements during the early decades of next century, however, have to factor not only total population growth (currently 1.8 percent) but also an increasing proportion of middle class with greater nutritional and appetising concerns. It is presumed that by 2025 India will have 1.4 billion people, majority of whom will have relatively higher living standards. To meet this demand, the strategists have set a growth target of 3 percent for the production and accordingly emphasised the need for action to achieve productivity from ever diminishing land resources. The solution lies clearly in the technology that aims at deriving best out of the configurations of genes and environments.

Dispensation of technology through genetic package i.e. seed, is the most cost effective strategy. Realising this, though belatedly, government of India liberalised vegetable seed imports by announcing the New Seed Policy, 1988. Tariff barriers were removed through an instrument of duty free Open General License (OGL). Thanks to the policy, that the farmers now have a very wide choice of planting materials available anywhere in the world.

A global trend of growers' shift into the fast track of hybrid technology is clearly visible in India too. The hybrids are being adopted for their: (a) greater productivity, (b) extended availability, (c) better adaptability, (d) selective capability. For the seed industry, constantly grappling with the onslaught of pirates, hybrids provide built-in safeguards in pre-programmed parent lines. Encouraged by these fundamentals, seed industry has started investing heavily in hybrid research while remaining an active partner in public institutional effort of an overall variety up gradation.

There is a necessity for continuous flow of value added planting materials employing conventional and/or biotechnological systems in order to match the ever changing needs of consumers and farms. An even greater participation and investment in biotechnological and applied research by both public and private sector is paramount. And, a consistent support-institutional, legislative and regulatory- has to be in place if the vast potential of the seeds, is to be unfolded.

Seeds form the fundamental and crucial input for sustained growth in farm production, often stimulating the use of new methods, machinery and yield-enhancing agro-inputs. The role of the seed sector is not only to ensure adequacy in seed quality but also to ensure varietal diversity. Today, the Indian seed programme boasts one of the biggest seed markets in the world, with annual sales at around US $920 million. Of this, domestic off take accounts for US $900 million and sales in the global market account for the remaining US $20 million.

The New Policy on Seed Development (NPSD), established in 1988 with the objective of augmenting productivity and output quality, stimulated major growth in the industry as it attracted a lot of investment in seed business from major domestic seed companies. Given the growth of the seed sector in recent years, India has the potential to become the foremost player in the seed export business in the developing world with prospective markets in Asia, Africa and South America.

STRUCTURE OF VEGETABLE SEED INDUSTRY

Public Sector: Generally, seed industry in India owes its strength to the public sector program. Several improved OP varieties were developed from public Institutes and these replaced the local varieties popular with the growers. In general, the Government deals with regulations and seed certification ensuring availability of high quality seeds to growers. The research in public sector is well spread out and organized. Work is carried out in over 25 agricultural universities, ICAR sponsored research Institutes and National Research Centres besides the All India Coordinated programs conducting trials in varied conditions. This network is one of the largest in the agricultural systems in the world.

Like many agriculturally developed Asian nations, India has sizeable public and private sector seed businesses. Giant public sector players include the National Seeds Corporation (NSC), the State Farms Corporation of India (SFCI) and the thirteen State Seed Corporations (SSCs). NSC was the first public sector organization, established in 1963, and remained virtually the only agency for seed production for around 13 years. Its role extended to several developmental programmes including training, quality control and extension activities in seeds. This was followed by the setting up of the SSCs under two consecutive plan periods, supported by the World Bank, and these largely adopted the role of the NSC in the Indian States. These corporations engage principally in production and marketing of seeds of high yielding and hybrid varieties developed by the public sector. The initial impetus to the vegetable variety development was from public institutes. Several high yielding varieties in many crops were released including some with disease resistances. These institutions continue to develop and release new varieties and hybrids. Popular varieties released by the Institutes are produced and marketed by many small and medium sized companies. These include Arka Anamika in okra, Arka Manik in watermelon, Arka Vikas in tomato, G4 in chillies, Hara Madhu in melons, Arka Komal in beans besides others.

The private seed companies have also been benefited as these releases formed the base material for the start of their breeding programs. Okra hybrids developed and sold by private companies today owe their success to releases resistant to YVMV like Arka Anamika, Parbani Kranti and A4. In tomato also, the private industry has successfully used the bacterial wilt resistant lines released from public institutes like IIHR, Bangalore to develop resistant hybrids. Many of the Institutes and Universities have formulated rules by which the seed companies can buy their varieties including parents of hybrids.

Biotechnology is an important growing area today with wide applications. The tools of molecular biology can be dovetailed with conventional breeding programmes enabling great advances in crop improvement. Many of the public Institutes have reasonably strong programs in this area. The objectives include marker - assisted selection (MAS), markers for use in purity tests and transgenics. Some of the companies have state of the art laboratories for molecular biology. Projects underway in Institutes and private companies include introduction of Bt gene into brinjal, tomato, cauliflower and chillies for insect resistance as well as engineering TLCV resistance in tomato. It would be important to prove the usefulness of the introduced gene(s) and also demonstrate biosafety aspects. With regulatory agencies in place, testing procedures and schedules worked out, it is expected that transgenics, when developed with the advantages demonstrated, will find favour with the growers. Strong linkages and joint operational projects in areas of molecular biology with public institutes will help medium sized private seed companies to utilize the scientific talent available in public institutes and benefit from costs of research.

Table 8.1: Public Sector Hybrids

Crop	Hybrid	Source
Tomato	Pusa Hybrid-1, PH-2, PH-4	IARI
	Arka Vishal, Arka Vardhan, Arka Abhijit	IIHR
	NDTH-1, NDTH-2, NDTH-4	Faizabad
	Pant Hybrid-1, 2, 10, 11	Pantnagar
Brinjal	Arka Navneet	IIHR
	Pusa Anmol, Pusa Hybrid-5, Pusa Hybrid-6, Pusa Hybrid-9	IARI
	Vijay Hybrid, Azad Hybrid	Kanpur
	NDBH-1, NDBH-6, NDBH-7	Faizabad
	PBH-1	Pantnagar
	Punjab Hybrid, BH-1	Ludhiana
Chilli	CH-1, CH-3	Ludhiana
Sweet pepper	Solan Hybrid-1	Solan
	Pusa Deepti, KT-2	Katrain
Okra	DVR-1, DVR-2	PDVR, Varanasi
	DOH-3, DOH-4	IARI
Onion	Arka Kirtiman, Arka Lalima	IIHR
Cauliflower	Pusa Hybrid-2	IARI
Cabbage	H-64, BRH-5	Katrain
Muskmelon	Punjab hybrid, MHL-10	Ludhiana
	Pusa Rasaraj, DMH-4	IARI
Watermelon	Arka Jyoti	IIHR
	RHRWH-2	Rahuri
Cucumber	Pusa Sanyog	Katrain
	AAUC-1, AAUC-2	Jorhat
	Pant Sankar Kheera-1	Pantnagar
Bottle gourd	Pant Sankar Lauki-1, Pant Sankar Lauki-2	Pantnagar
	Pusa Hybrid-2	IARI
	NDBGH-4, NDBGH-7	Faizabad
Pumpkin	Pusa Hybrid-1	IARI
Summer squash	Pusa Alankar	IARI
Bitter gourd	Pusa Hybrid-1	IARI

GOVERNMENT AND SEED INDUSTRY

During the last decade Governments, both central and state, and other related agencies have been supportive and proactive. It can be expected that further removal of controls and restrictions, which impede growth of the industry, will facilitate in making this sector stronger. India is also a signatory to WTO and the barriers for seed trade have been removed. PVP bill has been passed by the Parliament and this is expected to generate more investments in R&D. Government Institutes provide breeders seeds at reasonable prices. Private participation is also The policy framework hitherto has been regulatory with excessive legislation. Above plethora of legislation covering the seed sector is out of date and restrictive rather than progressive. The multiplicity of Acts, rules and administrative orders have resulted in over regulation of the nascent industry.

Private Industry: Technological skills and expertise in breeding, production and quality control along with marketing skills have put private sector as efficient developers, producers and marketers of hybrid seeds. The ultimate success of this enterprise can be measured from the profits that accrue to the grower. The private seed industry relying on varieties/ germplasm from public institutes and from international institutes, were quick to develop and deliver hybrids. It was soon clear that major vegetable crops imported from temperate countries cannot replicate similar yields in all agro climatic conditions demanding local and customized research. Imports are now made mostly in crops like cabbage, cauliflower, carrot, coriander and beetroot valued at 34 Mil USD.

Although private seed companies such as Poacha and Sutton have been established since the pre-independence era, accelerated growth of the private sector began only after the introduction of the new seed policy in 1988 which ushered in a liberal business climate. Currently there are over 200 private seed companies, together with a few multinational companies, and these tend to focus on low volume, high value crops with the principal effort being placed on creating hybrids for oilseeds, maize, cotton and vegetable crops. The private sector accounts for 70% of the market in terms of market turnover whereas the public sector has the greater share in terms of volume sales.

During the seventies, the advantages of hybrid vegetables were successfully demonstrated in growers' fields. In the same period, the vegetable seed industry became more organized. Initially, hybrids in tomato and capsicum made a mark with the growers. Since then, there has been a spurt of activity in the Indian vegetable seed scenario with the hybrid acreage soaring and a number of vegetable seed companies coming into existence. In the transformation of the largely unorganized seed sector to a more organized one, the policies of the Government of India played a significant role. In 1988, the private sector got a huge boost in growth with the removal of restrictions by a Government order liberalizing seed imports through open general license and removing tariff barriers. This move resulted in import of hybrid seeds in cabbage, cauliflower, chillies, etc. besides large quantities of seeds of carrot and beetroot by private seed companies. This Act also encouraged healthy competition in local research efforts leading to release of several hybrids by the private seed industry. Subsequently foreign direct investments flow increased, joint ventures (JVs) were set up and there was import of germplasm. Presently the private seed industry comprises of the following categories: (a) Local companies dealing predominantly with open pollinated varieties (b) Indian companies marketing hybrids sourced from abroad (c) Indian companies developing, producing and marketing hybrids.

INDIAN VEGETABLE SEED INDUSTRY

The lack of organized statistics in the vegetable sector has masked the contribution of the private seed industry. The hybrid vegetable seed market in India is estimated to be around Rs.1500 Crores (300 mill USD). Table 8.2 provides details of the major crops for hybrid seeds. It is reckoned that the Indian vegetable seed market is growing at a rate more than 10-15% a year. During the decade 1998-2008 there was a remarkable increase in market size of vegetable hybrid seeds (194%). It is anticipated that during the next five years also the growth will continue at a rapid pace (45.4%). Among the different crops vegetables are the fastest growing sector in the world (AVRDC 2006). No wonder that more and more arable land is being turned over to vegetable cultivation and the demand for quality seed is growing.

Table 8.2: Details of hybrid vegetable seed market in India

Crop	Estm. Market Size F 1 2009 (Tonnes)	Estm. Market Size F 1 2009 (Crore)
Watermelon	110	50
Melon	18	23
Tomato	55	165
Ridgegourd	35	11
Chilli Pepper	60	108
Cabbage	35	39
Cauliflower	40	60
Sponge gourd	25	5
Bottlegourd	100	18
Bittergourd	80	18
Cucumber	40	28
Okra	1400	140
Brinjal	35	18
Capsicum	1	4
Total	2,080	685

Source: Singh, 2010

Seed industry in India is very heterogeneous in terms of ownership, scales of operation and functioning and integration of research, production and marketing units. The private seed companies are structured in any one of the following ways.

1. Local companies trading in Op seeds; Indian companies selling F1 hybrids developed abroad.
2. Indian owned companies with production and marketing capabilities but have tie up with foreign companies for R&D.
3. Indian owned companies developing, producing and marketing of hybrid seeds. Some of them have enlarged their sphere of activity by opening offices in other countries.
4. Foreign companies (MNCs, transnational) with JV or subsidiary in India having R&D, production and marketing capabilities. They bring in germplasm and technology from abroad.
5. Foreign companies marketing hybrids developed by their parent organization abroad.
6. Indian companies relying on contract seed production for export and also or domestic market.

Operations by foreign seed companies have increased exponentially in India, directly or indirectly. Furthermore, need for new technologies like marker assisted selections, transgenics, phytopathological skills, induction of haploids, novel or new gene(s) for disease resistance, abiotic stresses or male sterility have intensified. Many of these global companies through their own research or through collaborative projects with foreign Universities of repute have access to these technologies. It is anticipated that many of these new technologies will be put into use in developing new hybrids by the seed companies.

DEVELOPING VEGETABLE HYBRIDS FOR INDIA

Developing hybrids for the Indian diversity is a challenge. Thanks to the major Indian vegetable seed companies who have been able to connect to this diverse requirement and evolved adaptable hybrids to the requirements. Below are the critical intersects.

Multiplicity of varieties in different regions of India: A critical insight is needed before decisions are made on research allocations on segments to concentrate. This also makes it difficult to market new varieties unless it conforms to the existing OP variety. This includes chillies, eggplant, besides cabbage and different maturity groups in cauliflower. Some of the available segments in major crops wherein hybrids have been introduced and are growing in popularity. In most crops the segmentation based on regions as in chillies, cabbages and now in tomato.

Tomato: Dual/Regular, Acidic, Acidic –TLCV resistant, Oval – TLCV resistant, BW resistant, Indeterminate.

Chillies: Fresh light green to dark green small, Fresh light green to dark green long, Red dry medium pungency small and long sized, Red dry high pungency, Red dry wrinkled, Bajji.

Melon: Cantaloupe, Yellow Canary, Galia, Honey dew.

Watermelon: Icebox, Sugar baby, Jubilee large oval, Jubilee large round, crimson sweet, Black Head.

Brinjal: Manjarigota - purple stripes, Small purple round/oval, Very dark purple small, Oval medium size, green purple stripes, Small round green, Small oval purple, Manjarigota - purple stripes with no spines, Long green.

Cabbage: Large flat tolerant to rain & heat, Round light green early 1-2kg, Round to green tight, 1.5kg, Small (1kg or less), Round to conical, Semi flat, 1.5-2kg, Very small and very early ; all with good adaptability & field holding.

Industrial needs: Segmentation can be complex in crops like chillies wherein, the industry has a dominant role to play in terms of required values for pungency and colour. Tomato for processing requires certain fruit biochemical traits like brix, viscosity and lycopene besides high yields and other fruit quality attributes.

Crop diversification: The Indian gourds, cucumber and acidic tomatoes popular in South India were anchored in OP varieties till a couple of years ago. However, now there has been a rapid shift to hybrids in these segments.

Transportability and shelf Life: In India the tomatoes, melons, travel distances more than 1000 km by road (Poor roads, poor packing and poor storage conditions) to reach the destination market. The Indian private vegetable seed industry could breed for successful hybrids, which have high LSL.

Pests and diseases of significance in tropics & sub tropics: Majority of them are specific to these regions and this is one of the major reasons for hybrids developed abroad not being successful.

There are reports of outbreak of new pests and diseases in most vegetable crops. Moreover, new races of the fungi and strains of the virus appear necessitating the need for local research. In tomato the TLCV is a major constraint in production. This is a devastating disease in summers but is now prevalent in other seasons as well. Differences in strains exist and different sources of resistances are required for North & South of India. Moreover available resistance is succumbing to the disease. GBNV causes serious economic losses in tomato and no source of resistance has yet been reported. Resistance breeding for late blight and bacterial wilt is confronted by prevalence of differences in races. Chilli harbors a multitude of viruses and breeding for multiple virus resistant is an important task. Chilli can be a major export earner if fruit rot resistance can be combined with tolerance to sucking pests and chemical sprays avoided. In watermelon, varieties resistant to *Fusarium* or Bud necrosis virus have not been developed yet. Similarly, in melons we need resistance to virus complex. In okra it is mandatory now to release hybrids with resistance to YVMV and ELCV (venation leaf curlvirus). Hybrids with combined and yet high stable resistance will be the target. The Private Indian seed Industry has invested significant funds in meeting these challenges and thereby creating a Win – Win situation for both growers and the entrepreneur.

ROLE OF PRIVATE VEGETABLE SEED INDUSTRY IN HYBRID SEED PRODUCTION

The National Seed Replacement Ratio (SRR) in vegetables which was only 20% in 1980's is today considered to be above 70% and growing with each year. Further, with the rapid pace of introducing innovative biotech technologies playing a prominent role in new product development, it is estimated that a significant and rapid conversion from OP cultivation to hybrids will happen in all most all the crops in vegetables. This shift to hybrids will lead to increased requirement for hybrid seed production in various vegetable crops. These challenges of higher production requirement have been tackled by well organized and developed production system in the private seed industry. Private seed industry has geared up to the challenge and started exploring various ways, like approaching new areas in India and other regions of the world, training man power for effective pollination, protected cultivation etc. In addition to this industry is also working on developing the hybrids based on CMS and gynoecious technologies.

PRESENT SCENARIO OF VEGETABLE PRODUCTION AND SEED REQUIREMENT

India is next only to China in area and production of vegetables and occupies prime position in the production of cauliflower, second in onion and third in cabbage in the world. The area and production of major vegetables during 2007-08 is estimated at 8.57 million ha with a production of 127.1 million tonnes (including chilli) and average productivity of 16.1 tonnes per ha. More than 40 kinds of vegetables belonging to different groups, namely, solanaceous, cucurbitaceous, leguminous, cruciferous (cole crops), root crops and leafy vegetables are grown in India in tropical, sub-tropical and temperate regions. Important vegetable crops grown in the country are tomato, onion, brinjal, cabbage, cauliflower, okra and peas. To meet the Nation's food and nutritional security needs, it is important to make available to Indian farmers a wide range of seeds of superior quality, in adequate quantity on a timely basis. The seed replacement rate of major vegetable crops (Table 8.3) in recent times is quite encouraging and there is a huge demand for quality seeds of vegetable crops within the country in addition to export opportunities.

Table 8.3: Seed Replacement Rate of major vegetables

Crop	SRR (%)
Brinjal	63.4
Cabbage	100
Cauliflower	86.4
Chilli	83.7
Gourds	73.5
Melons	89.2
Okra	92.4
Tomato	99.3
Beans	62.2
Onion	87.3
Peas	93.5
Others	72.6

Source: Agriculture Year Book, 2010

Table 8.4: Current demand of seeds of major vegetables

Vegetable	Area (ha)	Requirement (t)
Tomato	499449	249
Brinjal	49287	369
Chilli	420984	421
Cabbage	312861	156
Cauliflower	312861	156
Cucumber	22256	55
Gourds	420984	2104
Leafy vegetables	142207	5688
Melons	174197	696
Okra	382302	3058
Onion	399054	3990
Pea	233663	23366
Radish	306558	767
Beans	244402	24444
Others	1529938	3824
Total	5894530	69346

Souce: www.nsai.co.in

Table 8.5: Availability of quality seeds of vegetable crops in India

Vegetable Crop	Seed Availability (Tonnes)	Availability (%)
Beans	7983.4	67.2
Brinjal	151.9	63.4
Cabbage	197.1	86.4
Cauliflower	197.1	86.4
Cucumber	39.3	72.6
Chilli	1504.1	73.5
Gourd	1504.1	73.5
Leafy vegetables	2328.1	42.1
Melons	377.7	89.2
Okra	4292.7	92.4
Onion	4233.5	87.3
Peas	15929.7	93.5
Radish	719.7	97.5
Tomato	198.8	99.3
Others	2699.6	72.6
Total	42326.8	78.6

Source: Agriculture Year Book, 2010

Table 8.6: Estimated values (million US $) of the commercial markets for seeds

Sl. No.	Country	Value (million US $)
1.	U.S.A.	12,000
2.	China	6,000
3.	France	2,370
4.	Brazil	2,000
5.	India	1,500
6.	Japan	1,250

Source: ISF, 2011

CONCURRENT DEVELOPMENTS

1. Seed quality of commercial seeds is of a high order and there has been a continuous up gradation of quality of seeds indicating the self imposed regulation by the companies on quality of seeds supplied. They are fungicide treated coated with coloured polymers. Most of the companies have quality control labs of high standards. ISTA accredited labs are also now in place in India and helps in providing necessary documentation for exports.
2. In India most of the private companies sell seeds which have more than 90% germination and high degree of purity and this exceed the standards set out under the seed act. Besides the conventional GOT, many of the companies routinely use sophisticated molecular tools markers to assess seed purity.

3. Commercial seed production for export and domestic markets is carried out through contract production. Contract farming concept has been very successfully employed for benefit for both the parties in seed production. Seed production employs more than 7lakh people directly and indirectly.
4. Plant variety protection and farmer's act of 2001 and New Seed Policy of 2002 have been passed. According to the latter act, all varieties will have to be registered. Although there may be delays, it is expected that will benefit seed industry.

BIOTECHNOLOGY IN VEGETABLE CROPS AND ITS IMPACT

Considerable work on biotechnology related to vegetable crops is in progress in India. Research areas under this field include development of DNA markers and transgenics. The frontier area of biotechnology has opened up another avenue for enhancing productivity of crops through developing transgenics with tolerance/resistance to abiotic and biotic stresses. Work on transgenics is underway in both public sector and in the private sector. ICAR, DBT and Agricultural Universities have fully fledged projects on transgenics. Cotton hybrids with Bt gene(s) to counter boll worm attack have been successful in India and this technology is now being pursued in other vegetable crops for protection against fruit borers. Bt Egg plant from MAHYCO as well as IARI is in final stages of testing. Research on okra and tomato with Bt gene is being vigorously pursued and are already slated for field trials.

Many of the large seed companies intensively pursue their in-house biotech research projects. They work with gene constructs from abroad, from another company or from a public institute. The Government of India has been encouraging research on transgenics with funding and training programs. The Government is also proactive with policies and guidelines on release of transgenic crops. DBT has put in place a regulatory process with clear guidelines to follow while releasing transgenics. In cases where resistant gene(s) has not yet been sourced as in GBNV of tomato and bud necrosis of watermelon, transgenics could be an alternative approach. In vegetable crops abiotic stresses still pose a problem in terms of extending areas or seasons. Drought tolerance and salinity tolerance are important areas of research wherein traditional breeding efforts have not yet helped develop lines/hybrids. Work in M.S.Swaminathan Research Foundation has provided vital clues on useful genes for drought and salinity tolerance. Partnership with such research institutes will provide a strong platform for developing hybrids that can extend vegetable cultivation in water deficit and salinity prone areas.

REGULATORY ENVIRONMENT

Industry Regulation and Quality Control

The Ministry of Agriculture within the following legislative framework determines overall policy with regard to the seed industry.

1. The Seed Act, 1966 and Seed Rules, 1968

The Seed Act enacted in 1966, the Seed Rules framed under this Act and notified in 1968, and amendments from time to time provide the basic regulatory structure to ensure seed quality control. The Act provides for compulsory quality control of seed of any notified kind and variety; voluntary certification of seed of any notified kind or variety; and truthfully labeling of seeds. The Act specifies the function of various regulatory bodies associated with the industry as well as rules for notification of new varieties, specifications of minimum limits of germination and purity, regulation of sale of seeds, certification, labeling, etc.

2. Seed (Control) Order, 1983

A Seeds (Control) Order was issued in 1983 under the Essential Commodities Act of 1955, which required seed dealers to obtain a license valid for three years in order to operate, grants the Controller powers to regulate the sale and distribution of seed and provide additional power to the seed inspectors.

3. New Seed Legislation, 2002

The GOI is in the process of formulating a new seed legislation, which would ultimately replace the existing Seed Act, Rules, and Seeds (Control) Order, 1983. This legislation is aimed at regulating the quality of seeds for sale, imports, and exports. Various stakeholders are currently reviewing the draft bill. The salient features of the proposed legislation are:

1. Compulsory registration of all varieties being offered for sale by National Seed Board (NSB), to be constituted by the government
2. Registration to be valid for fifteen years for annual and biennial crops and 18 years for long duration perennial crops
3. Registration of genetically engineered crops subject to clearance under the Environmental (Protection) Act, 1986
4. Selling, bartering, importing/exporting of seed of any transgenic kind/ variety subject to declaration to this effect
5. Non-registration of a kind/variety of seeds containing any technology (including genetic use restriction technology and terminator technology), which is harmful, or potentially harmful
6. Registration of existing varieties on the basis of three years of agronomic performance data to be submitted by the applicant
7. Registration of new/exotic varieties only provisionally for two years

8. Registration of all seed producers and seed processing
9. Declaration of information on adaptability and expected agronomic performance by the breeder
10. NSB to decide the seed standards, to appoint private/public seed certification agencies and to formulate rules for compensation to farmers in the event of a crop failure due to defective seeds
11. Exemption of farmers' seed from the Seed Act and allowing them to save their own seeds and market it without branding.

4. Seed Bill, 2004

A bill to provide for regulating the quality of seeds for sale, import and export and to facilitate production and supply of seeds of quality and for matters connected therewith or incidental thereto. Combination of Seeds Act (1966), Seed Control Order (1983) and New Seed Policy (1988)

Salient features:

1. It includes all agricultural, horticultural, flowers, medicinal and aromatic plants seeds and planting materials.
2. Compulsory registration of varieties sold in market.
3. All public and private seed organizations should have Self certification for seed production
4. Compulsory labeling.
5. Each and every private seed company should have their own R & D.
6. Each and every private seed company should have seed quality testing laboratory.
7. Punishment and imprisonment has increased.
8. All registered varieties are eligible for certification.
9. Seeds of varieties or kinds not existing on "National Register of Seeds of kinds and varieties" shall not be permitted for marketing.
10. Horticulture nursery to be registered.
11. Registration of Seed Producers and Processing Units made compulsory.

5. Phytosanitary Regulations

The Destructive Insects and Pests Act, 1914 & Plants, Fruits and Seeds (Regulation of Import in India) Order, 1989. This Act and Order regulate the import into India of agricultural products including plants and seeds. Salient features are prohibit import of seeds for sowing and planting materials without a valid permit; clearance of consignments subject to inspection, fumigation, disinfection, and disinfestations as the case may be under official supervision; imports not permitted unless accompanied by an official Phytosanitary Certificate.

6. Plant Variety Protection and Farmers' Rights Act, 2001

To address concerns about the lack of effective intellectual property rights in the seed industry, the GOI enacted legislation in August 2001 named, "Plant Variety Protection and Farmers' Rights Act, 2001." This legislation provides for the establishment of a "Protection of Plant Varieties and Farmers' Right Authority" to implement the Act. Under the new legislation, farmers will continue to enjoy their traditional rights to save, use, exchange, share, and sell the produce of the protected variety with the only restriction that the farmer will not be able to sell branded seed of the protected variety for commercial purpose. The legislation contains several of the contentious issues such as the compulsory acquisition of parental material of a variety and granting production license to a third party to produce proprietary variety when there is a shortage of such seeds.

PROTECTED CULTIVATION

There has been significant increase the area under protected cultivation in the recent past and it is forecasted to grow rapidly because of the encouragement provided by the Government through subsidies for erection of plastic houses.

On the other hand growers are benefited by realizing a better price and productivity especially during the adverse weather conditions. The growth is also going to be driven by the demand from the consumers for better quality produce. Protected cultivation is expected to keep the price in check by ensuring availability during offseason also. Presently the seeds for protected cultivation are being provided by multinationals. Although in the future Indian private vegetable seed industry could gear up of this challenge of high precision.

INDUSTRY ISSUES

Assuring production **and** ***marketing:*** Priority policy formulation and regulatory changes for the 11th 5-Year plan aim to improve productivity, enhance farmer incomes, and stimulate agribusiness. Implementation at national, state, district, and farmer levels is the key to improving the rapidity and ease with which change can occur. Dialogue and active consultation at all levels are critical for avoiding overlap and for realizing national, state, and district initiatives. Implementation may be a challenge where political or sociocultural issues clash. Government focus on legal frameworks and funding for infrastructure, farmer, and SME incentives at local level will be paramount, especially in remote and marginalized areas.

Benefiting farmers and consumers: Enhancing food safety, quality, and supply chain management, and reducing postharvest loss reduction are key issues. Boosting literacy at village level, and enhancing practical skills, business knowledge, and "produce-care" capabilities of farmers, workers, and consumers are essential for agricultural modernization. Governments and communities must also devise opportunities for those who are marginalized by the changes within the farming and trading sectors.

Expanding trade and value adding: India could easily feed its entire population and expand trade if postharvest losses could be halved (from levels as high as 40%). More processing of vegetables will add value and reduce losses. Foster investment and ease regulatory controls while improving quality and food safety standards. Key challenges is to harness the strengths and achievements in research while paving the way through capacity and new modalities of training for the "new India" as the IT-savvy youth generation, who dominate the population now, become a more significant force in the economy.

Assuring quality and increasing consumption: Attention is needed not only to improve technical skills, logistics, and Good Agricultural Practice, but more critically to human resource development. The All-India coordinated projects for research and development, and the links between the Ministry of Agriculture Indian Council of Agricultural Research (ICAR) agencies and state and district level initiatives are impressive. However, R&D will be implemented more effectively by boosting partnerships with the private sector and with local and international NGOs.

RECOMMENDATIONS FOR DEVELOPMENT

Marketing and economics: Build capacity in agribusiness marketing and policy development for the vegetable sector. Improve collection and analysis of horticulture production and marketing data, and strengthen information flows for internet-based, community-level access. Develop cost-benefit and supply/demand models for transitional and high value production systems, particularly for rain-fed and remote areas, for use in decision making, state/district level investment, and promotion of the vegetable sector.

Industry development: Encourage demand-focused growth in domestic production while improving marketing and value-adding. Strengthen market-focused approaches to trade development. Streamline approaches to trade and agribusiness development, to optimize benefit flows to regions most in need/capable of benefiting from investment. Continue liberalization of market and trade regulation.

Systems and technology: Adopt systems and supply chain management approaches to planning and improvement. Increase developmental work for suitable varieties and productivity improvement under high temperatures. Foster uptake and improvement of low-cost structures, fertigation, and micro irrigation systems. Reduce overuse of chemical fertilizers and enhance precision application through fertigation and use of biofertilizers. Reduce pest and disease losses while minimizing reliance on chemicals for pest and disease management by improving pest management practices.

Collaboration and engagement: Engage with the private sector to streamline modernization of the retail and whole sectors. Focus government investment on logistic and infrastructure improvement and trade promotion, and policy reform on easing regulations and social disruption and increasing consumption.

CONCLUSION

The contribution of the Indian seed industry to provide India the food and nutritional security can be judged by significant increase in the rate of adoption of hybrids developed by the private sector. The Indian farmer considers seed as the most critical input among all the agricultural inputs and his decision making is purely based on the performance in his own field. The seed used has a direct impact on the net returns of the farmer. Now, High yielding hybrids, which are adaptable to various agro climatic zones and seasons, are in place. These hybrids are bred to produce uniform quality of fruits with better transport ability, disease resistance and taste for the consumers. The Government is also funding several projects for rural area development including increasing food supply and all these will generate higher and better seed usage. Shift from OPVs, increasing share of hybrid market, new areas coming under vegetable cultivation, growers irrespective of size of operations taking to hybrids and above all the inherent advantages of F1s in terms of yield, adaptability and fruit quality besides value addition like disease resistance are some of the major reasons for the growth of this industry. Growers are ready to invest in new hybrids and technology. Social gains from private hybrids can also be gauged from the benefits that accrued to small farmers using hybrid seeds. Adoption of improved hybrid technology is also contributing to the success. The private vegetable seed industry in India has set the ball rolling to arrive into an era of matching the world standard of productivity, nutritional security, year round availability.

REFERENCES

Anonymous. (2010): Agriculture Year Book, The National Agriculture Magazine, *Agriculture Today*, 4 (1): 56.

Anonymous. (2010): AVRDC, *Prog. Rep*, Taiwan, pp: 70-72.

Anonymous. (2011): Agriculture Year Book, The National Agriculture Magazine, *Agriculture Today*, 6 (8): 46-48.

Anonymous. (2011): Department of Agriculture and Co-operation., GOI, Report on Agriculture and Food Industry in India, pp: 108.

APEDA. (2007): HACCP and Residue Monitoring. Agricultural and Processed Food Products Export Development Authority, pp: 48.

APEDA. (2010): Agricultural and Processed Food Products Export Development Authority (APEDA), pp: 19.

Arora, R.S. (1998): Vegetable Seed Industry in India, In: National Symposium on Emerging Scenario in Vegetable Research and Development, December 12-14, IIVR, Varanasi, pp. 102-109.

Gadwal, V.R. (2003): The Indian Seed Industry: Its History, Current Status and Future, *Current Sci.*, 84 (3): 399-406.

Govindan, A. (2003): Indian Seed Industry Under Transition, *Gain Report-USDA Foreign Agricultural Service,* pp: 1-17.

Govindan, A. (2007): India FAIRS Country Report Annual 2007, GAIN (Global Agriculture Information Network) Report Number: IN7068, USDA Foreign Agricultural Service: USDA Foreign Agricultural Service, pp: 569.

Johnson, G.I., Weinberger, K. and Wu, M.H. (2008): The Vegetable Industry in Tropical Asia: An Overview of Production and Trade, with a Focus on Thailand, Indonesia, the Philippines, Vietnam,and India. Shanhua, Taiwan: AVRDC – The World Vegetable Center, pp: 56.

Kalloo, G., M.K. Banerjee, S. Kumar and C. Prakash. (1998): Hybrid Vegetable Technology in India: An Overview, In: National Symposium on Emerging Scenario in Vegetable Research and Development, December 12-14, IIVR, Varanasi, pp: 43-52.

Singh, B. (2003): Impact of Vegetable Research, Development and Future Prospects, In: Constraints and Priorities for Research and Development in Agriculture and Allied Sectors of Uttar Pradesh, Lucknow, UPCAR. pp: 145-158.

Singh, U. (2010): Indian Private Vegetable Seed Industry Impact on Food and Nutritional Security, *Agriculture Year Book, pp:* 112-116.

Pages: 139-151

Rural Development and Techno-Innovations
Edited by: Dr. Alka Chauhan; Er. Chhavi Kumar 'Bharti' & Dr. Pawan Kumar 'Bharti'
ISBN: 978-93-88854-07-8
Edition: **2019**
Published by: **Discovery Publishing House Pvt. Ltd., New Delhi (India)**

9

Application of Nanotechnology in Smart Agriculture Development and Future Prospects

A. Ramachandran*

ABSTRACT

The application of nanotechnology to agriculture and food industries is carrying increased weight because of the potential benefits ranging from improved food quality and safety to reduced agricultural inputs and improved processing and nutrition. Agriculture, food and natural resources sector is a part of those challenges like sustainability, vulnerability, human health and happy living. The aim of nanomaterials in agriculture is to reduce the amount of spread chemicals, minimize nutrient losses in fertilization and increased yield through water and nutrient management. Nanotechnology has the potential to develop the agricultural and food industry with novel tools for the molecular management of rapid disease detection, enhancing the ability of plants to absorb nutrients among others. The significant interest of using nanotechnology in agriculture includes specific applications like nanofertilizers and nanopesticides to track products and nutrients levels to increase the productivity without decontamination of soils and waters and protection against pest and diseases. The new chemical and physical properties of nanoparticles provide useful functions that are being rapidly exploited in medicine, biotechnology, electronics, material science and energy sectors among others. The nanoparticles like Ag, ZnO and CuO are relevant in the growth of agriculture by bioactivity and bio-modification. It has been suggested by the researchers that the carbon nanotube (CNT) fused mesh can remove water-borne pathogens, heavy metals like lead, uranium and arsenic. This sophisticated filtering machine removes microbial endotoxins, genetic materials, pathogenic viruses, and micro-sized particles. The carbon nanotubes plays a beneficial

* Assistant Professor, Department of Agronomy, Mother Terasa College of Agriculture, Mettusalai, Illuppur (Po), Pudukkottai - 622 102 Tamil Nadu (India)

role in mustard plant growth and the TiO_2 treatment by Nitrogen Photo-reduction leads to an improved growth of spinach. From many different technological innovations including hybrid varieties, synthetic chemicals and biotechnology nanotechnology seeks a new source of agricultural improvements benefitting from food processing, distribution, packaging and functional food.

The aim of nanoparticles in agriculture is to reduce the amount of sprayed chemicals to deliver active ingredients, minimize nutrient losses in fertilization and increase yield through optimized water and nutrient management. The delivered nanotechnology devices are also being explored in the field of plant breeding and genetic transformation. For the crop production and plant protection the nano-capsules nano-particles and nano-emulsion act as a smart delivery system of active ingredients for disease and pest control. Also this particle are used in fertilizers for the enhancement of nutrients adsorption by plants and delivery of nutrients.

The nanomaterials like zeolites plays a vital role in the agrochemical retention of water or liquid in the soil. The nanoparticles carrying DNA or RNA can be delivered to plant cells for genetic transformation hence plant breeding. The increased use of pesticides and herbicides in the agricultural system effectively utilizes modern technology for crop management called Controlled Environment Agriculture (CEA). The proficient use of agricultural naturals assets during farming as nanosensor is user friendly. For insect pest control a slow but efficient chemical like insecticide is released through a process called Nano-encapulation. Nano-encapsulation is currently the most promising technology for protection of host plants against insect pests. To enhance nutrient use efficiency and overcome the chronic problem of eutrophication, nano-fertilizer might be a best alternative. Nanofertilizers are synthesized in order to regulate the release of nutrients depending on the requirements of the crops, and it is also reported that nanofertilizers are more efficient than ordinary fertilizer. Nanofertilizers could be used to reduce nitrogen loss due to leaching, emissions, and long-term incorporation by soil micro-organisms. Organic farming has been a long-desired goal to increase productivity of crop yields with low input i.e. fertilizers, pesticides, herbicides among others through monitoring environmental variables. Nano-particles can be used in the preparation of new formulations like pesticides, insecticides and insect repellents. Another eco-friendly way to blend the soil without leaning any toxic residue and to prevent the growth of weed species is Nano-herbicide. Organic farming has also been a long desired goal to increase productivity with low input. Through monitoring environmental variables and applying targeted action.

Thus, nanotechnology promises a breakthrough in improving the nutrient use efficiency through nanoformulation of fertilizers, breaking yield and nutritional quality barriers through bionanotechnology, and control of pests and diseases, understanding the mechanism of host-parasite interactions at the molecular scale, development of new-generation pesticides and safe carriers, preservation and packaging of food and food additives, strengthening of natural fiber, removal of contaminants from soil and water bodies, improving the shelf-life of vegetables and flowers, and use of clay minerals as receptacles for nanoresources involving nutrient ion receptors, precision water management.

Despite of these potential advantages, agro-nanotech innovative products are experiencing difficulties in reaching agricultural market. This study provides the current challenges of sustainability, food security and climate change that are exploring by the researchers in the field of nanotechnology in the improvement of agriculture.

Keywords: Biomodification, Nanoformulation, Nanofertilizers, Eutrophication, Nano-encapulation, Nano-herbicide

INTRODUCTION

Nanotechnology, this vast field of the 21st century, is making a very significant impact on the world's economy, industry and people's lives [1,2]. It deals with the physical, chemical and biological properties of matter considered at nanoscale (1–100 nm) and their implications for the welfare of human beings [3]. Nanotechnology is a novel scientific approach that involves the use of materials and equipment capable of manipulating physical as well as chemical properties of a substance at molecular levels. On the other hand, bio-technology involves using the knowledge and techniques of biology to manipulate molecular, genetic and cellular processes to develop products and services and is used in diverse fields from medicine to agriculture[4].

Nanotechnology has the potential to revolutionize the agricultural and food industry with novel tools for the molecular management of diseases, rapid disease detection, enhancing the ability of plants to absorb nutrients, among others. On the other hand, nano bio-technology can improve our understanding of the biology of various crops and thus can potentially enhance yields or nutritional values, as well as developing improved systems for monitoring environmental conditions and enhancing the ability of plants to absorb nutrients or pesticides.[5] Agricultural and food systems security, disease management delivery systems, new techniques for molecular and cellular biology, new materials for pathogen detection and protection of the environment.[6] Nano biotechnology operates at the same level with virus or disease infecting particle, and thus holds the potential for primordial detection and eradication. It also holds out the possibility that smart sensors and delivery systems will help the agricultural industry combat viruses and other crop pathogens.[7] In the near future, nano-structured catalysts will be available which will increase the efficiency of pesticides and herbicides, allowing lower doses to be used. Nanotechnology will also protect the environment indirectly through the use of alternative (renewable) energy supplies, and filters or catalysts to reduce pollution and clean-up existing pollutants in soil and water.[8] In the agricultural sector, nanotech research and development is likely to aid and frame the next level of expansion of genetically modified crops, animal pro-duction inputs, chemical pesticides and precision farming techniques. [9]

NANOTECHNOLOGY AND AGRICULTURAL PRODUCTION DEVELOPMENTS

In the near future, nanostructured catalysts will be available which will increase the efficiency of pesticides and herbicides thus allowing lower doses to be used. An agricultural system widely used in the USA, Europe and Japan, which efficiently utilises modern technology for crop management is called Controlled Environment Agriculture (CEA). CEA is an advanced and intensive form of hydroponically based agriculture. Controlled-environment agriculture (CEA) is any agricultural technology that enables the grower to manipulate a crop's environment to the desired conditions. CEA technologies include greenhouse, hydroponics, aquaculture, and aquaponics. Controlled variables include temperature, humidity, pH, and nutrient analysis. Plants are grown within a controlled environment so that agricultural practices can be optimized. The computerized system monitors and regulates localised environments such as fields of crops and irrigated water. CEA technology provides an excellent platform for the introduction of nanotechnology to agriculture. Nanotechnological devices for CEA that provide "scouting" capabilities which could tremendously improve the grower's ability which will help in determining the best time to harvest the crop and the vitality of crop along with food security issues, such as microbial or chemical contamination. One area in particular is that of the cotton industry where current techniques of spinning cotton are quite wasteful. From harvesting the cotton to finalizing the fabric it's made into, over 25% of the cotton fiber is lost to scrap or waste [10] Margaret Frey, an assistant professor of textile science at Cornell University, has developed a technique called electrospinning that makes good use of the scrap material otherwise to make low-value products like cotton balls, yarn, and cotton batting [11]

NANOSENSORS FOR MONITORING SOIL CONDITIONS AND PLANT GROWTH HORMONE

The proficient use of agricultural natural assets like water, nutrients and chemicals during farming as nanosensors is user friendly. It makes use of nanomaterials and global positioning systems with satellite imaging of fields and might make farmers to detect crop pests or facts of stress such as drought. Nanosensors disseminated in the field are able to sense the existence of plant viruses and the level of soil nutrients [12]. They also minimize fertilizer consumption and environmental pollution. Nano-encapsulated slow- release fertilizers have been widely used [13] To check the quality of agricultural manufacture, nanobarcodes and nanoprocessing could be used the idea of grocery barcodes for economical, proficient, rapid effortless decoding and recognition of diseases. They created nanobarcodes that may tag perhaps multiple pathogens in a farm, which may simply be detected using any fluorescent based tools. Nanotechnocrates are capable of studying plant's regulation of hormones such as auxin, which is accountable for root growth and seedling organization. Nanosensors that react with auxin have been developed. This is a step forward in auxin research, as it helps scientists to know how plant roots acclimatize to their environment, particularly to marginal soils [14] For the improvement of soil retention of water or liquid by Nanomaterials, e.g. zeolites and nano-clays, for retention of water or liquid agrochemicals in the soil for their slow release to the plants.[15]

DETOXIFICATION OR REMEDIATION OF HARMFUL POLLUTANTS

Using synthetic clay nanomineral does not require expensive laboratory equipment for arsenic removal. The water to be filtered is percolated through a column of hydrotalcite (synthetic clay mineral). [16] suggests that this technology can be coupled with leaching through porous pots or filter candles, the technology available in many developing countries to filter organisms from drinking water. Zinc oxide nanoparticles can be used to remove arsenic using a point-of-source purification device. Nanoscale zero-valent iron is the most widely used the set of nanomaterials that could be deployed to remediate pollutants in soil or groundwater. Other nanomaterials that could be used in remediation include nanoscale zeolites, metal oxides, carbon nanotubes and fibers, enzymes, various noble metals (mainly as bimetallic nanoparticles) and titanium dioxide. Nanoparticle filters can be used to remove organic particles and pesticides (for example, dichorodiphenyl-trichloroethane (DDT), endosulfan, malathion and chlor-pyrifos) from water. A variety of nanoparticle filters have been used in remediation of waste sites in developed countries [17].

NANOCAPSULES FOR EFFICIENT DELIVERY OF PESTICIDES, FERTILIZERS AND OTHER AGROCHEMICALS

Nanoencapsulation is a process through which chemicals like insecticides are slowly but efficiently released to a particular host plant for insect pest control. Nanoencap-sulation with nanoparticles in the form of pesticides allows for proper absorption of the chemicals into the plants [18]. This process can also deliver DNA and other desired chemicals into plant tissues for protection of host plants against insect pests [19]. Release mechanisms of nanoencap-sulation include diffusion, dissolution, biodegradation and osmotic pressure with specific pH [20]. Nanoencapsulation is cur-rently the most promising technology for protection of host plants against insect pests. Now, most leading chemical companies focus on formulation of nanoscale pesticides for delivery into the target host tissue through nanoencapsulation. Fertilizer plays a pivotal role in agriculture production (35 to 40%). To enhance nutrient use efficiency and overcome the chronic problem of eutrophication, nano-fertilizer might be a best alternative. Nanofertilizers are synthesized in order to regulate the release of nutrients depending on the requirements of the crops, and it is also reported that nanofertilizers are more efficient than ordinary fertilizer [21]. Nanofertilizers could be used to reduce nitrogen loss due to leaching, emissions, and long-term incorporation by soil microor-ganisms. They could allow selective release linked to time or environmental condition. Slow controlled release fertilizers may also improve soil by decreasing toxic effects associated with fertilizer over- application [22].

Technologies such as encapsulation and controlled release methods have revolutionised the use of pesticides and herbicides. Pesticides inside nanoparticles are being developed that can be timely released or have release linked to an environmental trigger. Combined with a smart delivery system, herbicide could be applied only when necessary, resulting in greater production of crops and less injury to agricultural workers. Many companies make formulations which contain nanoparticles within the size ranges of 100-250 nm; they are able to dissolve in water more effectively than existing ones (thus increasing their activity). Other companies employ suspensions of nanoscale particles (nanoemulsions) which can be either water or oil-based and contain uniform suspensions of pesticidal or herbicidal nanoparticles in the range of 200-400 nm. These can be easily incorporated in various media such as gels, creams, liquids among others, and have multiple applications for preventative measures, treatment or preservation of harvested products. Syngenta, world's largest agrochemical corporation, is using nanoemulsions in its pesticide products. One of its successful growth regulating products is the Primo MAXX® plant growth regulator, which if applied prior to the onset of stress such as heat, drought, disease or traffic can strengthen the physical structure of turf grass and allow it to withstand ongoing stresses throughout the growing season. Another encapsulated product from Syngenta delivers a broad control spectrum on primary and secondary insect pests of cotton, rice, peanuts and soybeans. Marketed under the name Karate® ZEON this is a quick release microencapsulated product containing the active compound lambda-cyhalothrin (a synthetic insecticide based on the structure of natural pyrethrins) which breaks open on contact with leaves. In contrast, the encapsulated product "gutbuster" only breaks open to release its contents when it comes into contact with alkaline environments, such as the stomach of certain insects.[23]Application of nanotechnology in the agri-food sector is still a relatively new concept; the main reasons for its late incorporation are mainly due to issues relating to product labelling, potential consumer health risks, and a lack of unifying regulations and guidelines on nanotechnology governance[55] The nanoparticles like Ag, ZnO and CuO are relevant in the growth of agriculture by bioactivity and bio-modification[24] For Fertilizers the use of Nano capsules, nano particles and viral capsids is useful for the enhancement of nutrients absorption by plants and the delivery of nutrients to specific sites.[25]

NANOTECHNOLOGY IN ORGANIC FARMING

Organic farming has been a long-desired goal to increase productivity (that is, crop yields) with low input (that is, fertilizers, pesticides, herbicides among others) through monitoring environmental variables and applying targeted action. Organic farming makes use of computers, GPS systems, and remote sensing devices to measure highly localized environmental conditions, thus determining whether crops are growing at maximum efficiency or precisely identifying the nature and location of problems. By using centralised data to determine soil conditions and plant development, seeding, fertilizer, chemical and water use can be fine-tuned to lower production costs and potentially increase production all benefiting the farmer. Precision farming can also help to reduce agricultural waste and thus keep environmental pollution to a minimum.[26] The product for plant production with Nano capsules, nano particles, nano emulsions and viral capsids acts as smart delivery systems of active ingredients for disease and pest control in plants.[27] The carbon nanotubes plays a beneficial role in mustard plant growth and the TiO_2 treatment by Nitrogen[28]

NANOHERBICIDES

The easiest way to eliminate weeds is to destroy their seed banks in the soil and prevent them from germinating when weather and soil conditions become favourable for their growth. Being very small, nanoherbicides will be able to blend with the soil, eradicate weeds in an eco-friendly way without leaving any toxic residues, and prevent the growth of weed species that have become resistant to conventional herbicides. Weeds survive and spread through underground structures such as tubers and deep roots. Ploughing infected fields while removing weeds by hand can make these unwanted plants spread to uninfected areas. Whether the nano application is due to a nanosized active ingredient or the creation of a nanosized formulation through the use of an adjuvant, the use of nano application is same. If the active ingredient is combined with a smart delivery system, herbicide will be applied only when necessary according to the conditions of the agriculture field. Lower agricultural yields are obtained in soils contaminated with weeds and weed seeds. Improvements in the efficacy of herbicides through the use of nanotechnology could result in more crop production without causing any harmful effects to agricultural workers who are supposed to physically remove weeds if no application of herbicides is practised

NANOPARTICLES AND PLANT DISEASE CONTROL

Some of the nano particles that have entered into the arena of controlling plant diseases are nanoforms of carbon, silver, silica and alumino-silicates. At such a situation, nanotechnology has astonished scientific community because at nano-level, material shows different properties. The use of nano size silver particles as antimicrobial agents has become more common as technology advances, making their production more economical. Since silver displays different modes of inhibitory action to microorganisms [29], it may be used for controlling various plant pathogens in a relatively safer way compared to commercially used fungicides. Silver is known to affect many biochemical processes in the microorganisms including the changes in routine functions and plasma membrane [30]. The silver nanoparticles also prevent the expression of ATP production associated proteins [31]. In a nutshell, the precise mechanism of bio molecules inhibition is yet to be understood. [32] Nanoparticles from plants Production of nanomaterials through the use of engineered plants or microbes and through the processing of waste agricultural products.[56]

Thus, use of nanoparticles has been considered an alternate and effective approach which is eco-friendly and cost effective for the control of pathogenic microbes[33][34][35]. These nanoparticles have a great potential in the management of plant diseases compared to synthetic fungicides[36]. Zinc oxide (ZnO) and magnesium oxide (MgO) nanoparticles are effective antibacterial and anti-odour agents[37]. The increased ease in dispensability, optical transparency and smooth-ness make ZnO and MgO nanostructures an attractive antibacterial ingredient in many products. Both have also been proposed as an anti-microbial preservative for wood or food products [38][39][40]. Properly functionalized nanocap-sules provide better penetration through cuticle and allow slow and controlled release of active ingredients on reaching the target weed. The use of such nano-biopesticide is more acceptable since they are safe for plants and cause less environmental pollution in comparison to conventional chemical pesticides [41]. Nanosilver is the most studied and utilized nano particle for bio-system. It has long been known to have strong inhibitory and bactericidal effects as well as a broad spectrum of antimicrobial activities[34][35] Silver nanoparticles, which have high surface area and high fraction of surface atoms, have high antimicrobial effect compared to the bulk[39]. Fungicidal properties of nano-size silver colloidal solution are used as an agent for antifungal treatment of various plant pathogens; the most significant inhibition of plant pathogenic fungi was observed on potato dextrose agar (PDA) and 100 ppm of AgNPs [43]

NANOPARTICLES AS PESTICIDES

Nanoparticles are also effective against insects and pests. Nanoparticles can be used in the preparation of new formulations like pesticides, insecticides and insect repellants[41][44]. Torney reviewed that nanotechnology has promi-sing applications in nanoparticle gene mediated DNA transfer. It can be used to deliver DNA and other desired chemicals into plant tissues for protection of host plants against insect pests. Porous hollow silica nanoparticles (PHSNs) loaded with validamycin (pesticide) can be used as efficient delivery system of water-soluble pesticide for its controlled release. Such controlled release behaviour of PHSNs makes it a promising carrier in agriculture, especially for pesticide controlled delivery whose imme-diate as well as prolonged release is needed for plants[45]. According to[46], oil in water (nano-emulsions) was useful for the formulations of pesticides and these could be effective against the various insect pests in agriculture. Similarly, essential oil-loaded solid lipid nanoparticles were also useful for the formulations of nano-pesticides[45]. Nanosilica, a silica product, can be effectively used as a nanopesticide.[41] reviewed the use of nano-silica as nano-insecticide. The mechanism of control of insect pest using nano-silica is based on the fact that insect pests used a variety of cuticular lipids for protecting their water barrier and thereby prevent death from desiccation. But here, the nanosili caparticles when applied on plant surface, cause death by physical means of insects by being absorbed into the cuticular lipids. Modified surface charged hydrophobic nano-silica (~3-5 nm) could be successfully implemented to manage a variety of ectoparasites of animals and agricultural insect pests[47]. The insecticidal activity of poly-ethylene glycol-coated nanoparticles loaded with garlic essential oil against adult *Tribolium castaneum* insect was found in stored products.

It has been observed that the control efficacy against adult *T. castaneum* was about 80%; presumably due to the slow and persistent release of the active components from the nanoparticles [48]. The applications of diverse kind of nanoparticles viz. silver nanoparticles, aluminium oxide, zinc oxide and titanium dioxide in the management of rice weevil and grasserie disease in silk worm (*B. mori*) are caused by *Sitophilus oryzae* and baculovirus BmNPV (*B. mori* nuclear polyhedrosis virus, respectively[49][50] studied the insecticidal activity of nanostructured alumina against two insect pests viz. *S. oryzae* L. and *Rhyzopertha dominica* (F.), which are major insect pests in stored food supplies throughout the world. Significant mortality was observed after 3 days of continuous exposure to nanostructured alumina-treated wheat. Therefore, compared to commercially available insecti-cides, inorganic nanostructured alumina may provide a cheap and reliable alternative for control of insect pests, and such studies may expand the frontiers for nanoparticle-based technologies in pest management.

NANOTECHNOLOGY FOR CROP BIOTECHNOLOGY

Nanocapsules can facilitate successful incursion of herbicides through cuticles and tissues, allowing slow and regular discharge of the active substances. This can act as 'magic bullets', containing herbicides, chemicals origins which target exacting plant parts to liberate their substance[51][19] exploited a 3 nm mesoporous silica nanoparticle in delivering DNA and chemicals into isolated plant cells. Mesoporous silica nanoparticles are chemically coated and act as containers for the genes delivered into the plants; they trigger the plant to take the particles through the cell walls, where the genes are put in and activated in a clear-cut and controlled way, without any toxic side effects. This technique firstly has been applied to establish DNA fruitfully to tobacco and corn plants.[52] For breeding of Plant and genetic modification by Nanoparticles carrying DNA or RNA to be delivered to plant cells for their genetic transformation or to trigger defence responses, activated by pathogens.[53]

CONCLUSION AND PERSPECTIVES

Nanotechnology has great potential as it can enhance the quality of life through its applications in various fields like agriculture and the food system. Around the world it has become the future of any nation. But we must be very careful with any new technology to be introduced about its possible unforeseen related risks that may come through its positive potential. However, it is also critical for the future of a nation to produce a trained future workforce in nanotechnology. In this process, to inform the public at large about its advantages is the first step, which will result in tremendous increase in the interest and discovery of new applications in all the domains.With this idea in mind, this review has been written. The theme of the paper is based on the provision of basic knowledge about the applications of nanotechnology in agriculture and their prospects in the near future with reference to the current situation around the world. In this review, some of the potential applications of nanotechnology in agriculture for the welfare of humans and for sustainable environment, challenges and opportunities for developing countries have been identified. Finally, for their solution, collaboration among developed and developing countries, public and private sectors and between research institutions and international organizations have been identified and suggested.The future of nanotechnology is uncertain due to many reasons, such as negative reaction of the public towards genetically modified crops, lack of many of the requisite skills in public agricultural research organizations for this type of research and ill-equipped and somewhat hesitant regulatorystructures to deal with these new technologies. There is a dire need to tear down the sharp boundary present between the social and natural sciences and if we succeed in discarding this boundary, we may be able to develop a more desirable and more democratic sociotechnical future.[54]

REFERENCES

1. Gru'ere G, Narrod C and Abbott L 2011 *Agriculture, Food, and Water Nanotechnologies for the Poor Opportunities and Constraints* Policy Brief 19, June 2011 (Washington, DC, USA: International Food Policy Research Institute (IFPRI) http://www.ifpri.org/publication/agriculture-food-andwaternanotechnologies- poor/)
2. Scott N R and Chen H 2003 Nanoscale Science and Engineering or Agriculture and Food Systems *Roadmap Report of National Planning Workshop 2002 18–19 (November, 2002 Washington DC)* http://www.nseafs.cornell.edu/web.roadmap.pdf
3. Holdren J P 2011 *The National Nanotechnology Initiative Strategic Plan Report at Subcommittee on Nanoscale Science, Engineering and Technology of Committee on Technology, National Science and Technology Council* (Arlington, VA: NSCT)
4. Fakruddin Md, Hossain Z, Afroz H (2012). Prospects and Applications of Nanobiotechnology: A Medical Perspective. J. Nanobiotechnol. 10: 31.
5. Tarafdar JC, Sharma S, Raliya R (2013). Nanotechnology: Interdisciplinary Science of Applications. Afr. J. Biotechnol. 12(3): 219-226.
6. Welch RM, Graham RD (1999). A New Paradigm for World Agriculture: Meeting Human needs, Productive, Sustainable, and Nutritious. Field Crops Res. 60: 1-10.
7. Prasad KS, Pathak D, Patel A, Dalwadi P, Prasad R, Patel P, Kaliaperumal Selvaraj K (2011). Biogenic Synthesis of Silver Nanoparticles using *Nicotiana tobaccum* Leaf Extract and Study of their Antibacterial Effect. Afr. J. Biotechnol. 9 (54): 8122-8130.
8. Scrinis G, Lyons K (2007). The Emerging Nano-corporate Paradigm: Nanotechnology and the Transformation of Nature, Food and Agri-food Systems. Int. J. Sociol. Food Agric. 15: 22-44.
9. Prasad R, Bagde US, Varma A (2012a). Intellectual Property Rights and Agricultural Biotechnology: An Overview. Afr. J. Biotechnol. 11(73): 13746-13752.
10. "Electrospinning Nanofibres Can Turn Waste Into New Products." AZoNano - The A to Z of Nanotechnology. 10 September 2003. New York State College of Human Ecology at Cornell.
11. 25 March 2005 <http://www.azonano.com/details.asp?ArticleID=181>.
12. Ingale AG, Chaudhari AN (2013). Biogenic Synthesis of Nanoparticles and Potential Applications: An Eco-friendly Approach. J. Nanomed. Nanotechol. 4: 165. doi:10.4172/2157-7439.1000165.
13. DeRosa MC, Monreal C, Schnitzer M, Walsh R, Sultan Y (2010). Nanotechnology in Fertilizers. Nat. Nanotechnol. 5: 91-94.
14. McLamore ES, Diggs A, CalvoMarzal P, Shi J, Blakeslee JJ, Peer WA, Murphy AS, Porterfield DM (2010). Noninvasive Quantification of Endogenous Root Auxin Transport using an Integrated Flux Microsensor Technique. Plant J. 63: 1004-1016.
15. http://www.geohumus.com/us/products.html
16. Gilman GP (2006). A Simple Device for Arsenic Removal from Drinking Water using Hydrotalcite. Sci. Total Environ. 366: 926-931.
17. Karn B, Kuiken T, Otto M (2009). Nanotechnology and *in situ* Remediation: A Review of Benefits and Potential Risks. Environ. Health Persp. 117(12): 1823-1831.
18. Scrinis G, Lyons K (2007). The Emerging Nano-corporate Paradigm: Nanotechnology and the Transformation of Nature, Food and Agri-food Systems. Int. J. Sociol. Food Agric. 15: 22-44.
19. Suman PR, Jain VK, Varma A (2010) Role of Nanomaterials in Symbiotic Fungus Growth Enhancement. Curr. Sci. 99: 1189-1191.

20. Park HJ, Kim SH, Kim HJ, Choi SH (2006). A New Composition of Nanosized Silica-silver for Control of Various Plant Diseases. Plant Pathol. J. 22:25-34.
21. EC, Communication from the Commission to the European Parliament, the Council, the European Economic and Social Committee and the Committee of the Regions. 'A Euro-pean Strategy for Key Enabling Technologies - A Bridge to Growth and Jobs'. http://eur-lex.europa.eu/LexUriServ/LexUriServ.do?uri=COM:2012:0341:FIN:EN:PDF (2012
22. Suman PR, Jain VK, Varma A (2010) Role of Nanomaterials in Symbiotic Fungus Growth Enhancement. Curr. Sci. 99: 1189-1191
23. Vidhyalakshmi R, Bhakyaraj R, Subhasree RS (2009). Encapsulation the Future of Probiotics–A Review. Adv. Biol. Res. 3(3-4): 96-103.
24. Christian O. Dimkpa, Jaan E.Mclean, David W. Britt, and Anne J.Anderson.
25. N. Milani, et al., J. Agric. Food Chem. 60 (2012) 3991-3998.
26. Observatory NANO FP7, European Nanotechnology Landscape Report, 2011. http://www.scor.com/en/sgrc/pac/motor/item/1327-european-nanotechnology-landscape-report.html
27. C.H. Anjali, Y.Sharma, A.Mukherjee, N.Chandrasekaran, Pest Manage. Sci. 68 (2012) 158–163 Fertilizers.
28. Anindita Mondal, Ruma Basu, Sukhen Das, Papiya Nandy.
29. Young KJ (2009) Antifungal Activity of Silver Ions and Nanoparticles on Phytopathogenic Fungi. Plant Dis. 93(10): 1037-1043.
30. Pal S, Tak YK, Song JM (2007). Does the Antibacterial Activity of Silver Nanoparticles depend on the Shape of the Nanoparticle? A Study of Gram Negative Bacterium *Escherichia coli*. Appl. Environ. Microbiol. 73: 1712-1720.
31. Yamanka M, Hara K, Kudo J (2005). Bactericidal Actions of Silver ions Solution on *Escherichia coli* Studying by Energy Filtering Transmission Electron Microscopy and Proteomic Analysis. Appl. Environ. Microbiol. 71: 7589-7593.
32. R.K. Sastry, H.B. Rashmi, N.H. Rao, J. Intellect. Prop. Rights15 (2010) 197-205.
33. Kumar V, Yadav SK (2009). Plant-mediated Synthesis of Silver and Gold Nanoparticles and their Applications, J. Chem. Technol. Biotechnol. 84: 151-157.
34. Prasad KS, Pathak D, Patel A, Dalwadi P, Prasad R, Patel P, Kaliaperumal Selvaraj K (2011). Biogenic Synthesis of Silver Nanoparticles using *Nicotiana tobaccum* Leaf Extract and Study of their Antibacterial Effect. Afr. J. Biotechnol. 9 (54): 8122-8130.
35. Swamy VS, Prasad R (2012). Green Synthesis of Silver Nanoparticles from the Leaf Extract of *Santalum album* and its Antimicrobial Activity. J. Optoelectron. Biomed. Mater. 4(3): 53-59.
36. Park HJ, Kim SH, Kim HJ, Choi SH (2006). A New Composition of Nanosized Silica-silver for Control of Various Plant Diseases. Plant Pathol. J. 22: 25-34.
37. Shah MA, Towkeer A (2010). Principles of Nanosciences and Nanotechnology. Narosa Publishing House, New Delhi.
38. Aruoja V, Dubourguier H, Kasamets C, Kahru KA (2009). Toxicity of Nanoparticles of CuO, ZnO and TiO2 to Microalgae, *Pseudokirchneriella subcapitata*. Sci. Total Environ. 407: 1461-1468.
39. Huang L, Dian-Qing L, Yan-Jun W, Min David G, Xue ED (2005). Controllable Preparation of Nano-MgO and Investigation of its Bactericidal Properties. J. Inorg. Biochem. 99: 986-993.

40. Sharma VK, Yngard RA, Lin Y (2009). Silver Nanoparticles: Green Synthesis and their Antimicrobial Activities. Adv. Colloid Interface Sci. 145: 83-96.
41. Barik TK, Sahu B, Swain V (2008). Nanosilica-from Medicine to Pest Control. Parasitolol. Res. 103: 253-258.
42. Prasad R, Swamy VS (2013). Antibacterial Activity of Silver Nanoparticles Synthesized by Bark Extract of *Syzygium cumini*. J. Nanopart. http://dx.doi.org/10.1155/2013/431218
43. Kim SW, Jung JH, Lamsal K, Kim YS, Min JS, Lee YS (2012). Antifungal Effects of Silver Nanoparticles (AgNPs) against Various Plant Pathogenic Fungi. Mycobiology 40: 53-58.
44. Gajbhiye M, Kesharwani J, Ingle A, Gade A, Rai M (2009). Fungus Mediated Synthesis of Silver Nanoparticles and its Activity against Pathogenic Fungi in Combination of Fluconazole. Nanomedicine 5(4): 282-286.
45. Liu F, Wen LX, Li ZZ, Yu W, Sun HY, Chen JF (2006b). Porous Hollow Silica Nanoparticles as Controlled Delivery System for Water Soluble Pesticide. Mat. Res. Bull. 41: 2268-2275.
46. Wang L, Li Z, Zhang G, Dong J, Eastoe J (2007). Oil-in-water Nanoemulsions for Pesticide Formulations. J. Colloid Interface Sci. 314: 230-235.
47. Ulrichs C, Mewis I, Goswami A (2005). Crop Diversification Aiming Nutritional Security in West Bengal: Biotechnology of Stinging Capsules in Nature's Water-blooms. Ann. Tech. Issue of State Agri. Technologists Service Assoc. 1-18.
48. Yang FL, Li XG, Zhu F, Lei CL (2009). Structural Characterization of Nanoparticles Loaded with Garlic Essential Oil and their Insecticidal Activity against *Tribolium castaneum* (Herbst) (Coleoptera:Tenebrionidae). J. Agric. Food Chem. 57(21): 10156-10162.
49. Goswami A, Roy I, Sengupta S, Debnath N (2010). Novel Applications of Solid and Liquid Formulations of Nanoparticles against Insect Pests and Pathogens. Thin Solid Films 519: 1252-1257
50. Teodoro S, Micaela B, David KW (2010). Novel use of Nano-structured Alumina as an Insecticide. Pest Manag. Sci. 66(6): 577-579.
51. Pérez-de-Luque A, Rubiales D (2009). Nanotechnology for Parasitic Plant Control. Pest Manag. Sci. 65: 540-545.
52. N. Gupta, A.H. Fischer, S. George, L. Frewer, J. Nanopart. Res.15 (2013) 1-15.
53. F. Torney, B.G. Trewyn, V.S.Y. Lin, K. Wang, Nat. Nanotechnol. 2 (2007) 295-300.
54. Sugunan A, Dutta J (2008). Nanotechnology Vol. 2: Environmental Aspects (Krug Harald (ed.), Wiley-VCH, Weinheim.
55. Coles, D., & Frewer, L.J. (2013). Nanotechnology Applied to European Food Production - A Review of Ethical and Regulatory Issues. Trends in Food Science and Technology, 34(1), 32e43.
56. A. Alemdar, M. Sain, Bioresour. Technol. 99 (2008) 1664-1671

Pages: 152-167

Rural Development and Techno-Innovations
Edited by: Dr. Alka Chauhan; Er. Chhavi Kumar 'Bharti' & Dr. Pawan Kumar 'Bharti'
ISBN: 978-93-88854-07-8
Edition: 2019
Published by: Discovery Publishing House Pvt. Ltd., New Delhi (India)

10 Geoexchanger System for Buildings Heating and

A.M. Omer*

ABSTRACT

Geothermal heat pumps (GSHPs), or direct expansion (DX) ground source heat pumps, are a highly efficient renewable energy technology, which uses the earth, groundwater or surface water as a heat source when operating in heating mode or as a heat sink when operating in a cooling mode. It is receiving increasing interest because of its potential to decrease primary energy consumption and thus reduce emissions of the greenhouse gases (GHGs). The main concept of this technology is that it uses the lower temperature of the ground (approximately <32°C), which remains relatively stable throughout the year, to provide space heating, cooling and domestic hot water inside the building area. The main goal of this study was to stimulate the uptake of the GSHPs.

Recent attempts to stimulate alternative energy sources for heating and cooling of buildings have emphasised the utilisation of the ambient energy from ground source and other renewable energy sources. The purpose of this study, however, was to examine the means of reducing of energy consumption in buildings, identifying GSHPs as an environmental friendly technology able to provide efficient utilisation of energy in the buildings sector, promoting the use of GSHPs applications as an optimum means of heating and cooling, and presenting typical applications and recent advances of the DX GSHPs. The study highlighted the potential energy saving that could be achieved through the use of ground energy sources. It also focused on the optimisation and improvement of the operation conditions of the heat cycle and performance of the DX GSHP. It is concluded that the direct expansion of the GSHP, combined with the ground

* Energy Research Institute (ERI), Nottingham NG7 4EU, United Kingdom

heat exchanger in foundation piles and the seasonal thermal energy storage from solar thermal collectors, is extendable to more comprehensive applications.

Key words: Geothermal heat pumps; direct expansion; ground heat exchanger; heating and cooling

INTRODUCTION

The earth's surface acts as a huge solar collector, absorbing radiation from the sun. In the UK, the ground maintains a constant temperature of 11-13°C several metres below the surface all the year around Allan, and Philappacopoulus (1999). Among many other alternative energy resources and new potential technologies, the ground source heat pumps (GSHPs) are receiving increasing interest because of their potential to decrease primary energy consumption and thus reduce emissions of greenhouse gases (Anandarajah (2003).

Direct expansion GSHPs are well suited to space heating and cooling and can produce significant reduction in carbon emissions. In the vast majority of systems, space cooling has not been normally considered, and this leaves ground-source heat pumps with some economic constraints, as they are not fully utilised throughout the year. The tools that are currently available for design of a GSHP system require the use of key site-specific parameters such as temperature gradient and the thermal and geotechnical properties of the local area. A main core with several channels will be able to handle heating and cooling simultaneously, provided that the channels are thermally insulated to some extent and can be operated independently as single units, but at the same time function as integral parts of the entire core. Loading of the core is done by diverting warm and cold air from the heat pump through the core during periods of excess capacity compared to the current needs of the building ASHRAE (1995), and Bejan (2000). The cold section of the core can also be loaded directly with air during the night, especially in spring and fall when nighttimes are cooler and daytimes are warmer. The shapes and numbers of the internal channels and the optimum configuration will obviously depend on the operating characteristics of each installation. Efficiency of a GSHP system is generally much greater than that of the conventional air-source heat pump systems. Higher COP (coefficient of performance) is achieved by a GSHP because the source/sink earth temperature is relatively constant compared to air temperatures. Additionally, heat is absorbed and rejected through water, which is a more desirable heat transfer medium due to its relatively high heat capacity.

The GSHPs in some homes also provide:

- Radiant floor heating.
- Heating tubes in roads or footbaths to melt snow in the winter.

- Hot water for outside hot tubs and
- Energy to heat hot water.

With the improvement of people's living standards and the development of economies, heat pumps have become widely used for air conditioning. The driver to this was that environmental problems associated with the use of refrigeration equipment, the ozone layer depletion and global warming are increasingly becoming the main concerns in developed and developing countries alike. With development and enlargement of the cities in cold regions, the conventional heating methods can severely pollute the environment. In order to clean the cities, the governments drew many measures to restrict citizen heating by burning coal and oil and encourage them to use electric or gas-burning heating. New approaches are being studied and solar-assisted reversible absorption heat pump for small power applications using water-ammonia is under development Bergles (1988).

An air-source heat pump is convenient to use and so it is a better method for electric heating. The ambient temperature in winter is comparatively high in most regions, so heat pumps with high efficiency can satisfy their heating requirement. On the other hand, a conventional heat pump is unable to meet the heating requirement in severely cold regions anyway, because its heating capacity decreases rapidly when ambient temperature is below -10°C. According to the weather data in cold regions, the air-source heat pump for heating applications must operate for long times with high efficiency and reliability when ambient temperature is as low as -15°C Bowman and Maynes (2001). Hence, a great deal of research and development has been conducted to enable heat pumps to operate steadily with high efficiency and reliability in low temperature environments EPRI and NRECA (1997). For example, the burner of a room air conditioner, which uses kerosene, was developed to improve the performance in low outside temperature Fahlen (1997). Similarly, the packaged heat pump with variable frequency scroll compressor was developed to achieve high temperature air supply and high capacity even under the low ambient temperature of –10 to –20°C Fridleifsson (2003). Such heat pump systems can be conveniently used for heating in cold regions. However, the importance of targeting the low capacity range is clear if one has in mind that the air conditioning units below 10 kW cooling account for more than 90% of the total number of units installed in the EU Jo, Katsumi, Benson, and Edil (2001).

METHODS AND LABROTORIES MEAGUREMENTS

This section describes the details of the prototype GSHP test rig, details of the construction and installation of the heat pump, heat exchanger, heat injection fan and water supply system. It also, presents a discussion of the experimental tests being carried out.

The schematic of the test rig that was used to support the two ground-loop heat exchangers is shown in figure 10.1. It consisted of two main loops: heat source loop and evaporation heat pump. Three horeholes were drilled each 30 meters deep to provide sufficient energy. The closed-loop systems were laid and installed in a vertical well. The ground-loop heat exchangers were connected to the heat pump. The undertaken experimental work consists of three parts. The first step dealt with drilling three boreholes each 30 meter deep, digging out the pit and connection of the manifolds and preparation of coils. Holes were grouted with bentonite and sand. The pipes were laid and tested with nitrogen. Then, the pit was backfilled and the heat pump was installed. The second step was concerned with the setting up of the main experimental rig: construction and installation of the heat injection fan, water pump, expansion valve, flow meter, electricity supply, heat exchanger and heat pump. The third step was an installation of refrigerator and measurements.

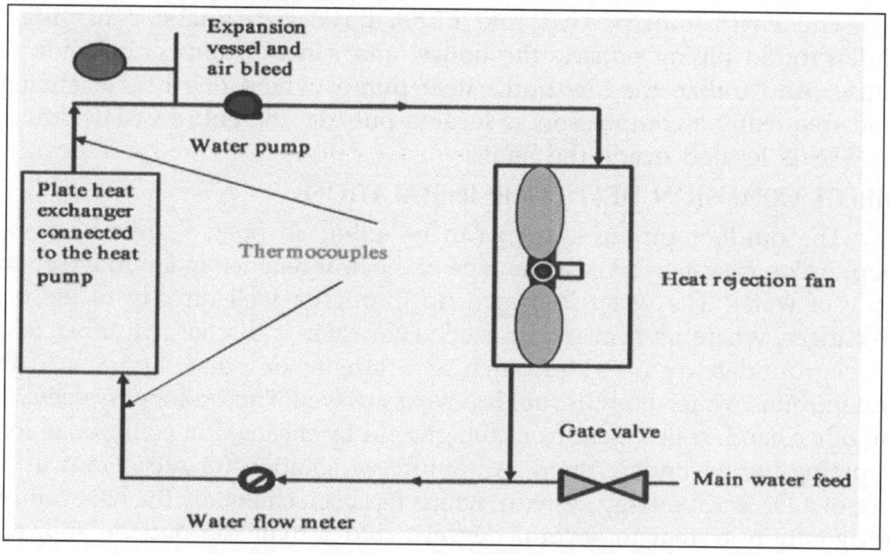

Fig. 10.1: Sketch of installing a heat pump

The aim of this project is to present and develop a GSHP system to provide heating and cooling for buildings (Figure 10.2). The heat source loop consisted of two earth loops: one for vapour and one for liquid. A refrigeration application is only concerned with the low temperature effect produced at the evaporator; while a heat pump is also concerned with the heating effect produced at the condenser.

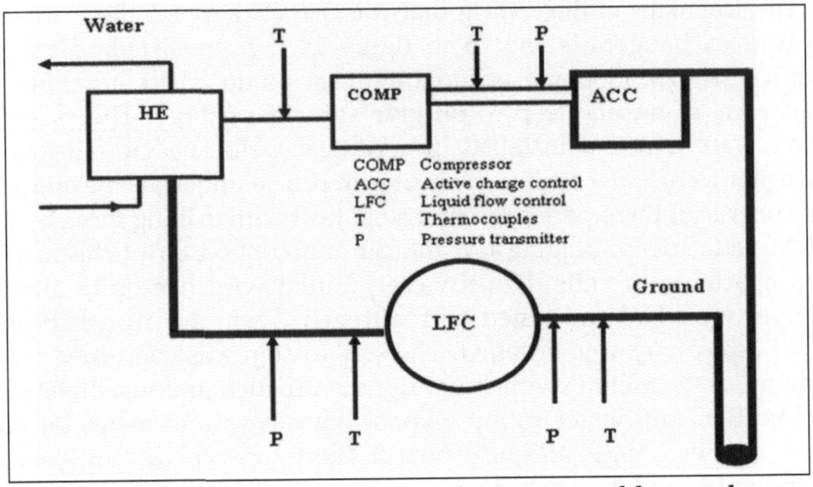

Fig. 10.2: Ground loops connections to heat pump and heat exchanger

The earth-energy systems, EESs, have two parts; a circuit of underground piping outside the house, and a heat pump unit inside the house. And unlike the air-source heat pump, where one heat exchanger (and frequently a compressor) is located outside, the entire GSHP unit for the EES is located inside the house.

DIRECT EXPANSION HEAT PUMP INSTALATION

The outdoor piping system can be either an open system or closed loop. An open system takes advantage of the heat retained in an underground body of water. The water is drawn up through a well directly to the heat exchanger, where its heat is extracted. The water is discharged either to an aboveground body of water, such as a stream or pond, or back to the underground water body through a separate well. Closed-loop systems, on the other hand, collect heat from the ground by means of a continuous loop of piping buried underground. An antifreeze solution (or refrigerant in the case of a DX earth-energy system), which has been chilled by the heat pump's refrigeration system to several degrees colder than the outside soil, and circulates through the piping, absorbing heat from the surrounding soil.

The direct expansion (DX) GSHP installed for this study was designed taking into account the local meteorological and geological conditions. The site was at the School of the Built Environment, University of Nottingham, where the demonstration and performance monitoring efforts were undertaken. The heat pump has been fitted and monitored for a one-year period. The study involved the development of a design and simulation tool for modelling the performance of the cooling system, which acts as a supplemental heat rejecting system using a closed-loop GSHP system. With the help of the Jackson Refrigeration (Refrigeration and Air Conditioning engineers) the following tasks were carried out:

- Connection of the ground loops to the heat pump
- Connection of the heat pump to the heat exchanger
- Vacuum on the system
- Charging the refrigeration loop with R407C refrigerant

Water Supply System

The water supply system consisted of a water pump, boiler, water tank, expansion and valve flow meter (Figure 10.4). A thermostatically controlled water heater supplied warm water, which was circulated between the warm water supply tank and warm water storage tank using a pump to keep the surface temperature of the trenches at a desired level.

The ground source heat pump system, which uses a ground source with a smaller annual temperature variation for heating and cooling systems, has increasingly attracted market attention due to lower expenses to mine for installing underground heat absorption pipes and lower costs of dedicated heat pumps, supported by environmentally oriented policies. The theme undertakes an evaluation of heat absorption properties in the soil and carries out a performance test for a DX heat pump and a simulated operation test for the system. In fact, these policies are necessary for identifying operational performance suitable for heating and cooling, in order to obtain technical data on the heat pump system for its dissemination and maintain the system in an effort of electrification.

In these circumstances, the study estimated the heat properties of the soil in the city of Nottingham and measured the thermal conductivity for the soil at some points in this city, aimed at identifying applicable areas for ground source heat pump system.

Design and Installation

Installation of the heat pump system and especially the ground heat exchanger needs to be carefully programmed so that it does not interfere with or delay any other construction activities. The time for installation depends on soil conditions, length of pipe, equipment required and weather conditions. The DX systems are most suitable for smaller domestic applications.

The most important first step in the design of a GSHP installation is accurate calculation of the building's heat loss, its related energy consumption profile and the domestic hot water requirements. This will allow accurate sizing of the heat pump system. This is particularly important because the capital cost of a GSHP system is generally higher than for alternative conventional systems and economies of scale are more limited. Oversizing will significantly increase the installed cost for little operational saving and will mean that the period of operation under part load is increased. Frequent cycling reduces equipment life and operating efficiency. Conversely if the system is undersized design conditions may not be met and the use of top-up heating, usually direct acting electric heating, will reduce the overall system efficiency. In order to determine the length of heat exchanger the piping material is needed. The piping material used affects the life; maintenance costs, pumping energy, capital cost and heat pump performance.

Heat Pump Performance

The need for alternative low-cost energy resources has given rise to the development of the DX-GSHPs for space cooling and heating. The performance of the heat pump depends on the performance of the ground loop and vice versa. It is therefore essential to design them together. Closed-loop GSHP systems will not normally require permissions/authorisations from the environment agencies. However, the agency can provide comment on proposed schemes with a view to reducing the risk of groundwater pollution or derogation that might result. The main concerns are:

- Risk of the underground pipes/boreholes creating undesirable hydraulic connections between different water bearing strata.
- Undesirable temperature changes in the aquifer that may result from the operation of a GSHP.
- Pollution of groundwater that might occur from leakage of additive chemicals used in the system.

Efficiencies for the GSHPs can be high because the ground maintains a relatively stable temperature allowing the heat pump to operate close to its optimal design point. Efficiencies are inherently higher than for air source heat pumps because the air temperature varies both throughout the day and seasonally such that air temperatures, and therefore efficiencies, are lowest at times of peak heating demand.

A heat pump is a device for removing heat from one place - the 'source' - and transferring it at a higher temperature to another place. The heat pumps consist of a compressor, a pressure release valve, a circuit containing fluid (refrigerant), and a pump to drive the fluid around the circuit. When the fluid passes through the compressor it increases in temperature. This heat is then given off by the circuit while the pressure is maintained. When the fluid passes through the relief valve the rapid drop in pressure will result in the cooling of the fluid. The fluid then absorbs heat from the surroundings before being re-compressed. In the case of domestic heating the pressurised circuit provides the heating within the dwelling. The depressurised component is external and, in the case of ground source heat pumps, is buried in the ground. Heat pump efficiencies improve as the temperature differential between 'source' and demand temperature decreases, and when the system can be 'optimised' for a particular situation. The relatively stable ground temperatures moderate the differential at times of peak heat demand and provide a good basis for optimisation.

The refrigerant circulated directly through the ground heat exchanger in a direct expansion (DX) system but most commonly GSHPs are indirect systems, where a water/antifreeze solution circulates through the ground loop and energy is transferred to or from the heat pump refrigerant circuit via a heat exchanger. This application will only consider closed loop systems. The provision of cooling, however, will result in increased energy consumption. The GSHPs are particularly suitable for new build as the technology is most efficient when used to supply low temperature distribution systems such as underfloor heating. They can also be used for retrofit especially in conjunction with measures to reduce heat demand. They can be particularly cost effective in areas where gas mains are not available or for developments where there is an advantage in simplifying the infrastructure provided.

Coefficient of Performance

Heat pump technology can be used for heating only, or for cooling only, or be 'reversible' and used for heating and cooling depending on the demand. Reversible heat pumps generally have lower COPs than heating only heat pumps. They will, therefore, result in higher running costs and emissions. Several tools are available to measure heat pump performance. The heat delivered by the heat pump is theoretically the sum of the heat extracted from the heat source and the energy needed to deliver the cycle. Figure 5 shows the variations of temperature with the system operation hours. Several tools are available to measure heat pump performance. The heat delivered by the heat pump is theoretically the sum of the heat extracted from the heat source and the energy needed to derive the cycle. For electrically driven heat pumps the steady state performance at a given set of temperatures is referred to as the coefficient pf performance (COP). It is defined as the ration of the heat delivered by the heat pump and the electricity supplied to the compressor:

$$COP = [\text{heat output } (kW_{th})]/[\text{electricity input } (kW_{el})] \quad (1)$$

For an ideal heat pump the COP is determined solely by the condensation temperature and the temperature lift:

$$COP = [\text{condensing temperature } (^{\circ}C)]/[\text{temperature lift } (^{\circ}C)] \quad (2)$$

Figure 10.3 shows the heat pump COP as a function of the evaporation temperature. Figure 10.4 shows the heat pump COP as a function of the condensation temperature. As can be seen, the theoretically efficiency is strongly dependent on the temperature lift (compressed). It is important not only to have as high a source temperature as possible but also to keep the sink temperature (i.e., heating distribution temperature) as low as possible. The achievable heat pump efficiency is lower than the ideal efficiency because of losses during the transportation of heat from the source to the evaporator and from the condenser to the room and the compressor. Technological developments are steadily improving the performance of the heat pumps.

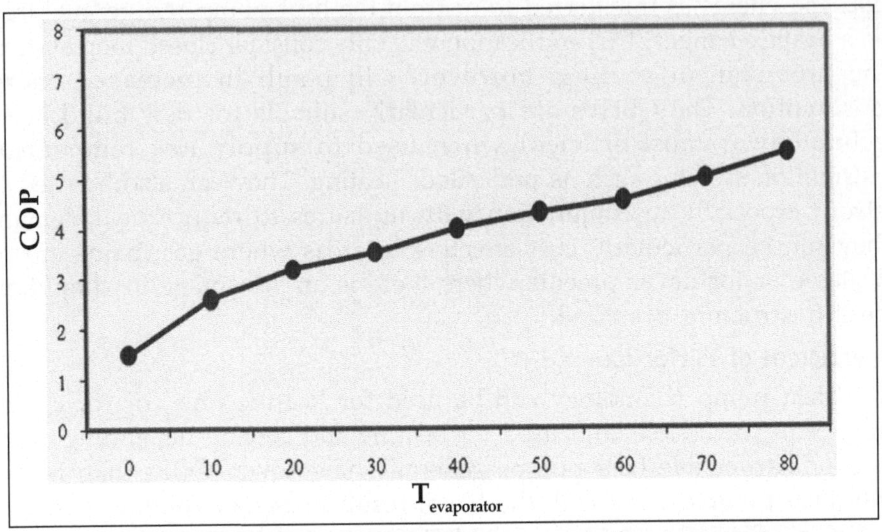

Fig. 10.3: Heat pump performance vs evaporation temperature

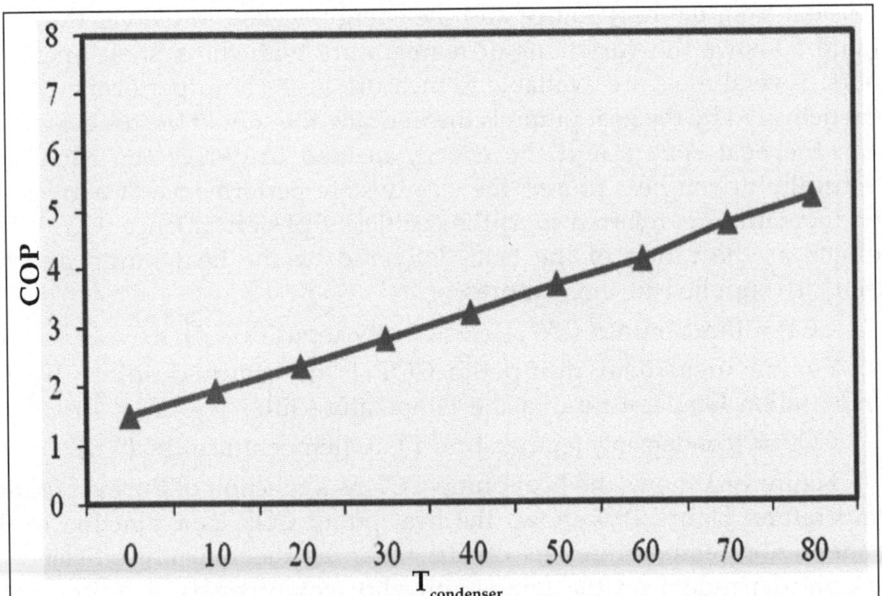

Fig. 10.4: Heat pump performance vs condensation temperature

The need for alternative low-cost energy has given rise to the development of the GSHP systems for space cooling and heating in residential and commercial buildings. The GSHP systems work with the environment to provide clean, efficient and energy-saving heating and cooling the year round. The GSHP systems use less energy than alternative heating and cooling systems, helping to conserve the natural resources. The GSHP systems do not need large cooling towers and their running costs are lower than conventional heating and air-conditioning systems. As a result, GSHP systems have increasingly been used for building heating and cooling with an annual rate of increase of 10% in recent years. While in some zones such as hot summer and cold winter areas, there is a major difference between heating load in winter and cooling load in summer. Thus the soil temperature increases gradually after yearly operation of the GSHP system because of the inefficient recovery of soil temperature as the result of imbalance loads (Figure 10.5). Finally, the increase of soil temperature will decrease the COP of the system.

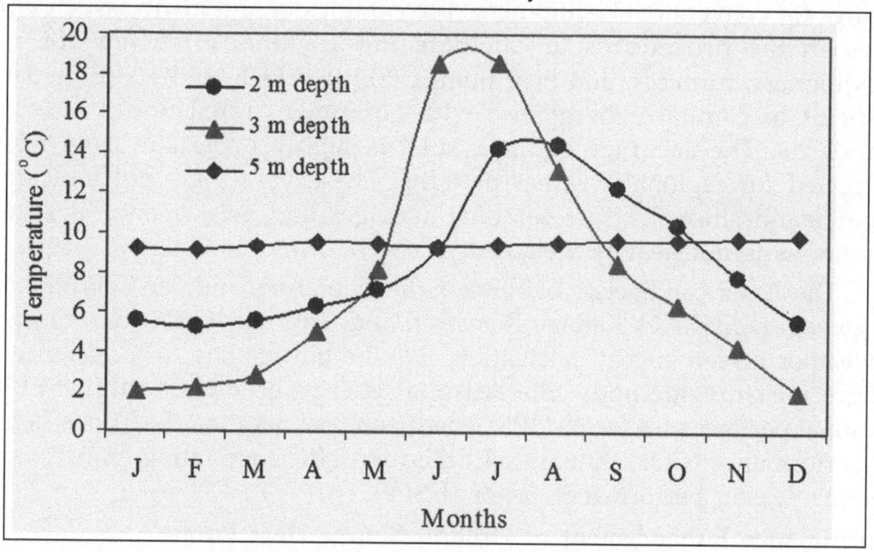

Fig. 10.5: Seasonal temperature variations

The first law of thermodynamics is often called the law of conservation of energy. Based on the first law or the law of conservation of energy for any system, open or closed, there is an energy balance as:

[Net amount of energy added to system] = (3)
[Net increase of stored energy in system]

Or

[Energy in] – [Energy out] = (4)
[Increased of stored energy in system]

In a cycle, the work reduction of produced by a power cycle (or the increase in work required by a refrigeration cycle) equals the absolute ambient temperature multiplied by the sum of irreversibilities in all processes in the cycle. Thus, the difference in reversible and actual work for any refrigeration cycle, theoretical or real, operating under the same conditions becomes:

$$W_{actual} = W_{reversible} + T_o \Sigma I \quad (5)$$

SIMULATIONS – RESULTS AND DISCUSSIONS

The GSHPs are generally more expensive to develop, however they have very low operating costs, therefore, it is necessary to have an idea of the energy use and demand of these equipments. The performances are normally rated at a single fluid temperature (0°C) for heating COP and a second for cooling EER (25°C). These ratings reflect temperatures for an assumed location and ground heat exchanger type, and are not ideal indicators of energy use. This problem is compounded by the nature of ratings for conventional equipment. The complexity and many assumptions used in the procedures to calculate the seasonal efficiency for air-conditioners, furnaces, and heat pumps (SEER, AFUE, and HSPF) make it difficult to compare energy use with equipment rated under different standards. The accuracy of the results is highly uncertain, even when corrected for regional weather patterns. These values are not indicators for demand since they are seasonal averages and performance at severe conditions is not heavily weighted.

The American Society of Heating, Refrigerating, and Air-Conditioning Engineers (ASHRAE) Kalbus, Reinstrof, and Schirmer (2006) recommends a weather driven energy calculation, like the bin method, in preference to single measure methods like seasonal energy efficiency ratio (SEER), seasonal performance factor (SPF), energy efficiency rating (EER), coefficient of performance (COP annual fuel utilisation efficiency rating (AFUE), and heating season performance factor (HSPF).

Performance Enhancement of Ground Source Heat Pump

The heat transfer between the GSHP and its surrounding soil is affected by a number of factors such as working fluid properties (e.g., 20% glycol) and its flow conditions, soil thermal properties, soil moisture content and groundwater velocity and properties, etc. The GSHP has a great potential to be one of the main energy sources in the future as it can be tapped in a number of different ways and can be used to produce hot water as well as electricity. It has a large spatial distribution with almost all countries having at least low enthalpy resources available (less than 125°C) and many countries around the world in both developing and developed countries are already harnessing it. It is a resource that has always been there and does not rely on specific factors such as the wind to be blowing or the sun to be shining, as is the case with other forms of renewable energies. The GSHP is inherently clean and environmentally sustainable and will soon become more economical than combustion (fossil fuel) plants as regulations on plant emission levels are tightened and expensive abatement measures such as carbon capture and storage become compulsory. This study urges the need for the GSHP to be considered much more strongly than it currently is in environmental policies as it has been overlooked as a main alternative to fossil fuels and other forms of renewable energies.

Geothermal power utilises the heat energy naturally produced within the earth. Its wide abundance and renewable nature make it an attractive alternative energy source to fossil fuels. The environmental impact of geothermal power plants is negligible in comparison to combustion plants and it is progressively becoming more financially viable as emission regulations are tightened. The technology is increasingly being utilised by countries all over the world, as there are many different ways in which geothermal energy can be harnessed. Geothermal power is very competitive with other sources of energy when it comes to energy costs. The geothermal is already generally more financially viable and cost-effective globally than other forms of renewable power, being on par with hydro-electricity (however, it is important to note that costs will vary between countries) Knoblich, Sanner, and Klugescheid (1993). The experiments and calculations are conducted for unsaturated soil without groundwater flow (US), saturated soil without groundwater flow (SS) and saturated soil with groundwater flow (SSG) under same conditions and their results are compared with each other in figure 10.6.

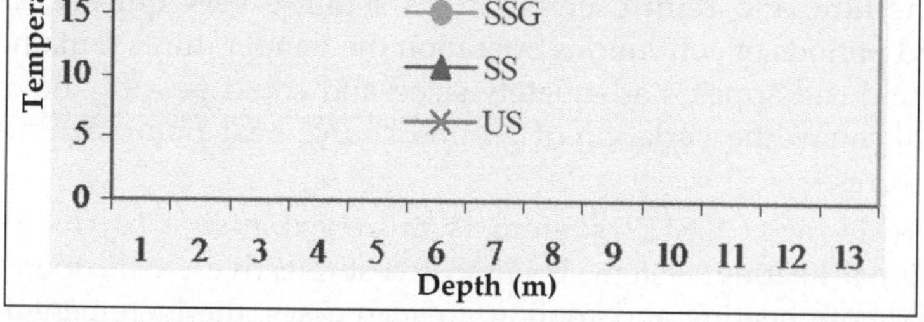

Fig. 10.6: Comparison of experiments for saturated soil with groundwater flow (SSG), saturated soil without groundwater flow (SS) and unsaturated soil without groundwater flow (US)

The GSHPs provide an effective and clean way of heating buildings worldwide. They make use of renewable energy stored in the ground, providing one of the most energy-efficient ways of heating buildings. They are suitable for a wide variety of building types and are particularly appropriate for low environmental impact projects. They do not require hot rocks (geothermal energy) and can be installed in most of the world, using a borehole or shallow trenches or, less commonly, by extracting heat from a pond or lake. Heat collecting pipes in a closed loop, containing water (with a little antifreeze) are used to extract this stored energy, which can then be used to provide space heating and domestic hot water. In some applications, the pump can be reversed in summer to provide an element of cooling. The only energy used by the GSHP systems is electricity to power the pumps. Typically, a GSHP will deliver three or four times as much thermal energy (heat) as is used in electrical energy to drive the system. For a particularly environmental solution, green electricity can be purchased. The GSHP systems have been widely used in other parts of the world, including North America and Europe, for many years. Typically they cost more to install than conventional systems; however, they have very low maintenance costs and can be expected to provide reliable and environmentally friendly heating for in excess of 20 years. Ground source heat pumps work best with heating systems, which are optimised to run at a lower water temperature than is commonly used in the UK boiler and radiator systems. As such, they make an ideal partner for underfloor heating systems.

The flow rate in the ground coil is 0.23 l/s. The heat collection rate varies from approximately 19 W to 27 W per meter length of collector coil. In winter, the ground coil typically operates with a temperature differential of about 5°C (i.e., a flow temperature from the ground of 2°C to 3°C and a return temperature to the ground coil of -1°C to -2°C). Icing up of the return pipework immediately below the heat pump can be quite severe. The ground coil temperatures are considerably higher in summer when, for water heating, the temperature differential is similar but flow and return temperatures are typically 11°C and 6°C respectively. When the heat pump starts, the flow and return temperatures stabilise very quickly. Even over sustained periods of continuous operation the temperatures remained stable. The ground coil appears adequately sized and could possibly be oversized. Figure 20 shows the variation of ground source heat pump against ground temperatures.

A residential GSHP system is more expensive to install than a conventional heating system. It is most cost-effective when operated year-round for both heating and cooling. In such cases, the incremental payback period can be as short as 3-5 years. A GSHP for a new residence will cost around 9-12% of the home construction costs. A typical forced air furnace with flex ducting system will cost 5-6% of the home construction costs. Stated in an alternative form, the complete cost of a residential GSHP system is $3,500-$5,500 per ton. Horizontal loop installations will generally cost less than vertical bores. For a heating dominated residence, figure around 550 square feet/ton to size the unit. A cooling dominated residence would be estimated around 450 square feet/ton.

Geoexchanger energy is a natural resource, which can be used in conjunction with heat pumps to provide energy for heating and hot water. CO_2 emissions are much lower than gas fired boilers or electric heating systems. Geothermal heating is more expensive to install initially, than electrical or gas fired heating systems. However it is cheaper to run, has lower maintenance costs, and is cleaner in use than other sources of heating.

The temperature of the earth under 2 metres of the surface is a fairly constant 10°C throughout the year. At a depth of about 100 metres, the temperature of any water or rock is at about 12°C throughout the year. The heat stored at this depth comes largely from the sun, the earth acting as a large solar collector. For very deep wells, in excess of about 170 metres, there is an added component of heat from the core of the earth. As an approximation, one can add 3°C of heat gain for every 100 metres of depth drilled into the earth.

A closed loop system takes the heat gained from the bedrock itself. In a vertical system a borehole of a diameter of about 150mm is drilled, depth varies between 32 and 180 metres but will depend on the energy requirements. Multiple boreholes can be drilled. A pair of pipes with a special U-bend assembly at the bottom is inserted into the borehole and the void between pipe and hole backfilled with a special grout solution so that the pipe is in close contact with the rock strata or earth. Fluid (referred to as 'brine' is then circulated through this loop and is heated up by the bedrock. Different rock types will give different results. In some cases a number of boreholes will be made (for example, over a car park) to provide sufficient energy for the heat pump supply. If the ground is not suitable, horizontal loops can be laid or even trench filled 'slinky' loops, which are very simple to install. However trench filled systems and horizontal systems require much more ground than vertical systems. If one has a pond or lake nearby then can lay a closed loop at the base of the pond (it needs to be about 2 metres deep), or simply extract the water directly out of the lake at low level and re-distribute it elsewhere in the lake.

DISCUSSION AND CONCLUSIONS

The direct expansion (DX) ground source heat pump (GSHP) systems have been identified as one of the best sustainable energy technologies for space heating and cooling in residential and commercial buildings. The GSHPs for building heating and cooling are extendable to more comprehensive applications and can be combined with the ground heat exchanger in foundation piles as well as seasonal thermal energy storage from solar thermal collectors. Heat pump technology can be used for heating only, or for cooling only, or be 'reversible' and used for heating and cooling depending on the demand. Reversible heat pumps generally have lower COPs than heating only heat pumps. They will, therefore, result in higher running costs and emissions and are not recommended as an energy-efficient heating option. The GSHP system can provide 91.7% of the total heating requirement of the building and 55.3% of the domestic water-heating requirement, although only sized to meet half the design-heating load. The heat pump can operate reliably and its performance appears to be at least as good as its specification. The system has a measured annual performance factor of 3.16. The heat pump system for domestic applications could be mounted in a cupboard under the stairs and does not reduce the useful space in the house, and there are no visible signs of the installation externally (no flue, vents, etc.).

The performance of the heat pump system could also be improved by eliminating unnecessary running of the integral distribution pump. It is estimated that reducing the running time of the pump, which currently runs virtually continuously, would increase the overall performance factor to 3.43. This would improve both the economic and the environmental performance of the system. More generally, there is still potential for improvement in the performance of heat pumps, and seasonal efficiencies for ground source heat pumps of 4.0 are being achieved. It is also likely that the unit costs will fall as production volumes increase. By comparison, there is little scope to further improve the efficiency of gas- or oil-fired boilers.

REFERENCES

Allan, M.L., & Philappacopoulus, A. J. (1999) 'Ground Water Protection Issues with Geothermal Heat Pumps', *Geothermal Resources Council Transactions*, 23, 101-105.

Anandarajah, A. (2003). 'Mechanism controlling permeability changes in clays due to changes in pore fluids', *Journal of Geotechnical and Geoenvironmental Engineering*, 129(2), 163-172.

ASHRAE, (1995) 'Commercial/Institutional Ground Source Heat Pump Engineering Manual', *American Society of Heating, Refrigeration and Air-conditioning Engineers, Inc.* Atlanta, GA: USA.

Bejan, A. (2000) 'Shape and Structure, from Engineering to Nature', Cambridge University Press: London. The many Faces of Protease-protein Inhibitor Interaction. *EMBO J.* 7, 1303-1130. 2000.

Bergles, A. E. (1988) 'Some Perspectives on Enhanced Heat Transfer - Second Generation Heat Transfer Technology', *Journal of Heat Transfer, 110,* 1082-1096.

Bowman, W.J. & Maynes, D. (2001) 'A Review of Micro-Heat Exchangers Flow Physics, Fabrication Methods and Application' Proc. ASME IMECE, New York, USA, HTD-24280.

EPRI and NRECA, (1997) 'Grouting for Vertical Geothermal Heat Pump Systems: Engineering Design and Field Procedures Manual', Electric Power Research Institute TR-109169, Palo Alto, CA, and National Rural Electric Cooperative Association, Arlington, VA.

Fahlen, Per. (1997) 'Cost-effective Heat Pumps for Nordic Countries, and Heat Pumps in Cold Climates', The 3rd International Conference, Acadia University, Wolfville, Canada. 1997.

Fridleifsson, I.B. (2003) 'Status of Geothermal Energy amongst the World's Energy Sources', *Geothermics*, 30, 1-27.

Jo, H.Y., Katsumi, T., Benson, C.H., & Edil, T.B. (2001) 'Hydraulic Conductivity and Swelling of Nonprehydrated GCLs Permeated with Single-species Salt Solutions', *Journal of Geotechnical and Geoenvironmental Engineering, 127*(7), 557-567.

Kalbus, E., Reinstrof, F., & Schirmer, M. (2006) 'Measuring methods for Groundwater Surface Water Interactions: A Review', *Hydrology and Earth System Sciences*, Vol. (10), pp. 873-887.

Knoblich, K., Sanner, B., & Klugescheid, M. (1993) 'Ground Source Heat Pumps', *Giessener Geologische Schriften*, 49, pp. 192, Giessen.

Pages: 168-189

Rural Development and Techno-Innovations
Edited by: Dr. Alka Chauhan; Er. Chhavi Kumar 'Bharti' & Dr. Pawan Kumar 'Bharti'
ISBN: 978-93-88854-07-8
Edition: 2019
Published by: Discovery Publishing House Pvt. Ltd., New Delhi (India)

11 Performance Effectiveness of Mahatma Gandhi National Rural Employment Guarantee Programme

Lawrence Prabu C
Esakkimuthu M
Shilaja S

ABSTRACT

Poverty eradication is a long term goal of India. Since independence number of poverty alleviation programmes were launched. It would be incorrect to say that all the poverty alleviation programmes had shown the result much expected. In this way the ongoing programme the Mahatma Gandhi National Rural Employment Guarantee Programme (MGNREGP) is a flagship programme of Government of India. It is launched on February 2006 with the aim of enhancing livelihood security and poverty reduction.

Key words: Alleviation, India, livelihood security, MGNREGP, performance effectiveness and Poverty eradication

INTRODUCTION

Jobless growth is a joy less growth of any country especially developing and population rich country like India. At overall level the unemployment rate is estimated at 94, which imply that 9.4 per cent of the labour force is unemployed and looking for jobs. In absolute terms about 40 million persons are found unemployed and majority of the estimated unemployed persons (80 per cent) is in the rural sector at overall level (Ministry of Labour & Employment 2010). In the midst of unemployment and distress migration the happy bells started to jingle in rural areas when the Government of India announced that "You have the right" to get an employment for hundred days in a financial year through "Mahatma Gandhi National Rural Employment Guarantee Programme".

[1,3] Kerala Agricultural University, COA, Vellayani, Kerala (India)
[2*] Kerala Agricultural University, RARS, Pilicode, Kerala (India)

The Rural India constitutes 72 per cent of the total population of India and scattered in more than six lakh villages. It plays a major role in shaping the democratic India economically, socially and culturally. The majority of the rural population depends on agriculture as a source of livelihood, however increasing real estate business, shrinkage of paddy cultivation, mechanization interventions, natural disasters etc., adversely affect the employment opportunity of casual women and men labourers who depend on agriculture and displace them for searching other employment sources. Due to inadequate employment opportunity the rural people become vulnerable to the possibility of sinking from transient to chronic poverty.

The poverty eradication is a challenging task which is placed before India when it freed from British rule. It is said to be that India still having the world's largest number of poverty affected people. It has been estimated that 350-400 million are below poverty line, of which 75 per cent of them in rural areas. Poverty and unemployment is not a straightforward issue, requires to be addressed by targeted, time bounded and specifically designed law or policy or else it could lead to multidimensional poverty and distress migration of rural poor people from villages to city. In order to address this crucial issue, the Government of India has taken various experiments such as five year plans, poverty alleviation and developmental programmes for the last five decades. The emerging threat such as poverty, distress migration, unemployment, inequalities etc., emphasis and invite the era of rural development.

In the context of poverty and unemployment, generation of productive and gainful employment with decent working conditions through the wage employment programmes in developed and developing countries are perceived as a boon for the unemployed rural poor and also as crucial strategy for 'inclusive growth' as well as it is equally important to make the employment opportunities accessible to all, especially poor and weaker sections of the society.

Since Independence, number of rural development programmes were implemented by the Government of India with the different perspectives and goals. But all the programmes did not bring the expected result and also some of the sections especially women, unskilled casual labourers remain unaffected by those programmes. Among those, the "Mahatma Gandhi National Rural Employment Guarantee Programme" is the flagship programme of the Government of India. The programme was launched by the Prime Minister Dr. Manmohan Singh on 2nd February 2006 based on the Mahatma Gandhi National Rural Employment Guarantee Act 2005. The historic legislation was passed by the Government of India on 23rd August 2005 and it was promulgated on 7th September 2005. It was enacted by the parliament to address the crucial issues of unemployment and poverty in rural India.

The ultimate objective of the programme is to enhance the livelihood security in rural areas by providing at least hundred days guaranteed wage employment in every financial year to every household whose adult members volunteer to do unskilled manual work. The programme provides unskilled manual works with the short term employment on public works, such as irrigation infrastructure, soil conservation, afforestation, road construction and land development. In such a way the programme acts as an income source to poor households especially during slack agricultural seasons or years.

It is quite interesting to realize that, the beautiful words of Mahatma Gandhi that "any effort for the development of India as a whole, should start from the villages of India" and also the important fundamental rights of Indian constitution that "Right to Livelihood" and "equal pay for equal work for both men and women" were fulfilled in this programme.

The MGNREGP was launched in two hundred selected districts on 2nd February 2006 in Phase I and it was extended to 130 more districts in 2007-08 in Phase II. It was further extended to 285 districts from 1st April 2008 onwards, in Phase III. In Kerala, the programme was initiated in February 2006 in the rural areas of two districts viz., Palakkad and Wayanad. The programme was extended to Kasaragod and Idukki districts by February 2007 and to the remaining districts by January 2009. The Government of Kerala issued detailed guidelines for implementing MGNREGP. The responsibility has been assigned primarily to Local-Self Governments. In Kerala, there are elected Village councils (Gram Panchayats) for an average population of thirty thousand. The agglomeration of a few neighbouring Grama Panchayats is called a Block Panchayat. For each revenue district, there is an elected district council (District Panchayat). Thus there is a three tier system of Local self governments in rural areas, each one with specific functions and responsibilities.

HISTORICAL PERSPECTIVE OF MGNREGP

The provision of gainful 'employment for all' was one of the policy goals of India. Accordingly after the Independence, the Government of India under the leadership of Pandit Jawaharlal Nehru, the then Prime Minister of India, had discussed with other senior minister and officials, the poverty conditions that existed in the rural areas of India and the factors which were responsible for it. They wanted to have a permanent solution to this social evil and find out how best the resources can be fully utilized for the future development of rural areas and also the India as a whole. Many of the experts expressed their view that laid a stone for the five year plans. In addition to this, number of rural development programmes were introduced by the Government of India for the upliftment of living standards of rural people by providing employment opportunities, insurance to agricultural crops, financial assistance to farmers like short term or medium term loans, modern tools to rural artisans and construction of houses to weaker section of the community etc. Some of the important national programmes are, Food for Work Programme (FWP) 1977; Integrated Rural Development Programme (IRDP) 1978; National Rural Employment Programme (NREP) 1980, Rural Landless Employment Guarantee Programme (RLEGP) 1983; Jawahar Rozgar Yojana (JRY) 1989; Employment Assurance Scheme (EAS) 1993; Swarna Jayanti Gram Swarozgar Yojana (SGSY) 1999; Pradhan Mantri Gram Sadak Yojana (PMGSY) 2000; Sampoorna Gramin Rogar Yojana (SGRY) 2001; National Food For Work Programme (NFFWP) 2004; Bharat Nirman programme (BNP) 2005. Although there has been an improvement in employment generation in rural areas over the years, some section of the rural population especially those unskilled, casual and manual labourers remain unaffected. This was mainly because, these programmes typically offered relief type employment opportunity, supply based, no guarantee of employment, no prescribed minimum wage pattern and mostly of trickle down approach. However, at the state level, the Government of Maharashtra formulated the Maharashtra Rural Employment Guarantee Scheme under the Maharashtra Employment Guarantee Act, 1977 to provide wage employment to those who demand for wage employment.

Based on the experience of these programmes, the National Rural Employment Guarantee Act 2005, a historic legislation passed by the Government of India on 23rd August 2005 and it was promulgated on 7th September 2005. It was enacted by the parliament to address the crucial issues of unemployment and poverty in rural India. Based on the Act the National Rural Employment Guarantee Programme was launched by the Prime Minister Dr. Manmohan Singh on February 2nd, 2006 and it was rechristened as Mahatma Gandhi National Rural Employment Guarantee Programme on 2nd October 2009, which confers legal right to guaranteed unskilled wage employment for hundred days to every household in a financial year at an equal wage rate for both male and female workers. It is a paradigm shift from other wage employment programmes since providing right based employment and building up of gender equality and pro-poor development as well as creating rural public assets, which has been largely neglected. It also has the capacity to tap the women force potentially and helps to enhance the purchasing power of rural households thereby contributing to poverty alleviation.

IMPORTANCE OF MGNREGP

India is still having the world's largest number of poverty affected people. An estimated 350-400 million people are below the poverty line; 75 per cent of them in rural areas. More than 40 per cent of the population is illiterate, women, tribal and scheduled castes. By scrutinizing these facts Agarwal (2010) cautions that India will not halve its 1990 poverty rate by 2015 as envisaged in the Millennium Development Goals, without more investment in agriculture and policy reforms in rural sector. The statement obviously notes the necessity and urgent need of policy reforms in rural areas, which should create employment opportunities to the neediest people without any kind of discrimination, creating community assets, considering natural resource management and having an extent possible touch with the vulnerable section of the people. By considering these objectives, it is perceptible that MGNREGP strives to realize these requirements. Hence, Roy and Dey (2010) asserted that the scheme (MNREGA) creates a social safety net for the vulnerable section of the people by providing a fall-back employment source, when other employment alternatives are scarce or inadequate. They validated their point by pointing that MNREGA has resulted in the generation of more number of person days than any other scheme that free India has ever seen. By observing the outstanding performance of the programme (MGNREGP) over a period, Harza (2009) came up with a valid point and he described that the programme (MGNREGP) has become a significant vehicle for regeneration of India's depleting natural resource base. Specializing on the impact of MNREGP upon natural resource management, Patel (2006) opined that it plays a vital role to mobilize and strengthen the untapped natural resources (physical, natural and human) for the development of village economy.

SIGNIFICANCE OF MGNREGP

The significance of MGNREGP having been topped because of its objectives and the way it is framed by the Government of India. The programme (MGNREGP) is structured in a 'Right- based and Need-based approach' getting employment under this programme is the Right of people and providing employment is based on the need of people. In such a way it shows the respect over the right and needs of the people. Having a thorough grasp over the structure of MGNREGP as he is one of the founding fathers of the scheme, Drèze (2008) opined that the MGNREGP is one of the greatest experiments to eradicate rural poverty. He further added that the scheme is both powerful and effective as the implementation of the scheme is styled in a genuinely democratic and decentralized manner in a rights based approach. The success of any developmental programme based on the active participation of the targeted group, in this way is worth to say that the MGNREGP succeeds on its goal. For instance, 2.10 crore households were provided employment during 2006-07; 3.39 crore during 2007-08; 4.49 crore during 2008-09 and 4.50 crore during 2009-10. These records illustrate the significance of MGNREGP.

CONCEPTS OF PERFORMANCE EFFECTIVENESS

According to Davis (1949) defined role performance as how an individual actually performs a task in a given situation as distinct from how he is supposed to perform. Hitt *et al.* (1983) wrote that effectiveness refers to how well an organization reaches its objectives over a period of time. Reddin (1987) observed that effectiveness is multidimensional and the extent to which managers achieve the output requirements of their position. He further stated that it is output, not input. Gosh *et al.* (1988) gave the measuring of effectiveness as the extent to which an action or activity achieves its stated purpose. Mohan (1988) stated that effectiveness is the measure of extent of contribution which an activity makes to the overall endeavour for the achievement of the pre-determined goal. Arora (1993) reports that success of any developmental measures is determined by the effectiveness of the administration system. Meadley and Shannon (1994) pointed out that the teacher performance effectiveness can be arrived through observational schedules, rating scale and student achievement test. Babykumari *et al.* (1998) defined performance as the pragmatic results that the organization is able to measure objectively.

According to Rao (2004) stated that performance is a result of both ability and effort. A highly capable individual may need to put in only marginal effort to give high performance, whereas another individual with low ability may need to put in a lot of effort to produce even an average level of output. Bella (2006) in her study performance on effectiveness of teachers, defined performance effectiveness of the teacher means the degree to which a teacher does right things in a creative way to achieve the intended and desired results through optimum utilization of resources in teaching, research and extension education. Sharma *et al.* (2009) in their study on evaluating performance of NREGA, reported that, there was significant variations in performance of NREGA *vis a vis* SGRY. The regional level performance of eastern region was poor and other regions have witnessed reduction in cost per day of employment generated. Mehta (2010) in his study on management of MGNREGP reported that a very poor performance was indicated in providing 100 days of employment to the applicant households. Shah (2010) reported that 98 per cent the beneficiaries and 73 per cent of the non – beneficiaries of MGNREGS created useful assets at the village level.

EXTENT OF STAKEHOLDER PARTICIPATION

It is defined as the extent of actual involvement of people both physical and mental in different stages of programme. French (1960) referred participation as a process in which two or more parties influence each other in making certain plans, policies and decisions. According to Soyal (1966) participation refers to the convergent action by which the citizens take part in the accomplishments of administrative services without belonging to the governing or managing body. Acoording to Davis (1969) participation is a mental and emotional involvement of a person in a group situation which encourages him to contribute to goals and shares responsibility in them.

According to Nandal (1972) participation of the people in the planning process at different stages of decision making, deision implementation and evaluation is needed for the success of planning. Baetiz (1975) observed that participation in development means how community members can be assured the opportunity to contributing the creation of communitie's goods and services. Pearse and Stiefel (1979) referred participation as an organized effort to increase control over resources and regulative institutions in a given social situation as the part of groups and movement of those hitherto executed from such control. Jayavelu (1980) found that lack of knowledge about the economies of the development programme might result in the non participation of the people in it. According to Mishra (1984) participation means direct involvement of people and not involvement through representatives.

According to Saiyadain (1988) participation refers to sharing in an appropriate way the decision making power with subordinates. In the opinion of Mishra (1994) the term participation has three conditions. Participation means cooperation, taking part in something, the mere presence, even silence presence of individuals or representatives of an organization at different levels. According to him participation can be direct or indirect, passive/active and it is one of the important techniques to achieve the desired goal. State Planning Board of Kerala (1996) reported that only through decentralization of power we could ensure the participation of people in various developmental activities. Parker (1997) observed that participation ranges from local people being involved in implementing development or conservation of programmes to being actively involved in all stages of the development process including decision making process.

According to Ray (1997) defined participation as the process of getting oneself involved in thoughts, feelings and actions with others. It may be perceived as a continuum varying between positive listening to active involvement in benefit sharing. Veluswamy and Manoharan (1998) found that majority of the beneficiaries participated in all activities of NGO. Situation survey was the activity in which more participation was found, followed by selecting problems for action and analyzing the situation, problem assessment and prioritizing problems. According to Blackburn and Holland (1998) participation is the full involvement of local population in identification of priorities, problems and potential solutions with team of scientists, planners and development specialists. Kareem and Jayaramaiah (1998) defined participation as the degree to which the members of the beneficiary families involved themselves in different stages of the programme, starting from their selection of beneficiary to deriving benefits from assistance provided under programme.

According to Rehman and Rehman (1998) defined participation as a process of learning and sharing. Participation process is a goal directed, objective focused on activity of an organization. Suthan (2003) in his study on the analysis of farmer's participation in the Participatory Technology Development (PTD), found that 64 per cent of farmers had high extent of participation in PTD and correlation analysis showed that extent of participation in PTD was positively and significantly related with social participation and need satisfaction. Padhi *et al.* (2010) reported that there is little participation in MNREGA on the part of the households belonging to household income range of less than Rs.10,000 and also reported that extent of women participation is much higher than the targeted 30 per cent. Mehta (2010) in his study on management of MGNREGP in U.P found that the participation of women in NREGA has been very unsatisfactory in the state. Thus the overall share of women in getting employment under MGNREGA has declined by 45.56 per cent during first phase, nearly 18 per cent during the second phase and 12 per cent during third phase; but increased to 14 per cent during the fourth phase at the state level.

EXTENT OF BENEFICIARY SATISFACTION

The beneficiary satisfaction is operationalised as the set of responses of the beneficiaries which shows the satisfaction or dissatisfaction towards Mahatma Gandhi National Rural Employment Guarantee Programme. Katzell (1964) defined job satisfaction as the verbal expression of the incumbent's evaluation of his job. Perumal and Rai (1978) reported that maximum number of Agricultural Extension officers in Tamilnadu were in average job satisfaction category and rest in low and high categories. Also there was no relationship existed between job satisfaction and job performance. Nelson (1992) in his study on role of Krishi bhavan reported that job satisfaction of AAOs was found to be significantly and positively related with their attitude towards Krishi bhavan. Datar (2007) in his study on NREGA revealed that there was dissatisfaction about the measurement practices in work allocation. Adhikari and Bhatia (2010) in their study on NREGA wage payments reported that a large majority (77 per cent) of the sample workers preferred NREGA wages to be paid through banks or post offices rather than in cash. Shah (2010) reported that 50 per cent of the respondents preferred cash payment whereas three-fourth of them preferred time based against piece rate work. Mehta (2010) states that very high majority (76 per cent) of respondents were preferred to undertake piece rate of work over the time based.

SOCIO-ECONOMIC AND COMMUNICATION CHARACTERISTICS OF STAKEHOLDERS

Age

It refers to the number of calendar years completed by the respondents at the time of interview. Sherin (1997) in her study on analysis of the characteristics of women's group and their role in rural development reported a positive and significant correlation between age and need satisfaction of women. Haorei and Kumar (2010) in their study on impact of MGNREGS on Rural women empowerment, observed that majority of scheme beneficiary respondents comes under the age group of 39-65 (58 per cent) followed by age group of 18-35 (42 per cent) with no respondents were above 65 years old. Sharma *et al.* (2010) in their study on Management of MGNREGS observed that the participants within the age group of 21 years to 35 years were higher in number as compared to the age group of 30-60 years.

Sex

It is a dichotomized variable having only two categories namely 'male' and 'female'. Sulaiman (2004) remarked that, the term 'sex' denotes the physical and biological differences between men and women, whereas the 'gender' describes the socially determined attributes of men and women. This includes male and female roles in economic functions, differential access to control over resources and differences in knowledge and skills. The sexual division of labour for both agricultural and domestic tasks varies greatly by community and ethnic group and it is difficult to make generations about the roles that men, women and children play.

According to Vijayanand and Jithendran (2008) in their study on "Implementation of NREGA– Experience" of Kerala, observed that there are enthusiastic women participation under this MGNREG programme, nearly 80 per cent of workers have been women. Galab *et al.* (2009) in their study on management of NREGS reported that demand for the work from women is higher than from men. Nair *et al.* (2009) in their study on NREGP in three gram panchayat of Kasaragod district, observed that 60.8 per cent in Madikkai, 62.1 per cent in Ajanoor and 54.1 per cent in Trikarpur were women. Adhikari and Bhatia (2010) observed that 78 per cent of the respondents were men and 28 per cent were women in MGNREGA. Banerjee and Saha (2010) found that female participation was higher than male participation in MGNREGP. Haorei and Kumar (2010) reported in their study on Impact of MGNREGS on Rural women empowerment, women beneficiaries contributed 78 per cent whereas 22 per cent were men.

According to Shah (2010) in his study on MGNREGS observed that female workers constituted 57 per cent of the total work force. Sharma *et al.* (2010) reported that 92.5 per cent male and 7.5 per cent female. This distribution of participating households shows that the percentage of male outnumbers that of female. Galab *et al.* (2010) in their study reported that NREGS helped in reducing male – female wage inequality, thereby enabling women to control more money, leading to equity in food consumption and schooling of children and also women workers were found to have participated more (58 %) compared to men (50 %) in the sample districts.

Caste

According to Nair *et al.* (2009) in their study on NREGA of three grama spanchayats of Kesaragod district observed that the extent of SC households registered in NREGA in Trikarpur was 54.9 percent whereas in Madikkai and Ajanoor it was 41.9 and 23.8 per cent respectively. Madikkai has the highest ST registration with 73.8 percent and Ajanoor stands second with 66.3 per cent. Adhikari and Bhatia (2010) found that tribal population was predominant under MGNREGA. Dalapati (2010) in his study on MGNREGS found that majority of beneficiaries (42 %) were from scheduled tribes and 21.5 per cent belonged to scheduled caste category. The participants of other backward castes were reported to be 32.1 per cent, whereas only 4 per cent general castes people participated in the wage employment programme.

According to Galab *et al.* (2010) observed that the proportion of SC, ST and BC household participation was around 64 per cent and only 15 per cent among other castes. Mehta (2010) in his study revealed that highest proportion of 80 per cent SC and lowest proportion of 40.45 per cent general caste households participated in MGNREGA. Shah (2010) found in his study on MGNREGS in Gujarat that 57 per cent of sample households belonged to scheduled tribes and 23 per cent scheduled castes. Sharma *et al.* (2010) reported that 68.8 per cent of the participants belonged to scheduled castes and 16.3 per cent were other backward castes. Padhi *et al.* (2010) observed that the portion of SC households among participants is much greater than their share in total population for all the four surveyed districts of Orissa.

Education

It refers to the extent of literacy obtained by the respondent at the time of study. Babykumary *et al.* (1998) in their study observed that the educational qualification had non-significant association with job performance of farm scientist. Halakatti and Sundaraswamy (2003) in their study on agricultural assistants organizational commitment in training and visit system found that educational background of the respondents did not show any significant relationship with organizational commitment. Rezvanfar and Vaisy (2006) in their study found that educational level had positive and significant relationship with job satisfaction. Singh and Mishra (2006) reported that NREGA is operated in such area where most of the people are uneducated. Adhikari and Bhatia (2010) in their study observed that education level among the MGNREGA workers were relatively low. Almost half (45%) of the workers were illiterate, with only 21 per cent having completed 10th class.

According to Dalapati (2010) found that majority (60%) of participating respondents on MGNREGS were illiterate, 14 per cent were educated up to class 9th, 4.6 per cent had the high school level education and only 2.5 percent were above class 10th. Haorei and Kumar (2010) in their study on the impact of MGNREGS observed that majority of respondents completed 10th standard and 8 per cent had completed 6-10th standard and 32.35 per cent of respondent had completed 1-5th standard. Sharma *et al.* (2010) in their study observed that among the participating households the proportion having lower primary qualifications was the highest while those having senior secondary qualification were the lowest.

Family Type

In this study family type means, nuclear family or joint family. Nuclear family is one which consists of husband, wife and their unmarried children whereas joint family is one which composed of grand parents and their children including married sons and daughters with their spouses.
Shilaja (1981) operationalised family type as family composition in which families were classified into nuclear and joint families depending upon the composition of the family. A nuclear family consists of husband, wife and their unmarried children if any. Two or more nuclear families living in the same household and sharing the same kitchen constituted a joint family.

Family Size

In the present study family size was measured by taking into consideration the specific number of members in the family of the respondents. Tea Board (1962) in its study on survey of the living conditions of tea plantation labour in Tripura found that families with three members constituted (29.3%) of the sample, followed by two member families (18.6%). The average size of labour family was 4.01. Deepali (1979) in her study revealed that small families were having high participation score in agricultural operations when compared to big families. Kumar (1982) observed in his study on profile of agricultural labourers that, the sample households of agricultural labourers were small family. Ingle and Dharmadhikaraj (1987) reported that the average size of the family among agricultural labourers households was 4.6 persons and among landless agricultural labourers it was 4.48 persons.

Occupation

Majority (58.4 %) of the participants household's main occupation was agriculture labourer, 19.3 per cent households were agriculture self-employed, 15.6 per cent households were non agricultural labourer and 5.0 per cent households were non agricultural self employed Dalapati (2010).

According to Sharma *et al.* (2010) in their study on MGNREGS reported that occupation wise proportion of participating household showed that casual labourer doing MGNREGS works was the highest as compared to the other categories of respondents. The casual labourer in agriculture is the dominant occupational group among participant households in all the surveyed districts, followed by casual labourer in non-agriculture or self employed in agriculture (Padhi *et al.*, 2010).

Annual Income

The annual income of the family was the total earnings of the household for one year including the income through MGNREGP and all other sources. The income from various practices of MGNREGP work and from all other sources were added up to get the total income. The MGNREGP has suddenly increased the purchasing power of poor and there is visible local economic development and also lays foundation of livelihood security through hundred days wage employment (Vijayanand and Jithendran, 2008). The NREGP was successful enough in raising the level of employment and income of the rural households, thereby enhancing their purchasing power and it has substantially increased their credit worthiness (Nair *et al.*, 2009).

The MGNREGP become a beacon of light in empowerment of rural women and contributed substantially for the increased living and economic condition by generating employment and also providing equal wages to both male and female workers (Ramesh and Krishnakumar, 2009). An average household generated a total annual income and total wage income of Rs.22999 and Rs.14151 respectively during 2007-08. Out of which MGNREGS income was around 14.7 per cent of the total income and 23.9 per cent of the total wage income of a household. Thus shows that MGNREGS increased the income of the beneficiary households (Dalapati, 2010). Participant women were contributing 11 per cent additional income over the non-participant women to their household by way of getting NREGA employment (Mehta, 2010).

Performance of NREGS in Kerala revealed there has been substantial change in the household income after the introduction of NREGA. The change in the average income was found to be much higher in Idukki with Rs.2601/- followed by Alapuzha with Rs.2093/- (Narayanasamy *et al.*, 2010); NREGS was seen to contribute maximum to household income, surpassing even agricultural and non agricultural sources. The proportionate contribution of NREGS to household income was the highest in Rajasthan and in Bihar with most families having a lower income base to begin with in the first place, NREGS earnings contributed to about 8 per cent of the household income (Reddy *et al.*, 2010). Socio-economic conditions of MGNREGA found that 59 per cent of workers surveyed belonged to BPL family (Yadav and Gargh, 2010).

Expenditure Pattern

It is defined as the total amount spent on food, non-food consumptive items, agriculture, livestock etc. Agricultural crisis, credit and indebtedness of farmers reported that 32 per cent of total expenditure was on medical treatment, 25.60 per cent for purchasing of consumer durables, 16.20 per cent expenses on repair of house, 7 per cent on educational expenses and 5.60 per cent on construction of house. The largest proportion of participants, 27.6 per cent utilized MGNREGS income for purchasing food items. Around 23 per cent of them spent the income from NREGS on health. Small proportion ie 20 per cent has also been able to save some amount from the income gained from employment under MGNREGS. An additional income earned through MGNREGA-related work was mostly spent on consumption of food grains. Maximum (75.3%) beneficiaries used the MGNREGS income for purchasing food items and who had very significant income (16.6 percent) were able to invest the MGNREGS wages on building durable assets for them. Over 78 per cent women were utilizing their wage income for purchasing of food items, while the lowest proportion of 19 per cent of them were using it for personal purpose (Prakash, 2007; Sharma *et al.*, 2010; Banerjee and Saha, 2010; Dalapati, 2010; Mehta, 2010).

Mass Media Exposure

It refers to the degree to which the respondent was exposed to various mass media channels. It has positively and significantly related with the extent of participation in agricultural and allied fields (Pradeepkumar, 1993). Open meeting of Gram Panchayat and information given through Radio, T.V, News paper, Notice board of Gram panchayat and local officials were the prominent sources of bringing awareness among the villagers about prescribed wage rates and other matter of NREGA to the villagers (Mehta, 2010). According to Dey and Bedi (2010) in their study on MGNREGP observed that 99.4 per cent of surveyed households were aware of the existence of MGNREGP and it was by far the best known programme, whereas 60-65 per cent of surveyed households were aware of the social schemes such as IAY, SGSY which have been in operation since 1985-1999. In terms of information source 32 per cent of respondents mentioned that the most common sources of information on MGNREGP was the Gram panchayats and 25 per cent of respondents mentioned through affiliated political party. The MGNREGS in Gujarat reported that the extent of awareness was found to be relatively higher (Shah, 2010).

Contact with Officials

It is a degree to which the respondent is having contact with officers for obtaining information regarding MGNREGP. It had positive and significant relationship with attitude of farmers toward Krishibhavan. People had contact with sarpanch and they were the main source of information the sarpanch, the NGOs became an important source of information (Nelson, 1992; Jaswal and Mistry, 2007).

Social Participation

It is a degree to which the respondent participates in various social activities. Social participation of farm women had significant and negative association with the extent of involvement in farm activities. Old farmers were likely to loose interest in active participation within and outside the social system. Majority of the respondents had medium level of social participation due to lack of credible institutions and extension contacts. Over 93 per cent of the respondents reported to have participated in the Gram Sabha meeting convened specially to discuss the matters related to MGNREGS (Govind, 1984; Sindhu, 2002; Sasankan, 2001; Narayanasamy *et al.*, 2010).

Level of Aspiration

It is a individual's desire or need to acquire better in life. The level of aspiration as the standard by which a person judges his own performances as a success or failure or as being up to what extent he expects of himself (English and English, 1958); individual as his overall assessment of his concern for wishes and helps for the future in his own reality world (Cantril and Free,1962); one's personal and socio-economic attributes to a great extent contributed to one's level of aspiration which increased the adoption of new idea (Muthayya, 1971); level of aspiration had no significant relationship with role performance (Seema, 1986); it is the performance level of future attainment that the person sets himself to reach in some extent to gravitate towards his achievement (Kannayan, 1998).

Economic Motivation

It refers to the extent to which an individual is oriented towards achievement of the maximum economic ends. Positive and significant relationship between economic development and attitude of pepper growers in Pepper Development Programme (Chandran, 1989); An economic motivation was significantly related to extent of participation in primary milk producers co-operative societies (Krishnaiah and Maraty, 1989). It is an important character that persuades people to adopt improved agricultural practices for sustainable returns from farm (Sivaprasad, 1997); most of the people motivated by economic ends, they try to adopt the practices which are aimed at increasing sustainable returns (Thomas, 1998).

Attitude of Stakeholders towards MGNREGP

Attitude as the degree of positive or negative effect associated with some psychological object towards which people can differ in varying degrees. The adopters of new ideas had favourable attitude towards government programmes. Farmer's attitude towards the package programme had positive and significant influence on the level of adoption of package of practices. Attitude as a summary statement or label for the individuals entire learning history with respect to attitudinal object (Sureshkumar, 1989); significant difference in the level of attitude among beneficiaries towards pepper development programmes (Sajeevchandran, 1989); agricultural labourers had favourable attitude towards welfare schemes for agricultural labourers implemented by the Government of Kerala (Fathimabi,1993). It can be concluded from the above studies that favourable attitude towards development programme, new ideas, technology or innovation, is prime requirement for the participation and success (Thurstone, 1946; Rai, 1965; Singh *et al.*,1966).

Perception of Stakeholders on MGNREGP

It refers to a process which leads to fixation of certain ideas, belief, image or opinion over an object by the result of how an individual see, listen and understand particular object. It is operationalised as the meaningful sensation of the respondent about Mahatma Gandhi National Rural Employment Guarantee Programme. Perception is the factor that shapes and produces what we actually expresses. Over 75 per cent of participants of Intensive Agriculture District Programme (IADP) perceived that methods of availing benefits were more complicated. Lab to Land Programme found that about 55 per cent of the non-tribals and 75 per cent of tribals belonged to the high perception group. Over 90 per cent of households felt that as a result of IRDP, their family employment had increased. majority of the women beneficiaries of IRDP perceived enhanced income through participating in the programme

(Mitchel,1978; Balu,1980; Sudha,1987; Khanna,1987; Sharma,1989).

The right kind of perception is highly essential for successful programme implementation and organizational climate adds considerably to the perception and success of any extension programme. Over 67 per cent of farmers perceived that employment through National Rural Employment Guarantee Programme was very useful. Over, 54.7 per cent of participants perceived that MGNREGS is very important for their family and over 43 per cent households accepted that MGNREGS has brought significant changes in their life. A three-fourth proportion of respondents perceived that the assets created in their Gram Panchayat was very useful in the interest of village communities and 72 per cent participants perceived that implementation of MGNREGA has been important in the interest of the welfare of their village people. Above 88 per cent of households perceived that MNREGA was 'very important' and 37 per cent 'somewhat important in all three surveyed districts. However, 92 per cent of the beneficiary households perceived that MNREGS was important because it gives work at door step and 11 per cent of the respondents indicated that

MNREGS was important because it provided better wages (Mangaraj,1999; Kumaran, 2008; Dalapati, 2010; Mehta, 2010; Padhi *et al.*, 2010; Shah, 2010).

Constraints perceived by the Stakeholders

Constraint is operationalised as difficulties or problems faced by the stakeholders of the MGNREGP which hinders the successful implementation of the programme and avail the benefits. Pandya and Trivedi (1988) defined constraints as "those items of difficulties or problems faced by individuals in the adoption of technology". Gogoi and Talukdar (1989) defined constraints as those factors which have repressive efforts on a desired and or purposive action. Asiabaka and Bamisile (1991) in their study on assessing the performance level of agricultural extension agents in Logos state agricultural development project found that lack of transportation, lack of incentives and ultimately distribution of inputs to farmers, lack of office space, problem of payment of traveling allowance and lack of promotions were the major constraints influencing their performance level. Nelson (1992) reported that lack of clerical support in office work was the most important constraint perceived by Agricultural officers in the effective functioning of Kishi bhavan followed by lack of conveyance facilities, lack of funds to meet traveling expenses and lack of office facilities. Singh and Sharma (1998) found illiteracy to be rampant among the farm women in both hills and plains. The women are mostly involved in repetitive and monotonous operations.

According to Chathukulam and Gireesan (2007) in their study on impact assessment of NREGS in Kerala observed that paucity of technical staff delays in wage payment and other NREGS activities as major constraints. Das and Pradhan (2007) reported that contractors were involved in NREGA and they had taken all the wage earners' job cards and it is noticed in Talandangadang of Koraput District in Orissa. Khera (2008) observed extremely low wages, deficiencies in work measurement at the worksite, coupled with lack of co-ordination among NREGS staff undertaking measurement as major constraints. Vijayanand (2008) in his study on NREGA reported that there is clashing with agricultural season during implementation of the programme works. Shah and Mehta (2008) reported that some of the problem of supply side management, observed during most of the employment generation/ guarantee programmes, including Maharashtra Employment Guarantee Scheme (MEGS), seems to loom large in this early phase of NREGS.

According to Adhikari and Bhatia (2010) in their study on NREGA wage payments observed that there is growing complexity in the maintenance of records, which was making difficult to match work attendance details with wages paid and received. Chhabra *et al.* (2010) in his study reported that untimely payment of wages by gram panchayat and banks and time taken in releasing funds to the gram panchayat were reported as a major problems existing in proper implementation of NREGS.

In addition to these problems inadequate staff, difficult procedures adopted for measurement of works, criteria fixed for selection of works and provisions for payment of wages through bank/ post office were also adversely affecting proper implementation of the programme. Dalapati (2010) observed that lack of adequate number of sub –engineers and Gram Rojgar Sahayaks, measurement and payment of wages to work getting delayed are the major constraints.

According to Mehta (2010) found that at majority of (56 %) worksites, the labourers had complained untimely payment of wages or the ongoing practices of paying less than prescribed amount of wages as the major constraints. Padhi *et al.* (2010) reported that serious problem of concern is the inordinate delay in wage payment. Raman (2010) noticed that the problem on the worksites is apparent that very few civil society institutions really monitor MGNREGA and there are not enough programme officers. Shah (2010) observed that 18-23 per cent of the households reported that the scheme has resulted in scarcity of labour during peak agricultural season and also administrative delays in starting the work, continuity and more importantly predictability, seasonality and transparency in payment all these remains teething trouble at least during the initial phase of implementation of the scheme. Vendan and Murugavel (2010) found that there is discrimination in allotting works under this programme. The study reported that favouritism and discrimination against people in allotting type and location of work.

CONCLUSION

The MGNREGP is the first ever law internationally, that guarantees wage employment at an unprecedented scale. It is the flagship programme of the Government of India. It aims at enhancing livelihood security of households in rural areas of the country by providing hundred days wage employment in a financial year whose adult members volunteer to do unskilled manual work. Unemployment is a major problem in rural areas. This programme is employment generation, public and private asset creation and empowerment of rural people economically, politically and socially.

REFERENCES

Adhikari, A. and Bhatia, K. (2010): NREGA Wage Payments: Can we Bank on the Banks?, *Econ. & Polit. Weekly,* XIV (1): 37.

Agarwal, M. (2010): Is India's Inclusive Economic Growth: A Reality?, *The Hindu Survey of Indian Agriculture,* pp: 111-114.

Arora, S. (1993): Organizational Effectiveness and Participatory Management, *J. Rural. Dev.,*5 (1): 87-106.

Asiabaka, C.C and Bamisile, (1991): An Assessment of the Performance of Agricultural Extension Agents: A Case Study of Logos State Agricultural Development Projects (ISADP), *J. Rural. Dev.,* 10(6): 705-714.

Babykumary, P. Rathakrishnan,T. and Seetharaman,N.R. (1998): Factors Affecting the Job Performance of the Farm Scientists, *J. Extn. Edu.*, 9: 2025-2026.

Baetiz, R.C. (1975): Development and Participation, Operation, Implications for Social Welfare, *Columbia University Press*, New York.

Balu, S.R.A. (1980): A Study on the Functioning of Integrated Dryland Agricultural Development Project, Tamil Nadu Agricultural University, Coimbatore, pp: 40-60.

Banerjee, K and Saha, P. (2010): The NREGA the Maoists and the Developmental Woes of Indian States, *Econ & Polit. Weekly*, XLV (28): 42-47.

Bella, M. (2006): Performance Effectiveness of Teachers in the Agriculture Colleges of Kerala Agricultural University, College of Agriculture, Vellayani, pp: 72.

Blackburn, J and Holland, J. (1998): Who changes? Institutionalising Participation in Development, *Intermediate Technology publication Ltd.*, London.

Cantril, H and Free, L.A. (1962): The Pattern of Human Concerns, *Rudgers University Press*, New Brunswick.

Chandran, S.A. (1989): Impact of Development Programme of Promoting Pepper Production in Kerala, Kerala Agricultural University, Vellayani, pp: 141.

Chathukulam, J and Gireesan, K. (2007): Impact Assessment of NREGS in Kerala Evaluation of System and Processes, *The Gazette of India*, Ministry of Rural Development, 48: 174-176.

Chhabra, S., Raina, R.L and Sharma, G.L (2010): MGNREGA-A Step towards Meeting the Challenges of Inclusive Growth: A Study of Six States, *LBS. J. Mgt & Res.*, VIII (1): 123-149.

Dalapati, T.K. (2010): MGNREGS in Madhya Pradesh: Loopholes, Silver Linings and Ways Ahead, *LBS. J. Mgt & Res.*, VIII (1): 73-84.

Das, V. & Pradhan, P. (2007): Illusions of Change, *Econ & Polit. Weekly*, XLII (32): 12-15.

Datar, C. (2007): Failure of National Rural Employment Guarantee Scheme in Maharashtra, *Econ & Polit. Weekly*, XLII (34): 3454-3457.

Davis, J.H. (1969): Group Performance: Reading Mass, *Addison Wesley*, New York.

Davis, K. (1949): Human Society, *The Mc Milan Co.*, New York, pp: 676.

Deepali, M.N. (1979): A Study on the knowledge and Participation of Rural Women in Agricultural Operations with Respect to Paddy Crop and their Value Orientation in Dharwad District, University of Agricultural Sciences, Dharward, pp: 77.

Dey, S. and Bedi, A.S. (2010): The National Rural Employment Guarantee Scheme in Birbhum, *Econ & Polit. Weekly*, XLV (41): 19-24.

Dreze, J. (2008): Act Fair give Rural Workers their due, *The Times of India*, April 4, 2008, pp: 10.

English, H.B and English, A.C. (1958): A Comprehensive Dictionary of Psychological and Psychological and Psycho-analytical Terms, *Logmans Green and Co.*, New York, 625p.

Fathimabi, P.K. (1993): Welfare Scheme for Agricultural Labourers- A Multi Dimentional Analysis, College of Agriculture, Vellayani, pp: 108.

French, J.R.P. (1960): An Experiment in Participation in Norwegian Factory, Human *Relations*, 13 (3): 46.

Galab, S., Reddy, P.P., Revathi, E and Revathi, C. (2009): A Report on Management of NREGS, Issues and Challenges: The Case of Andrapradesh, CESS, Hyderabad, pp: 14-34.

Gogoi, D.K and Talukdar, R.K. (1989): The Concept, Constraint and Problem: Need for Constraint Analysis and Typology of Constraints in Transfer of Technology, Paper Presented at the Workshop on Methodologies and Approaches to Constraint Analysis in the Transfer of Agricultural Technologies (Aug 8-10), National Academy of Agricultural Research Management, Hyderabad, pp: 454.

Gosh, P.K., Sharma, S.D. and Raj, G.D. (1988): Encyclopaedia Dictionary of Management, Vol. III, *Anmol Publications*, New Delhi, pp: 36-37.

Govind, S. (1984): Participaation of Farm Women in Farm and Home Activities, Tamil Nadu Agricultural University, Coimbatore, pp: 140.

Halakatti, S.V and Sundaraswamy, B. (2003): Agricultural Assistants Organizational Commitment in Training and Visit System, *J. Ext. edu.*, 14(3 & 4): 3508-3511.

Harorei, W and Kumar, P.A. (2010): Impact of Mahatma Gandhi National Rural Employment Guarantee Scheme on Rural Women Empowerment, *J. Extn. & Res.*, XII (2): 124-125.

Harza, A. (2009): Transforming Rural India, *Kurukshetra*, 58 (2): 7-10.

Hitt, M.A, Middlemist, R.D. and Mathis, R.L. (1983): Management Concept and Effective Practice, *West Publishing co.*, Minnesota, pp: 110.

Ingle, P.O and Dharmadhikaraj, N. (1987): Personal and Socio-economic Status of Agricultural Women Labour, *Maharashtra J. Extn. Educ.*, 6: 27-32.

Jaswal, A and Mistry, P. (2007): Will NREGA Ensure Security on against Hunger?., *Indian Institute of Management*, Ahmadabad, pp: 1-8.

Jayavelu, N. (1980): An Analysis of Factors Responsible for Participation of Cotton Growers in Regulated Market, Tamil Nadu Agricultural University, Coimbatore, pp: 402.

Kannayan, S. (1998): Job Satisfaction of Graduates Engaged in Selected Avenues of Employment in Alleppy District, Kerala Agricultural University, Thrissur, pp: 89.

Kareem, K.M and Jayaramaiah, K.M. (1998): Participation of Beneficiaries in Integrated Rural Development Programmes, *Madras Agrl. Journal*, 85(1): 20-23.

Katzell, R.A. (1964): Personal Values, Job Satisfaction and Job Behaviour, In: Man in a World at Work, Borrow, H. (ed) Boston Massachsetts, *Houghton Mifflin Company*, London, pp: 49.

Khanna, I. (1987): IRDP is having a Positive Impact, *Yojana*, 3 (5): 12.

Khera, R. (2008): Group Measurement of NREGA Work: The Jalore Experiment Rajasthan-Jalore District, Paper Presented at NREGA: Impacts and Implementation Experiences, *Institute for Human Development Press, New Delhi*, 16 and 17 September, pp: 452.

Krishnaiah, G. and Maraty, P. (1989): Impact of Primary Milk Producers Co-operative Societies on Beneficiaries in Nalgonda District of Andra Pradesh, *Indian Co-operative Review*, 26(8): 278-282.

Kumar, B. (1982): Profile of Agricultural Labourers in Mau Tahsil of Bunda District, G.B Pant Social Science Institute, Allahabad.

Kumaran, V. (2008): Survival Stress for Livelihood Security of Farmers in Palakkad District: The Case of Nalleppilly Panchayat, College of Agriculture, Vellayani, pp: 63-64.

Mangaraj, A.K. (1999): Perception of AEO on Agricultural Extension Programme in Orissa, *Ind. J. Extn. Edu.*, 35 (1&2):146-147.

Medley, D.M and Shannon, D.M. (1994): Teacher Evaluation, The International Encyclopedia of Education, *Oxford Press*, USA.

Mehta, G.S. (2010): Management of Mahatma Gandhi National Rural Employment Guarantee Programme in U.P.: Issues and Challenges, *LBS. J. Mgt & Res.*, VIII (1): 99-122.

Ministry of Labour & Employment. (2010): Report on Employment & Unemployment Survey, Ministry of Labour & Employment, *Labour Bureau,* Delhi, pp: 151.

Mishra, S.N. (1984): Participation and Development, *NBO Publications*, New Delhi.

Mishra, Y. (1994): People's Participation in Production Process under Watershed, *Kurukshetra,* 12 (11): 2830-2833.

Mitchel, B. (1978): An Analysis of Perception of the Role of Subordinates with Respect to Authority Responsibility and Delegation in the Community Schools of Pliant at the Attendance Centre Level, *Mitchigon State University*, Mitchigon, pp: 220.

Mohan, S. (1998): The meaning of Managerial Effectiveness- A Synthesis of some Modern Management, *J. Extn. Edu.*, 5(2): 49-56.

Muthayya, B.C. (1971): Farmers and their Aspiration: Influence of Socio-economic Status and Work Orientation, National Institute of Rural Development, Hyderabad, pp: 243.

Nair, K.N., Sreedharan. T.P and Anoopkumar. (2009): A Study of National Rural Employment Guarantee Programme on Three grama Spanchayats of Kasaragod District (Working Paper Series 413), *Centre for Development Studies*, Thiruvananthapuram, pp: 1-47.

Nandal, R.S. (1972): Planning for Development of Agriculture, *Ind. J. Extn. Edu.*, 16(1&2): 15-17.

Narayanasamy, N., Boraian, M.P., Manivel, S., Saji, M.P., Sebastian, P., Dhavamani, R., Lalan, A.,Geethanjali and Pandian, M. (2010): A Study on the Performance of NREGS in Kerala, pp: 14. (Available at http://www.crd.kerala.gov.in/2010/sept/consolidaton, Pdf. 175p.)

Nelson, A.S. (1992): Role of Krishi Bhavan in Agricultural Development Thiruvnanthapuram District, Kerala Agricultural University, Thrissur, pp: 134.

Padhi, S.P., Meher, S and Panigrahi, N. (2010): Management of MG National Rural Employment Guarantee Act: Issues & Challenges in Orissa, *LBS. J. Mgt & Res.*, III (1): 85-98.

Pandya, R.D and Trivedi, J.C. (1998): Constraints in Adoption of Gobar Gas Technology, *Rural India,* 5(7): 123-126.

Parker, S. (1997): Annapurna Conservation Area Project- In Pursuit of Sustainable Development?, In: Richard, M.A and Katrina, B. (eds.) Approaches to Sustainable Development, *PRINTER,* London, pp: 144-166.

Patel, A. (2006): Role of PRI's in Implementing Rural Employment Guarantee Scheme, *Kurukshetra,*12: 24-29.

Pearse, A and Stiefel, M. (1979): Inquiry into Participation, *UINRISD*, Geneva, pp: 459.

Perumal, G. and G.C. Rai (1978): Job Satisfaction and Job Performance of Agricultural Extension Officers Working in Rural Development Blocks of Tamilnadu, *Madras. Agric. Journal,* 65(2): 96-99.

Pradeepkumar, (1993): Aspiration of Educated Unemployed Youth for Self-employment in Agriculture and Allied Fields, College of Agriculture, Vellayani, pp: 49.

Prakash, B.A. (2007): Agricultural Crisis, Credit and Indebtedness of Farmers in Wayanad District: Findings of a Survey, University of Kerala, Thiruvananthapuram, pp: 45-49.

Rai, H.N. (1965): Diffusion of Information and Farmers Response in Relation to an Improved Farm Practices, *Indian. J. Extn. Edu.*, 1:140.

Ramesh, G and Krishnakumar.T, (2009): NREGA: Facet of Rural Women Empowerment: A Case Study in Karimnagar District in Andra Pradesh, *Kurukshetra*, 58(2): 29-30.

Rao, T.V. (2004): Readings in Human Resource Development, *Oxford and IBH Publishing Co. Pvt. Ltd.*, New Delhi, pp: 435.

Ray, G.C. (1997): Facilitating People's Participation in Rural Development Programmes, In: Samanta, R.K. and Arora, S.K (eds.) Management of Agricultural Extension in Global Perspective, *BR publishers*, New Delhi, pp: 171-187.

Reddin, W.J. (1987): Effectve Management, *Tata Mcgraw Hill Publishing Company Ltd.*, New Delhi, pp: 270.

Reddy, N.D., Alakh N., Sharma., Tankha. R. and Upendranadh, C. (2010): Institutions and Innovations in the Implementation Process of Mahatma Gandhi National Rural Employment Guarantee Scheme (MGNREGS) in India, SPA Working Papers 2010, Institute for Human Development, New Delhi. pp: 44.

Rehman, K and Rehman, M.M. (1998): Participation to Development, A Resource Book on Strategy, Programmes and Procedures, *Manak Publications Pvt. Ltd.*, New Delhi, pp: 24.

Rezvanfar, A and Vaisy, H. (2006): Job Satisfaction amongst Agricultural Extension Personnel in Kurdistan Province of Ira, *J. Ext. System*, 22 (1): 23-35.

Roy, A and Dey, N. (2010): MNREGA: Breeding New Grounds, *The Hindu*, February 5, 2010, pp: 6.

Saiyadain, M.S. (1988): Human Resource Management, *Tata Mcgraw Hill Company Ltd*, New Delhi, pp: 200-203.

Sajeevchandran, A. (1989): Impact Development Programmes in Promoting Pepper Products in Kerala, College of Agriculture, Vellayani, pp: 43.

Sasankan, V.R. (2001): Production System Typology and Technology Utilization Pattern in Cassava Cultivation in Thiruvananthapuram District, Kerala Agricultural University, Thrissur, pp: 94.

Seema, B. (1986): Role of Farm Women in Decision making Process of a Farming Community in Trivandrum District, Kerala Agricultural University, Vellanikkara, pp: 95.

Shah, A and Mehta, A.K. (2008): Experience of the Maharashtra Employment Guarantee Scheme: Are these Lessons for NREGS?, *Ind. J. Labour Economics*, 51(2): 191-206.

Shah, A. (2010): MGNREGS in Gujarat: Initial Experience and Early Signals, *LBS. J. Mgt & Res.*, VIII(1): 46.

Sharma, A., Ghate, P., Joshi, L., Sahu, A. (2009): NCAER Study on Evaluating Performance of National Rural Employment Guarantee Act, NCAER, Parisila Bhavan, New Delhi.

Sharma, D. (1989): Implementation of IRDP in Ganganagar District of Rajasthan, *J. Rural. Dev.*, 8(1): 109-112.

Sharma, G.L., Balamurugan, P., Kumar. S and Bajipai, S.K. (2010): Management of Mahatma Gandhi National Rural Employment Guarantee Scheme in Haryana: Issues and Challenges, *LBS. J. Mgt & Res.*, VIII(1): 63.

Sherin, M. (1997): Analysis of the Characteristics of Women's Groups and their Role in Rural Development, Kerala Agricultural University, Thrissur, pp: 257.

Shilaja, S. (1981): Influence of Leaders in the Development of Rural Areas, Kerala Agricultural University, Thrissur, pp: 269.

Sindhu, S. (2002): Social Cost Benefit Analysis in Vegetable Production Programmes in Kerala through Participatory Approach, Kerala Agricultural University, Thrissur, pp: 145.

Singh, B.N., Jaiswal, N.K. and Thakur, R.S. (1966): Attitude of Farmers towards Intensive Agricultural District Programme, *Ind. J. Extn. Edu.*, 2(3&4): 150-162.

Singh, J.N. and Mishra, A. (2006): Backward Linkages of Rural Employment Guarantee Scheme, *Kurukshetra* 8: 30-34.

Singh, M.P and Sharma, N. (1998): Hill Women of Uttar Pradesh, *A Survey of Ind. Farming*, 36(8): 8.

Sivaprasad, S. (1997): Problems and Prospects of Self-employment of Trained Rural Youth in Agriculture, Kerala Agricultural University, Thrissur, pp: 123.

Soyal, M. (1966): Public Relations in Administration II: The Influence of the Public on the Operation of Public Administration and Excluding Electoral Rights, *International Institute of Administrative Sciences*, Brussels, pp: 25-80.

State Planning Board. (1996): Jankeeyasutarana Purusthanam, Government of Kerala, Thiruvananthapuram, pp: 35.

Sudha, V.K.(1987): A Study on the Impact of Lab to Land Programme on Tribal and Non-tribal Participants, Kerala Agricultural University, Thrissur, pp: 45.

Sureshkumar. (1989): Attitude Formation and Change, *Jaico Publishing House*, Bombay, pp: 65.

Suthan, L. (2003): Analysis of Farmer's Participation on the Participatory Technology Development (PTD) Process vis-à-vis Plant Protection in Vegetables at Kunnathukal Panchayat, College of Agriculture, Vellayani, pp: 76-78.

Tea Board. (1962): Survey of the Living Conditions of Tea Plantation Labour in Tripura, Tea Board, Calcutta, pp: 3.

Thomas, P. (1998): Fisherman Development through Thrift and Credit. Indo-German Reservoir Fisher Development Project, Kerala Agricultural University, Thrissur, pp: 126.

Thurstone, L.L. (1946): Comment. *Amer. J. Sociology*, 52: 39-50.

Veluswamy, R. and Manoharan, M. (1998): Extent of Participation of Beneficiaries in the Activities of NGO, *Ind. J. Extn. Edu.*, 9(1): 1912-1914.

Vendan, M and Murugavel. (2010): NREGS: Key Issues, *Agrl. Finance*, 42(1): 26-29.

Vijayanand, S.M and Jithendran, V.N. (2008): Implementation of NREGA – Experience of Kerala, *The Gazette of India*, Ministry of Rural Development, 48: 179-184.

Yadav, H.R and Garg, N. (2010): Socio-economic Conditions of MGNREGA Workers in District Rewari, *Social Welfare*, 57 (5): 24-26.

Pages: 190-201

Rural Development and Techno-Innovations
Edited by: Dr. Alka Chauhan; Er. Chhavi Kumar 'Bharti' & Dr. Pawan Kumar 'Bharti'
ISBN: 978-93-88854-07-8
***Edition:* 2019**
***Published by:* Discovery Publishing House Pvt. Ltd., New Delhi (India)**

12

Gender Empowerment from Millennium Development Goals to Sustainable Development Goals

Suraiya Nazeer

ABSTRACT

Millennium Development Goals was the world's biggest agreement to reduce poverty and human deprivation at unrecorded rate through collaborative action of major countries among the world. They differ from other Global promises of poverty reduction in their comprehensive nature and systematic effort taken to finance, implement and monitor them. They have galvanized efforts to meet needs of poorest of the poor. The Goal of "promoting gender equality and empowering women" is the third on the list after "Eradicating extreme poverty and hunger" and "achieving universal primary education". The Millennium Developmental Goals are gender responsive because among all the eight Goals, three are directly related to gender equality and the other five goals go beyond equality to incorporate components of equality between men and women. However, the Goals can be criticised in the following ways. The Goals framed in the MDGs are not comprehensive and they lack many dimensions. But MDGs have in general the power to mobilize the International Community to raise money and take action for developmental issues that still had to be implemented. Since MDGs expired in 2015.In the post MDGs period if the UN will agree to came with the targets that follow the frame work of MDGs so that the problems of Gender Empowerment will be addressed once and of all. To create a new, people-cantered, development agenda, UN came out with Sustainable Development Goals. The SDGs include 17 goals and 169 targets.

In this context the study would attempt to access to much extent MDGs helped in obtaining Gender Empowerment. It is thus significant in analyzing the how Sustainable Development Goals will carry forward the

PhD Student, Central of Central Asian Studies, University of Kashmir, Hazratbal, Srinagar, Jammu and Kashmir - 190 006 (India)

unfinished agenda of MDGs in obtaining the Gender Empowerment. The study will also make a humble attempt to analyse the differences between Millennium Development Goals and Sustainable Development Goals.

Key words: "International Community", "Injustice", "Millennium Development Goals", "Poverty", "Gender Empowerment", "Sustainable Development Goals", "United Nations".

SIGNIFICANCE

The term Gender Justice refers to equality between the sexes. The Gender Justice may be defined as a political ideology or a set of conventions about what is 'right' and 'good' in human relationships and how these desirable outcomes may be attained. In the name of gender, women have been discriminated as compared to men throughout the world. In the words of Wilchins "Gender is not what culture created out of my body's sex; rather; sex is what culture makes when it genders my body"

We are living in a world which is characterized as a 'compression of time and space'. Individual has changed in this new world of Globalization, new informational technologies and multinational capitalism. In this frame of Globalization social process is reshaped, reconstruct and reinvent. But the condition among women remains same. Because of her gender women have been subjugated by many ways as women throughout the Globe lack support for fundamental functions of a human life. They are under nourished than men, less healthy, more susceptible to physical cruelty and sexual abuse. They In order to tackle these problems, the United Nations passed many declarations related to the rights of vulnerable groups such as women, children, persons with disabilities and other minorities. The outcome of these treaties and declarations is that they helped to create a 'culture of human rights' throughout the world and is providing an influential tool to defend and encourage all rights.The major aim of the present study is to find out how international Legislation is helpful in tackling the problem, what are the lacunas and what is the way to go forward is.

METHODOLOGY

The study relies on secondary data including books, research journals, newspapers and opinions generated therein by the relevant experts and officials. The study has also focused the reports of various international organizations regarding women empowerment. The study is also based on the conceptual and theoretical framework regarding different issues and aspects including Feminism, Gender, Sex, and Women Empowerment. Historical, analytical, interpretative and descriptive methods have been followed to reach to the conclusion.

Objectives:

- To analyse the role of MDGs in obtaining Gender Empowerment.

- To analyzing that how Sustainable Development Goals will carry forward the unfinished agenda of MDGs in obtaining the Gender Empowerment.

INTRODUCTION

"It is more difficult to murder a phantom than a reality-Virgina Woolf 2002" The term Gender[1] Justice is defined as equality[2] between the different Sexes. The Gender Justice may be defined as a Political Ideology or a set of Convention about what is 'Justice' and 'Good' among the humans in relation to fellow beings and how these desirable outcomes may be attained. Gender Justice cannot be achieved unless socio-political needs are satisfied. Throughout the World Gender Justice has gained and is gaining strength over the years, as it has been realized that there cannot be development in states if half of its population is held back[3]. In the name of Gender, women have been discriminated as compared to men throughout the world.[4]

The Movement which has been going on to end the women's oppression is known by the name of Feminism[5]. Feminists have understood Women not on the basis of the term Sex, but in terms of Gender which depends on social and cultural factors.[6] Women had been discriminated and continue to discriminate throughout the World in the name of Gender. As in most parts of South Asia, Central Asian, Africa and Latin America, about 70 to 90 percent of women work and lived in rural areas in the late 20th century. They were the world's largest group of the food producers using Traditional Means while as in Technologically Advanced world, rural women were trying to strike a balance between hunger and nutrition.[7] In case of political rights they also face discrimination as regarding their seats in parliament are concerned they take up 18% of parliamentary seats throughout the whole world. There is also a lot of diversity related to percentage in the parliament as it is indicated by the fact averages of the percentage of women in parliament in different regions of the world as Nordic countries contain 41.4%, Americas have almost 21.8% in case of Europe it is 19.1 and Asia - 17.4%.[8] Their discrimination is also indicated by the fact that Females consists of half of the World's Population, Women's makes up 70 percent of the world's poor and two-thirds of the world's illiterate population.[9]

GLOBALIZATION AND ITS IMPACT

The rise of the Globalization[10] brought new changes at international level while some countries had been benefiting from this reformation; many others in the North and South have seen their economies weaken as the developing and underdeveloped countries. The world enters into the phase in which liberalism dominate other ideologies, and laissez-fair economy dominate the other economies to which Fransus Fukayama alluded to as End of History.[11]

The rapid socio-economic changes taking place in the world economy have a direct impact on women's status. According to the various surveys during the last decade, the participation rates of women in the labour force have dramatically increased. This increase has serious implications, beyond the economy, for social policy. Whatever new employment opportunities have appeared, women have frequently been channelized into the service sector, into low status and low-income jobs.[12] The female jobs were characterized short term with small pay, no option of progress, and few, if any benefits and men continue to get more than their fair share of the better jobs.[13]

INSTITUTIONAL IMPACT OF GLOBALISATION

Creation of Corporate Realities

The creation of Feministic Discourse emerged from a critique of biologically deterministic and culturally essential Gender constructive discourses. The unintentional side effects Feminist Gender de/construction has contributed to the reproduction of a dichotomous understanding of biological sex and socio-cultural gender.[14] In the present context where the Feminism is in the Fourth Wave[15] it seems that "feminism" in 2017 is more concerned with promoting superficial trappings of genuine equality than with doing the tough work required to address the hard, cold facts of gender and racial inequality.[16] For instance females represent half of the world's population, women flock make up 70 percent of the world's poor and two-thirds of the world's illiterate population. If the status of women improves the quality of life will improve automatically. The subordinate position of women prevents them from having control over their lives and bodies. The parents see daughters as burdens rather than valuable members of the family. Gender inequality has serious consequences because it impedes progress of global health, economic stability and human rights.[17]

In spite of the above discrimination the quantity of Cosmetic Procedures increased by 44 percent from 2003 to 2004, according to the American Society for Aesthetic Plastic Surgery. Plastic surgeons conducted a record 11.9 million procedures last year, including nonsurgical procedures like Botox and surgical procedures like breast augmentation or liposuction.[18] The bigger reason for that is the present culture is dominated by the cultural images of Sexualisation, which is increasingly evident in sexualised imagery and discourses. The sexualisation is invading mainstream culture rapidly and the increasing volume and availability of pornography; interest in the porn industry from real life media genres.[19]

NEW SENSE OF INDIVIDUALISM

The Problems which the social critics identify in the present context are the highly organised capitalistic society, and a highly centralised state crushing the individual under the dead weight of uniformity. Society has become more and more advanced, the output of goods are enormous but the common man is engaging all the time in nothing but the exacting task of trying to, or worrying in order to improve his economic status. The individual finds himself or herself more and more alienated, alienation from state, from who with he/she is working and from himself/herself.[20]

Women have also become the victim of this individualism, as a breed of women attractive and qualified is having plastic surgeries-'boob job', 'bump job' etc. The Plastic Generation are unfaltering belief that, 'The body can be shaped and remoulded over and over again, regardless of the price.'[21] UN notes that basic education for all who live in the developing countries would cost somewhere in the region of $ 6 billion a year. However, the US alone already spends a staggering $ 8 billion annually on cosmetics.[22]

ADDRESSING THE ISSUE BY UNITED NATION

Considering the present context achieving Gender Equality is a Goal it has been accepted by Governments, Regional and International Organizations to achieve the Goal. Any new developmental structure must prioritize Gender Empowerment primarily because of the persistent injustice faced by Women around the World with Women disproportionately representing among the poorest and most marginalized. It is enshrined in International Agreements and Commitments. The greatest achievement is the construction of a body of International Human Rights Law of United Nations also other negotiations, Treaties and Declarations which focused on the rights of vulnerable groups such as women, children, persons with disabilities, minorities and indigenous peoples. All this will help to create a 'Culture of Human Rights' throughout the world.[23]

Far reaching commitments to Women Rights contained in different conventions and programs of United Nations the UN Convention on the Elimination of All Forms of Discrimination against Women, Beijing Declaration and UN Security Council Resolutions 1325, 1820, 1888 and 1889.[24]

However, the greatest Programme was United Nations Millennium Development Goals. In the year 2000 it was adopted by United Nations. This Declaration was signed by 189 countries, and then it was translated into a road map by setting out Goals to be reached by 2015.The Goals were set out for development and poverty eradication they were known as Millennium Development Goals. These eight goals represent commitments to reduce poverty and hunger, to take ill health, Gender Inequality, lack of education, lack of access to clean water, and environmental degradation.[25]

MILLENNIUM DEVELOPMENT GOALS

In September 2000 the General Assembly adopted the UN Millennium Declaration. This Declaration was signed by 189 countries, they were translated into a roadmap by setting out Goals to be reached by 2015.That Goals were eight in number. All the Goals were constructed on the United

Nations Conference of 1990s and represent commitments to reduce the poverty, hunger, Empower Women and achieve other sustainable goals. The Eight Millennium Development Goals commit world leaders to an ambitious agenda for change. For all of the Goals, a set of time-bound targets and indicators have been proposed as a means of tracking progress. However, the Goal to promote Gender Equality and Women Empowerment can be seen as a significant indicator vis-à-vis women status as it has initiated the process to 'Engender' the developmental progress.[26]

Source: Google Images

ASSESSING THE ACHIEVEMENTS

- An increase in the number of girls in school in 2015 compared to 2000. The developing world as a whole has achieved the goal of eliminating gender disparity in all levels of education, including primary, secondary, and tertiary.
- In Southern Asia, the number of girls enrolled in primary school was 74 for every 100 boys in 1990. By 2015, there were 103 girls enrolled for every 100 boys.
- The proportion of women in vulnerable employment compared to total female employment has reduced by 13 percent in the period between 1991 and 2015, compared to a 9 percent decrease for men.
- Significant gains in women's parliamentary representation in nearly 90 percent of 174 countries for which data has been available in the past two decades. At the very least, the average proportion of women in parliament has increased by nearly 100 percent during the last 20 years, yet this still translates to one woman for every five men.[27]

Goals and Targets	Africa		Asia				Oceana	Latin America and the Caribbean	Caucasus and Central Asia
	Northern	Sub-Saharan	Eastern	South-Eastern	Southern	Western			
GOAL 3	Promote gender equality and empowerment								
Equal girl's enrolment in primary school	Close to parity	Close to parity	Parity	Parity	Parity	Close to parity	Close to parity	Parity	Parity
Women's share of paid employment	Low share	Medium share	High share	Medium share	Low share	Low share	Medium share	High share	High share
Women's equal represantation in national parliament	Moderate representation	Moderate representation	Moderate representation	Low representation	Low representation	Low representation	Very low representation	Moderate representation	Low representation

Target met or excellent progress	Good progress	Fair progress	Poor progress or deterioration	Missing or insufficient data

Source: Millennium Development Goals Reports

FAILURES

With developed experiences towards MDG, we came to know that how we could crystallise the global agreements to acknowledge change, and what are the loop holes. The MDG goals can be criticised in the following ways. The goals framed in the MDG are not comprehensive and they lack many dimensions, as according to Jan Vandemoortele,[28] the dimensions of Climatic change, infrastructure, good governance, quality of education. In the words of Jan, the overburdening of MDG may weaken them.[29] Some Human rights advocates were of the opinion that the targets of MDGs were narrow since it does not contain the good governance goals. Also, the environmentalist activists also complained that the goals are not comprehensive as they do not contain the issues as climate change, land degradation, ocean management, and air pollution. If we look at the Millennium Developmental Project, there were several issues as narrowly defined as Gender equality environmental sustainability. The focus of the educational goal is also limited to the primary schooling.[30]

There are some apparent contradictions in the goals and targets, and raises general question of what the goals should be about and for.[31] The first question is why these particular goals and targets have been chosen and not others.[32]

SUSTAINABLE DEVELOPMENT GOALS

Since MDGS expired in 2015.In the post MDGS period if the UN will agree to came with the targets that follow the frame work of MDGS the problem of gender injustice will be addressed once and of all. The United Nation came with Sustainable Development Goals to reflect further strengthening convergence of the development agenda. The SDGs include 17 goals and 169 targets. The progress would be measured now in the next 15 years. How SDGs would mobilize the resources and efforts. So as to make the world a better place to live. The SDGs can be broadly divided into three categories: First, an extension of MDGs that includes the first seven SDGs; second group is inclusiveness (jobs, infrastructure, industrialization, and distribution). It includes goals 8, 9, and 10; and the third group is on sustainability and urbanization that covers the last seven goals: sustainable cities and communities, life below water "consumption and production; climate action; resources and environment; peace and justice; and the means of implementation and global partnership for it".[33]

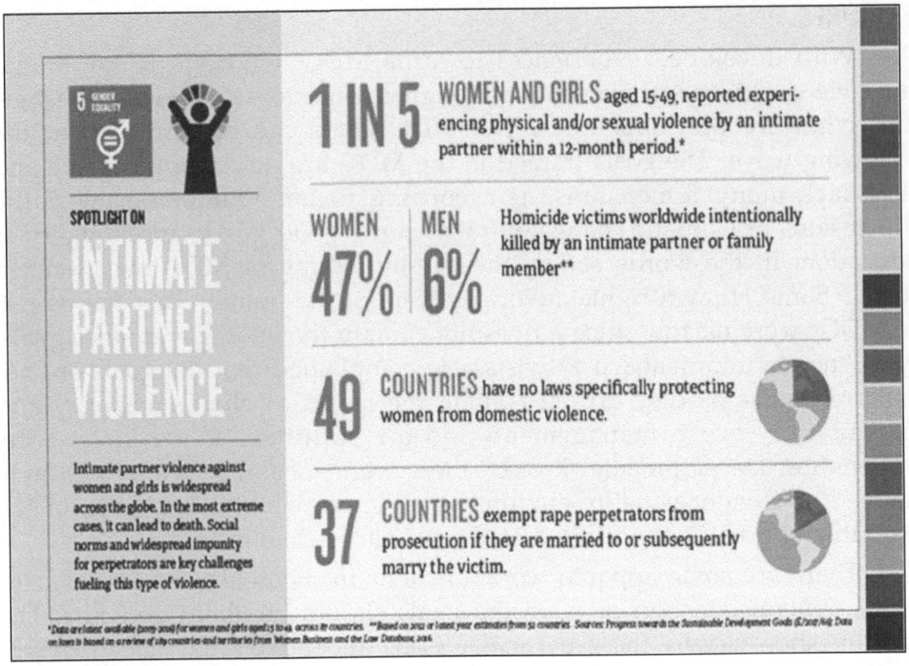

Source: Google Images

CONCLUSION

On the basis of Gender, women are being denied of their rights, opportunities or resources. Throughout the Globe, Women are being treated unequally and also less value is placed on their lives as compared to men because of their Gender. Women's degree of difference, right to use to power and control of possessions is central to this discrimination in all institutional spheres, i.e. the family circle, community, market, and state.

Millennium Development Goals of ensuring gender justice and promoting women status in all spheres. Although gender issues are not sufficiently addressed in the policy provisions of MDGS, but MDGS have in general the power to mobilize the International Community to raise money and take action for developmental issues that still had to be implemented. Since MDGS will expire in 2015.In the post MDGS period if the UN will agree to came with the targets that follow the frame work of MDGS the problem of gender injustice will be addressed once and of all. The UN came out with SDGs. They will guide developmental programmes in all countries for the next fifteen years. To overcome the lacunas which were found in MDGs for making Gender Empowerment an achievable goal?

SUGGESTIONS

- All the practices which lead to discrimination against women if may not be controlled wholly with the formulation and application of the relevant social legislation. Then there is need of organizing broader social support through the organization of social movement against these inhuman practices. In spite of these both the measures can work together at various levels jointly that may lead to the resolution.

- Social Legislation if implemented sincerely and completely without any bias may provide an effective measure.
- Establishment of plenty courts which will deal with the issues related to problems of Gender Justice.
- Empower Women and create among them awareness about their rights and obligations. This process may be carried out in the schools, Families and education.
- There is a greater need to increase the involvement of the women of younger generation in women's rights, development and social justice works is absolutely necessity.
- The ideology of feminism should be promoted and all the negativities associated with it should make clear. Also feminists should solve the problems related to different ideologies within it. So that they may gave a uniform message to the world.

REFERENCES

1. The term "Gender" was used and defined for the First Time in International Criminal Law Treaty that is the Rome Statute of the International Criminal Court in the Year 1998. The Term "Gender" was then used and Continue to be using by the United Nations in the Areas of International Human Rights and Refugee Law. Oosterveld, V. (2005). The Definition of Gender in the Rome Statue of the International Criminal Court: A Step Forward or Back for International Criminal Justice?. *Harvard Human Rights Journal*, Volume 18, University of Massachusetts: Boston, pp. 55.
2. With the adaptation of UN Conventions on Human Rights that Starts from 1948, Equality becomes the basis for Political Statements and Developmental Plans at National and International Level. Then after in Series of UN Conferences in 1990s on Children, Population, Human Rights, Women, Environment and Habitat all Literature used Equality and Equity in their Reports. Ahoojapatel, K. (2001). *Development has a Women's Face: Insight from within the UN*. S.B. Nangia, A.P.H. Publishing Corporation: New Delhi.
3. Gupta, G.R., Khan, Z. and Grown, C. (2003). Achieving Gender Equality and the Empowerment of Women, International Centre for Research on Women, Washington, D.C.
4. Fatima, T. (2010). Gender Justice: A Conceptual Analysis. *Excellence International Journal of Education and Research*. India, Volume 1, Issue 4, p. 275.
5. The Term Feminism was First Introduced by Elizebth Candy Stranton in 1848. It is a Self Conscious and Systematic Movement which began in the late Eighteenth Century. The Word Appeared First in France in the 1880, Great Britain in 1890s and United States in 1910. Its Understanding includes Women Acting, speaking and Writing on Women's Issues and Rights, Identifying Social injustice in the Status quo and bringing their own Unique Perspective to the issues. Tendon, N. (2008). *Feminism: A Paradigm Shift*, Atlantic Publisher and Dist.: India.

6. Stanford Encyclopaedia of Philosophy, (2011). *Feminist Perspectives on Sex and Gender.*
7. "International Women's Democracy Centre, (2008). *Fact Sheet: Women's Political Participation, Women in Parliaments.*
8. International Women's Democracy Centre, (2008). *Fact Sheet: Women's Political Participation, Women in Parliaments.*
9. Edmounds, M. (2013). *Examples of Gender Inequality Around the World.* Afriqtalk.
10. Globalization has at least two Common meanings: The Increased Integration of Various Places into the World Economy, and the Effects of Vastly Improved Transportation and Communication Systems on Multidirectional Cultural Flows. Many Anthropologists Emphasize Globalization as Cultural Flows, Leaving as Shadowy or Invisible the Economic and Political Processes and Institutions that both Shape and are Shaped by those Flows. Edelman, M. and Haugerud, A. (Ed). (2005). *The Anthropology of Development and Globalization from Classical Political Economy to Contemporary Neo liberalism.* Wiley-Blackwell, p. 3.
11. In his Theory, 'End of History' Fransis Fukayama said there is Remarkable Consensus Concerning the Legitimacy of the Liberal Democracy as a system of Government and as a World form of Government. The Liberal Ideology Conquered Rival Ideologies like Hereditary Monarchy, Fascism and most Recently Communism. The Fukayama argued that Liberal Democracy may Constitute the "End Point of Mankind's Ideological Evolution," and the "Final Form of Government" and as such Constitute "End of History." Blunden, A. (2005). *The End of History and the Last Man.* Penguin, p. 99.
12. Ahoojapatel, K. (2001). *Development has a Women's Face: Insight from within the UN.* New Delhi: S.B. Nangia A. P.H. Publishing Corporation, p. 143.
13. Jannet, L.J., Connelly, J. and Barriteau, E.(2000). *Theoretical Perspective on Gender and Development.* International Development Research Centre. Canada.
14. Lykke, N. (2010). *Feminist Studies,* Rutledge: UK.
15. Jennifer Baumgardner identified Fourth Wave of Feminism as Starting in 2008 and Continuing into Present day. The Fourth Wave becomes Possible by the use of New Technological Tools that helps Women to Build a Strong, Popular, Reactive Movement online. The Fourth Wave of Feminism is Characterized by its Reliance on the Internet. Kategagliano, (2014). *Social Media and the Fourth Wave of Feminism.* available at: https://manshipmassmedia.wordpress.com/.../social-media-and- the-fourt,(accessed on July 7, 2015.)
16. Alexander, A.(2017). Today's Feminism: Too Much Marketing, Not Enough Reality, Code Switch Race and Identity, Remixed, accessed on 23-9-2017, available at *www.npr.org/sections/.../21/.../today-s-feminism-too-much-marketing-not-enough-realit...*
17. Edmounds, M. (2013). *Examples of Gender Inequality Around the World.* Afriqtalk.
18. Dittmann, M. (2005). "Plastic Surgery: Beauty or Beast?", *American Psychological Association,* Vol. 36, No. 8.
19. Coy, M., Wakeling, J. and Garner, M.(2007). "Sexualised Popular Culture as Symbolic Violence", *Women Studies and International Forum,* Vol. 34.
20. Varma, S.P.(2007). *Modern Political Theory,* Vikas Publishing House: India.
21. Elliott A. and Lemert, C. (2006). *The New Individualism,* Rutledge: UK.
22. Ibid.
23. 'MDG-3: Promote Gender Equality and Empower Women in Tajikistan', available at www.tj.undp.org/content/tajikistan/en/home/.../mdgoverview/.../mdg3.ht.,(assesed on 13 April,2015)

24. Report of UNDP,(2010). *Millennium Development Goals about Tajikistan* available at: www.tj.undp.org/content/tajikistan/en/home/mdg overview.html.(assessed on 24 March, 2015).

25. UNICEF, (2002). The UN Role in Human Rights Respect, Convention on the Rights of Child, available at: www.unicef.org/crc/index_30198.html,(accessed on December 2, 2015.)

26. Andy Haines and Andrew Cassels, "Can the Millennium Developmental Goal be Attained", Vol. 324, 2004.

27. MDG Monitor, available at www.mdgmonitor.org/mdg-3-promote-gender-equality-and-empower-women/,accesed *on 3-2-2018*

28. Vandemoortele, J. (2015). *Advancing the Global Development Agenda Post-2015: Some Thoughts, Ideas and Practical Suggestions*. UN Task 'Team on the Post-2015 UN Development Agenda, New York, pp. 8-9.

29. Melamed, C. and Scott, L. (2011). After 2015: Progress and Challenges for Development. Overseas Development Institute. London: 2011, available at *http://www.odi.org/resources/docs/7061.pdfhttp://www.odi.org/resources/docs/7061.pdf*. (accessed on 17, February 2015)

30. McArthur, J. (2013). Own the Goals: What the Millennium Development Goals have Accomplished. *Foreign Affairs*, Volume 29, Number 2.

31. As Goal 1 is to "Eradicate Extreme Poverty and Hunger" and this Translates into Two Quantitative, Time-bound targets - to Halve the Proportion of People with an Income of Less than $1 a day and to Halve the Numbers of People who Suffer from Hunger by 2015. Goal 2 is Educational, with the Target of Full Primary Schooling by 2015 for Boys and Girls alike. Goal 3 Promotes Gender Equality, Overlapping with the Previous Goal, but Extending the Gender Equality Targets to Secondary and all Levels, by 2005 and 2015 Respectively. Goal 4 is to Reduce under-five Mortality by Two-thirds and Goal 5 is to Reduce the Maternal Mortality Ratio by Three-quarters, also by 2015. Goal 6 is to Combat HIV/AIDS, Malaria and other Diseases, with the Target of Halting, and beginning to Reverse the Spread of HIV/AIDS by 2015. Goal 7 is to "Ensure Environmental Sustainability". This Breaks Down into Three Targets: The Integration of Sustainable Development, Halving the Proportion of Poor People without Sustainable Access to Safe Water and Sanitation, and Achieving a Significant Improvement in the Lives of at least 100 Million Slum Dwellers, the Latter Two by 2015. Goal 8 is to "Develop a Global Partnership for Development". New York, (201I). The Millennium Development Goals Report, *United Nations*, pp. 6-67.

32. Khoo, S.M. (2005).The Millennium Developmental Goals: A Critical Discussion. *Trocaire Developmental Review*, pp. 46-48.

33. Stephen Mortan, David Penchen and Neil Squires, Sustainable Development Goals and their Implementation: A Natural Goal Framework for Health, Development and Equity needs a Systems Approach at Every Level, British Medical Bulletin, and Vol. 124. Issue1, 2017.

Index

S

T

U

V

❑❑❑❑❑❑